The Utterm

# The Uttermost Part of the Earth

## A GUIDE TO PLACES IN THE BIBLE

Richard R. Losch

WILLIAM B. EERDMANS PUBLISHING COMPANY
GRAND RAPIDS, MICHIGAN / CAMBRIDGE, U.K.

© 2005 Wm. B. Eerdmans Publishing Co.
All rights reserved

Wm. B. Eerdmans Publishing Co.
255 Jefferson Ave. S.E., Grand Rapids, Michigan 49503 /
P.O. Box 163, Cambridge CB3 9PU U.K.

Printed in the United States of America

09 08 07 06 05     7 6 5 4 3 2 1

ISBN 0-8028-2805-1

www.eerdmans.com

# Contents

# Introduction

When Jesus gave his apostles the Great Commission, he commanded them to go and be witnesses "both in Jerusalem, and in all Judaea, and in Samaria, and unto the uttermost part of the earth" (Acts 1:8). This must have been a daunting challenge to them, as the diversity of strange races, religions, and cultures seemed to them as broad as the modern science fiction buff's ideas of the diversity of beings throughout the universe.

This book is designed to be an introduction to the stories of the many fascinating places that are mentioned in the Bible, as well as some nonbiblical places that played a significant role in Bible times. It is not intended to be an in-depth study or encyclopedia of biblical sites. Rather, it is designed as an aid to readers of the Bible to give them a broader picture of the places and cultures that influenced biblical events, and, I hope, to encourage them to seek more information about them. In short, it is intended to be nothing more profound than a collection of information for the curious.

It would be unreasonable to study a single ancient city or region without also considering its interplay with the others of its time, including those that influenced its development, and those that were influenced by it. This would be like studying a single verse of the Bible out of context, with no consideration of the religious, social, and cultural influences that led to the thought behind that verse. History is the account of a complex network of forces, sometimes in concord, but more often in conflict. For this reason there are many stories and events that appear again and again in this volume.

Readers of this book may have never heard of some of these places. The Galilean city of Sepphoris, for example, is never mentioned in the Bible. It is rarely mentioned in accounts of Jesus' life, yet it very probably played a major role in the culture of Nazareth and in Jesus' early education. On the other hand, I have not attempted to include every single place mentioned in the Bible. Some played such a minor role in the development of the history and religion of the area that I have chosen to omit them rather than clutter the pages with tiny bits of information about insignificant places.

There are a few places that played enormous parts in the early development of Western civilization and religion, including Mesopotamia, Jerusalem, Greece, and Rome. For a huge portion of European history and of the early Christian timeline, the driving force and irresistible influence was that of Rome, and I have thus dedicated by far the longest section of the book to that great city and the empire it ruled. Information on ancient Greece can be found particularly in the sections on Athens and Corinth, and information on Mesopotamia in sections including Babylon, Nineveh, and Ur of the Chaldeans.

Modern archaeology is a fascinating science, as it involves almost equal portions of advanced technology and cognitive reasoning. As difficult as it may be for the layman to understand, even tiny fragments of broken pottery can provide huge amounts of information about the date, culture, and practices of an ancient town or civilization. Fortunately for us, the survivors or descendants of the vast majority of ancient cities that were destroyed or fell into decay did not clear away the rubble and rebuild. Frequently they would simply rebuild on top of the old ruins. Often they would build beside the ruins, using them for their trash heap, thus covering them with a layer of their middens. When their city fell, the next would build on top of the trash heap, now a relatively smooth mound, using the new set of ruins for their trash. Thus over the centuries was deposited layer after layer of very telling evidence of their cultures. We can find city upon city, and civilization upon civilization, in great mounds made up of excavatable layers that reveal a vast amount of information about the way of life in those places. Throughout the world archaeologists are exploring these mounds, called *tells* in the Middle East (from the Arabic for "heap"), creating an ever growing body of knowledge about ancient times. In many cases they have substantiated biblical stories previously considered mythological, and in others they have challenged what we thought to be true, causing us to re-evaluate our positions on many points of history, culture, and religion.

My sources of information were manifold, and even though not all agree on some details, they are sources in which I have confidence. They include two volumes specific to the subject, L. F. DeVries, *Cities of the Biblical World* (Peabody, Mass.: Hendrickson, 1997), and J. J. Bimson, ed., *Baker Encyclopedia of Bible Places* (Leicester: Inter-Varsity Press, 1995). I also gleaned huge amounts of information from the 1967 Encyclopedia Britannica, the 1914 *Catholic Encyclopedia*, the 1957 and 1998 *Interpreter's Bible*, and the 1967 *Interpreter's Dictionary of the Bible*. A valuable but somewhat less reliable resource is the Internet, which provides an enormous number of articles, as well as the sites of various national boards of tourism. The Internet cannot be considered quite as trustworthy as the aforementioned resources, however, because it requires the ability to discern true experts from self-appointed experts, of whom there are many.

Some readers may read this volume cover-to-cover, while others may simply dip in to find out more about a particular town or city. Either way, I hope it will provide a helpful and interesting introduction to the lands of the Bible.

# A Brief History of the Holy Land

Many readers may not be familiar with all the Bible stories and historical events that shaped the history of the part of the world we call the Holy Land, or Palestine. It therefore seems appropriate to present here a brief sketch of that history as it relates to those stories. It is obviously impossible to present a comprehensive account of ten thousand years in a few pages, so I ask the forgiveness of the historians and other scholars for the necessary lack of detail and the omission of many events.

The region we call Palestine is tiny, yet it has left an indelible mark on world history and human culture. Located on the eastern coast of the Mediterranean Sea, it is a strip of land only about two hundred miles long, and averaging fifty miles in width. It contains a huge variety of terrains, including fertile coastal plains and two mountain chains, between which are found the Jordan River and two bodies of water. The northern body is a freshwater lake abundant in fish, the Sea of Galilee (often called the Sea of Tiberias today). The Jordan flows from it almost due south to where it drains into the Dead Sea, an inland sea so salty that no plants or animals can live in or beside it. Palestine's elevations range from thirty-five hundred feet at the top of Mount Hebron to thirteen hundred feet below sea level at the shore of the Dead Sea, the lowest land point on earth. It is surrounded by lands of the Fertile Crescent (today's Lebanon and Syria) in the north, Mesopotamia (today's Iraq and Jordan) in the northeast, the northern Arabian desert on the east and southeast, and Egypt (the Sinai Peninsula) on the southwest. Because of its location, Palestine was for millennia the passageway for most of the commerce and the aggression between Egypt, Mesopotamia, and Syria. This brought it countless migrations, as well as great prosperity during the times that it was not under occupation by invaders.

The first known settlers of Palestine were the Canaanites, a Semitic people about whose origins little is known. The Bible identifies them as the descendants of Canaan, the son of Ham, Noah's son.[1] By 3000 BCE, the be-

---

1. The Jews considered the Canaanites to be cursed by God. Genesis 9:20-27 tells the story that Ham saw Noah drunk and naked, and ran out to tell his brothers. Because of this Noah cursed Ham's son Canaan and all his descendants, saying that they would be slaves to

ginning of the middle Bronze Age, they had developed city-states all
through the region, one of the first of which was Jericho. They developed a
simple alphabet, perhaps the first in the world. Its characters represented
individual sounds, unlike the Mesopotamian cuneiform or Egyptian hi-
eroglyphics, whose characters represented syllables.[2] Their religion was
polytheistic, although many of their religious practices had a strong influence on Judaism, and thus on Christianity and Islam as well.[3] The
Canaanites were well established as the primary inhabitants of the land by
the time of Abraham (early second millennium BCE), and the region was
known as the land of Canaan. Tradition paints them as crude barbarians,
but this is a false representation. Not only were they literate, they produced
beautiful arts, and were technologically as advanced as any people of their
time.

Although the Canaanites inhabited the region, it was conquered by
Egypt as early as 2000 BCE, and it remained under Egyptian control until
the late fourteenth century BCE, by which time the Egyptian grip on the
land had weakened sufficiently that it was no longer of importance. During that period the Egyptians did not attempt to settle the land but were
content simply to control it and reap a profit from its prosperity. Their
control was not unchallenged, however. Canaan was constantly being attacked by other peoples, primarily the Amorites, Hittites, and Hurrians.
The Canaanites, with Egyptian help, were able to defeat each of these at-
tackers, and then absorbed the people into their own culture.

The Bible says that Abraham came into Canaan from Ur of the
Chaldeans, a city in Mesopotamia. There is archaeological evidence that a
people from Mesopotamia migrated into Canaan sometime before 1500
BCE, and Egyptian records of a Canaanite tribe called the Habiru are consistent with this to the extent that it is not at all unreasonable to argue that
the Habiru and the Hebrews were the same people.

---

the descendants of Shem (the ancestor of the Jews) and of Japheth. It was because of this
curse that the Jews believed that God gave them the land of the Canaanites.

2. The other major type of writing is the ideogram, where each character stands for a
complete word or idea, but does not represent any actual sounds. Ideograms can be read by
people who speak many different languages.

3. In many cases the influence of foreign religions on Judaism, although strong, was
negative. For instance, there was a pagan custom of seething a baby goat in its own mother's
milk, then eating the meat as a religious ritual. It is believed that the Jewish prohibition of
eating dairy foods and meat at the same meal arose from this, rather than its being a matter
of health such as the ban on pork and shellfish.

Around 1700 BCE a Semitic tribe called the Hyksos[4] swept out of the north and conquered Egypt, holding it until about 1550, when Amhose I drove them out. It would have been about the time of the Hyksos rule that Jacob and his sons, fleeing a famine in Canaan, were invited by Joseph to move to Egypt. No Egyptian pharaoh would have elevated a Semite (Joseph) to be his second in command, but a Semitic pharaoh might. Also, the Egyptians would not have given some of their richest land, the land of Goshen, to foreigners. The Hyksos, however, might have welcomed their fellow Semites in. When the Hyksos were defeated and driven out of Egypt by Amhose, their friends the Hebrews in Goshen would have been considered by the Egyptians to be consorts of their enemies, and thus themselves dangerous enemies, and they were therefore enslaved. This fits the time line quite well for Ramses II to have been the pharaoh when Moses led the Hebrews out of Egypt in the thirteenth century BCE.[5] Ramses did an enormous amount of building in the area where Goshen was believed to be, and the Bible says that the main work of the Hebrew slaves was the making of brick. There is no Egyptian record of Joseph and the moving in of the Hebrews, but this is not surprising. The Egyptians kept excellent records, but the Hyksos kept very few. Therefore most of what we know of the 150 years of Hyksos rule comes from archaeological excavations and the records of other nations, many of whom were equally bad record-keepers.

The Israelite conquest of Canaan began in about the late thirteenth century, after the Hebrews wandered in the Sinai Peninsula for forty years.[6] Because of his lack of trust in God, Moses was allowed to see the Promised Land but not to enter it (Num. 20:12). He died, and Joshua became the people's leader. In the course of time the Israelites conquered most of Canaan and entered into the period of the Judges, a time of a simple governmental

4. Their true name is unknown. The name "Hyksos" is Egyptian for "foreign rulers."

5. There are some scholars who argue that the story of slavery in Egypt is purely legendary, and that the Hebrews were a tribe of Canaanites who started expanding their territories sometime before the thirteenth century BCE. The only major inconsistency with the story, however, is that the Bible says the Hebrews were slaves for 430 years to the day (Exod. 12:40-41), and this does not fit the time line. If this number is held to be accurate, there is little to lend authority to the stories of Joseph and Moses. The very fact that it is emphasized to have been exactly 430 years to the day, however, indicates that there may well be a bit of imaginative thinking in the estimation of the number.

6. The timing of forty years may also be exaggerated. In the Hebrew idiom, forty is an expression that means "a lot." To say that they wandered forty years means only that they wandered for a very long time. This idiomatic exaggeration is similar to our expression, "I've done it a thousand times."

system ruled by tribal judges selected by the people and the prophets. As they gained greater and greater control of the region, each of the twelve tribes was assigned a specific area. There was squabbling and jealousy between the tribes, and occasionally it broke out into open warfare, such as when the Ephraimites attacked the tribes of Gilead and lost forty-two thousand of their warriors (Judg. 12:1-6). For the most part, however, the tribes coexisted reasonably amicably as a loose federation of Jews.

At some point in the early twelfth century BCE a tribe of Hellenic people from the Aegean and Crete, called the "Sea People," invaded from the Mediterranean. They were highly civilized, with well developed art and literature. They settled primarily in the southeast coastal region, in what today is called the West Bank and the Gaza Strip, and named the region Philistia. The Bible calls them Philistines,[7] and the name "Palestine" is a corruption of that. They captured many of the cities that the Israelites had taken from the Canaanites, and during the period of the Judges they oppressed and harassed the Israelites. The story of Samson, a judge of the tribe of Dan, gives much information about the relationship between the Philistines and the Israelites (Judg. 14:1–16:30).

By the eleventh century BCE, the Israelites felt the need for a more centralized leadership and demanded a king over the twelve tribes. The prophet Samuel reluctantly anointed Saul, prophesying God's warning that they would regret wanting a human instead of God as their king. Saul warred against the Philistines, but with little significant success. In his later years he became more and more paranoid and despotic, trying to kill David, whom he saw as a rival. It is quite apparent that if he was not mad at the end of his life he was close to it.

In about 1000 BCE David ascended the throne, and he soon managed to unify all twelve tribes into a single nation, called the United Monarchy of Israel. He finally defeated the Philistines and soon after established his capital city at Jerusalem. Jerusalem was on the border between the tribal lands of Judah and Benjamin, who were constantly bickering, and David eased their mutual jealousy by selecting the city as his capital. He built a palace and moved the ark of the covenant to a tent tabernacle he erected there.[8] David's reign was a turbulent one, tainted by rape, adultery, mur-

---

7. It is ironic that today we use the term "Philistine" to describe a boor or barbarian, since the Philistines were in reality a highly civilized (although often cruel) people. This conception probably arose because they were bitter enemies of the Israelites, and the Bible does not paint them in a very favorable light.

8. The ark had been captured by the Philistines, but after a plague struck Gaza they re-

der, and rebellion. He is nevertheless revered by Jews as the greatest king ever to rule in Israel. He ruled for thirty-nine years, and by his death Israel could be counted as one of the great nations on earth, and Jerusalem as one of the world's leading cities.

David was succeeded by his son Solomon, who also reigned thirty-nine years, adding wealth, beauty, and majesty to the nation to which David had given strength. For all his achievements, Solomon is best remembered for having built the temple, a magnificent edifice. He did it, however, at the expense of the unity of the nation. He enslaved twenty thousand Jews to build the temple and his palace, and he taxed the people oppressively to pay for them. The unrest that this engendered resulted in a rebellion, in which his chief overseer Jeroboam attempted a coup d'état. When it failed he and his fellow conspirators fled to Egypt, where they were given sanctuary. When Solomon died in 922 BCE, his son Rehoboam ascended the throne. Jeroboam soon returned from Egypt with Egyptian forces, however, and tried again to take the throne. He had the support of the disgruntled northern tribes, but Rehoboam held the support of Judah and portions of the southern tribes. Finally, after a long conflict, the United Monarchy was broken into two kingdoms. Jeroboam took the northern tribes and declared himself king of Israel, with his capital at Shechem. Rehoboam retained the throne at Jerusalem as the monarch of the southern kingdom, Judah. The northern tribes had long been flirting with paganism, and Jeroboam encouraged this. The result was that a relatively small remnant of the people remained faithful to the Levitical Law, while the majority allowed their religion to be badly polluted with paganism, and this became worse with subsequent kings. Also, social injustice slowly increased to the point that most of the wealth was controlled by a handful of people, with the vast majority living in abject poverty.

During the period following Solomon's death, the Assyrian Empire in Mesopotamia grew in strength. By the eighth century BCE the northern kingdom, Israel, had become so weakened that the Assyrians swept down and destroyed it, carrying most of the leaders and educated population back to Assyrian captivity. They also sacked Jerusalem and some of the northern cities of Judah, but did not hold them. The southern kingdom

---

turned it. For twenty years it was secretly held for safekeeping at the home of a priest named Abinadab at Kiriath Jearim. When David moved it to Jerusalem he placed it in a tabernacle, which was actually a huge tent. God had forbidden him to build a temple, because he had been a man of war.

survived for another two centuries. During those centuries the Assyrian power weakened, and the Babylonian Empire was on the rise. By the middle of the sixth century BCE Nebuchadrezzar[9] II's Babylon was the controlling kingdom in Mesopotamia. In 597 BCE the Babylonians swept through Palestine, securing what had been the Assyrian holdings and moving further south to capture Judah. They carried all of Judah's artisans, teachers, nobles, and warriors into captivity in Babylon. They returned in 586, when they destroyed Jerusalem and the temple and carried off the rest of the leaders. Those left were unable to organize or rebuild, and thus were no threat to Babylon.

In 536 BCE Cyrus of Persia (today Iran) defeated the Babylonians and released the Assyrian and Babylonian captives to return home. Most of them, especially the long-term Assyrian captives, had become so absorbed into Mesopotamian culture that they preferred to stay, with only the "remnant" returning (cf. Isa. 10:20-23). The Persians continued to rule Palestine until the late fourth century BCE. Theirs was a reasonably benevolent rule, however. They assisted the Jews in the rebuilding of Jerusalem and the temple and protected them from foreign invaders.

In 333 BCE Alexander the Great defeated the Persians and became the ruler of Palestine. Upon his death he left no heirs. He had often said that his heirs would be whoever was strong enough to take and hold his empire, and this eventually fell to three of his generals, Ptolemy, Seleucus, and Antipater. Ptolemy took Egypt, north Africa, and much of the Middle East, including Palestine. Seleucus took the rest the Middle East, and Antipater became the king of Macedonia and Greece. In 198 BCE Seleucus's descendants were able to take and hold the rest of the Middle East from the Ptolemies, establishing what came to be known as the Seleucid Empire. This was oppressive to the Jews, especially by 168 BCE when Antiochus IV Epiphanes became emperor. He devoted himself to the destruction of Judaism, ravaging Jerusalem, dedicating the temple to Zeus Olympius, and sacrificing a pig on the high altar. That turned out to be a grave mistake. The desecration so infuriated the Jews that they revolted, and under the

9. His name is more commonly written as Nebuchadnezzar, although Nebuchadrezzar appears to be more correct. His name was either *Nabû-kudurri-usur,* "Nabu Defend My Boundaries," or *Nabû-kuduni-usur,* "Nabu Defend My Crown." Today the consensus among scholars is that the former is correct. In the early Hebrew script, the symbols for "r" and "n" are similar, and can be easily confused if not carefully written. Also, the Mesopotamian cuneiform, in which the characters stand for syllables, is easily confused between *kuduni,* "crown," and *kudurri,* "boundary stone."

leadership of Judas Maccabaeus they defeated and expelled the Seleucids in 165 BCE. The Maccabees ruled for just over a century, until they were overrun by the Romans in 63 BCE.

In 63 the general Gnaeus Pompeius Magnus (Pompey the Great) swept through the Middle East, capturing everything that Alexander had held and more. His rival and sometime friend was Gaius Julius Caesar, who was doing the same thing in western Europe. Together they more than tripled the size of the Roman holdings in just a few years. Soon thereafter Caesar defeated Pompey in a civil war and gained power over the whole empire.[10] In 47 BCE he appointed Antipas, who came from the territory of Idumea and whose family were converts to Judaism, as procurator (governor) of Judea. After Caesar's assassination in 44 BCE Marc Antony was given authority over Palestine, and in 37 BCE he placed Antipas's son Herod on the throne in Jerusalem as king of Judea. Although king, he was a puppet of Rome. This was satisfactory to him, because he loved everything Roman and held the Jews in contempt. Herod, who came to be known as "Herod the Great," was a cruel and tyrannical king, hated by his subjects. Trying to curry their favor, he embraced Judaism as his father had (but only for show) and built a new temple on the site of the old. Herod's temple was an extraordinarily magnificent edifice, eclipsing even the glory of Solomon's temple. While the Jews accepted it as their center of worship, it did not in any way ingratiate them to Herod. The Romans were content to let Herod do what he wanted, as long as it did not interfere with their interests.[11]

When Herod the Great died in 4 BCE,[12] the Romans divided his kingdom between three of his sons, Herod Antipas, Archelaus, and Philip. These three were not kings in the proper sense (as their father was), but tetrarchs. A tetrarch was a local leader appointed by Rome who served

10. Although the term is apt, Rome was not yet technically an empire. That would not happen until the first emperor, Augustus, ascended the throne in 27 BCE. Even then it was not officially a monarchy, but Augustus would become in effect an absolute ruler.

11. It was Herod the Great who ordered the massacre of the infants in Bethlehem at the time of the birth of Christ. There is no record of it in the Roman annals, but that does not mean it didn't happen. Such massacres were common among Middle Eastern despots, and the Romans, who had little reverence for life, would not have taken much notice of it as long as it did not threaten their power, interfere with Roman taxes and tributes, or endanger any Romans. Despite the Christian tradition, the population of Bethlehem at the time would indicate that no more than fifteen to twenty children would have been slaughtered.

12. Because of the correction of an error in the calendar, Jesus was born between 6 and 4 BCE, not in 1 CE. His birth, therefore, coincided with the end of Herod's reign.

somewhat like a governor with limited royal powers.[13] Archelaus, a tyrant, was tetrarch of Judea and Samaria when Mary and Joseph brought Jesus back from Egypt, which is why they decided to settle in Galilee. Herod Antipas ruled Galilee for forty-three years, but only a few details are known of his rule. He was the Herod who killed John the Baptist, and before whom Jesus stood at his trial. Antipas was eventually banished to Gaul by Caligula, and by the time of Jesus' trial Judea was ruled by a Roman governor, Pontius Pilate,[14] rather than by a tetrarch.

By the middle of the first century CE Palestine, particularly Judea, was in turmoil. Revolts were bursting out regularly, and there was a major one brewing. In 66 CE a full-scale rebellion erupted, and the Romans responded in full force. After three years of severe suppression of the uprisings, Rome was fed up. The general who had commanded the Roman forces, Flavius Vespasian, had recently become emperor of Rome. He authorized his son Titus, now in command, to do whatever was necessary to restore calm to Palestine. Titus responded brutally in 70 CE. He destroyed Jerusalem and razed the temple to the ground. He demolished every city that had supported the revolutionaries and slaughtered Jews by the thousands. The Jewish historian Flavius Josephus reported that Titus barricaded Jerusalem and starved hundreds to death, then crucified Jews until there was no wood left to make crosses.[15] Huge sections of the population fled Judea, some seeking refuge in Galilee but the majority leaving Palestine altogether.[16] This calmed things for a while, but local revolts contin-

13. The term actually means ruler of a fourth, although by this time tetrarchies could be in anything from two to five parts. Originally the Romans often diluted the power of local kingdoms by dividing them into fourths, with a tetrarch over each section. This way the regions could still think of themselves as self-governing monarchies rather than occupied territories, yet Rome could keep a strong control over them.

14. The New Testament is reasonably kind to Pilate. In fact he was a cruel and petty demagogue who had no understanding of the Jews or their religion, and cared even less about them. He came from a rich and powerful Roman family. He was appointed procurator of Judea, in the Romans' eyes a God-forsaken outpost of the empire, because the Romans did not trust him to rule an important post. In 36 CE he was recalled to Rome where he later committed suicide. The Coptic (Egyptian) Church reveres him as a martyr. They believe that he became a Christian and was for this condemned to death by the Senate, but there is no documentary evidence of this.

15. Customarily the Romans left a body on the cross until it decayed to the point that it fell off. This was thought to be a deterrent to other criminals. Because of this, a cross might be in use for some time. Wood was in scarce supply in that arid region, so it is possible that Josephus's claim that they ran out of wood could be true.

16. Titus succeeded his father as emperor of Rome in 79 CE. Despite his cruelty to the

ued for another sixty years. In 132 CE a second major rebellion broke out. This time the Romans again massacred thousands of Jews and tried to drive the rest out of Palestine. Most of the remaining Jewish population fled Palestine, either north, eventually settling in western Asia and Europe, or across the Mediterranean into Iberia and north Africa. Only a small percentage of the original Jewish population remained in Palestine. The emperor Hadrian built a Roman city on the site of Jerusalem, naming it Aelia Capitolina.

As the Roman Empire slowly split into the Western and Eastern (Byzantine) empires, Palestine remained a part of the Roman, and eventually Byzantine, province of Syria. In 313 CE the emperor Constantine legalized Christianity and it was soon declared the official religion of the Roman Empire. Constantine's mother, St. Helena, traveled through Palestine trying to identify the specific locations of biblical events, particularly those in the life of Christ, and as a result Palestine became a focus of Christian pilgrimage. It entered a golden age of peace, growth, and great prosperity, and most of the population became Hellenized and converted to Christianity. In 614 the golden age collapsed, however, when Rome's (and Christianity's) old archenemy Persia invaded and occupied Palestine until 629. The Persians were violently anti-Christian, and launched a brief but cruel persecution of Palestinian Christians. The Romans regained control in 629, but held it only nine years. In 638 Muslim Arab armies invaded Palestine, drove out the Romans, and captured Jerusalem. They called the city *al-Quds al-Sharîf,* "the Noble Sanctuary,"[17] and the country Filistin. The Muslim rulers did not force their religion on the Palestinians. They respected Jews and Christians as "people of the Book," and allowed them freedom to worship, although they tried to encourage conversion by example. Within a century the majority of the population had voluntarily become Muslim, and the people rapidly adopted the Arabic language and culture. The tolerance of the early Muslims is rare in religious history. Un-

---

Jews he was a very good emperor during his short reign, and when he died in 81 CE he was one of Rome's most popular and beloved emperors. His brother Domitian built a huge triumphal arch in the middle of Rome to celebrate his victory over the Jews. On it are reliefs showing the taking of the sacred vessels out of the temple and the carrying of them to Rome. The Arch of Titus still stands today, and by tradition Jews will not walk under it. By an unwritten international understanding, whenever the army of a free nation parades in Rome the Jewish soldiers are permitted to fall out of rank and march around the arch instead of under it.

17. Jerusalem is the third holiest city to Muslims, after Mecca and Medina in Arabia. They believe that Mohammed ascended into heaven from the mount of the temple.

fortunately, by 750 CE fanatic Muslims from Turkey and Baghdad began to wrest power from the moderate Arabic Muslims. They began to take power in Palestine, and with them came persecution and forced conversion of Jews and Christians. Although their rule was brutal and intolerant, it must be said for the Muslims that they preserved the great learning, literature, and art of the ancient Greeks and Romans. As the Roman Empire decayed and collapsed, Europe entered the period known as the Dark Ages, during which an advance of barbarism and violence brought about the loss of most of the Roman and Greek cultures. During this time the Islamic world enjoyed a golden age of intellectual achievement while Europe wallowed in ignorance and brutality. The Muslims' oppression of Christians and the desecration of their holy places incurred the wrath of the Europeans, however, and in 1095 the First Crusade was launched to drive the Muslims from Palestine.

The barbarism of the Crusaders was no less than that of the Muslim fanatics, and under Christian rule the Muslims suffered as much as the Christians had under their rule. The Jews suffered under both. Under the harsh rule of the fanatic Muslim Mamelukes, Palestine declined into neglect, while much of the ancient learning, of which the Muslims had become stewards, crept back into Europe to nourish the birth of the Renaissance. In 1517 CE the Turkish Ottoman Empire captured Palestine and drove out the Mamelukes, and a new era of reasonable religious tolerance began. As much as possible the Ottomans placed the descendants of the ancient Canaanites in power in Palestine. The modern Middle Eastern residents who now call themselves Palestinians claim to be descendants of these people. The region had a resurgence of prosperity for a couple of centuries, but by the end of the seventeenth century the Ottomans were in decline, and Palestine again slipped into neglect. It remained a poor but surviving region through the remainder of the Ottoman rule. At the outbreak of World War I in 1914, in an attempt to shore up their power, the Ottomans unwisely chose to ally with the Germans instead of the British. With the defeat of the Kaiser the Ottoman Empire also fell, and Palestine came under British control. In 1917 the British Parliament authorized the Balfour Declaration, stating an intent to take a part of Palestine and designate it as a homeland for the Jews. In 1922 the League of Nations adopted the Balfour Declaration, and designated the British, under what was called the British Mandate, to expedite the plan. Nothing significant came of this until after World War II, when Europe and the Middle East were flooded with displaced Jews who had lost their homes and families in the Holocaust.

In 1948 the United Nations partitioned Palestine, establishing the State of Israel. The Muslims of the region, who later organized as the Palestinian Liberation Organization (PLO), resisted the partition with terrorism and guerilla warfare. In 1967 several of the neighboring Arab states, under the leadership of Egypt and Jordan, formed a coalition to attack and destroy Israel. The war lasted only six days, with Israel gaining a resounding victory and taking huge amounts of Egyptian and Jordanian territory. Over the course of the following years several treaties were drawn up returning most of the captured territory, although Israel has held on to control of a few strategically important regions such as the West Bank and the Gaza Strip. To this day Palestine is in great turmoil as the conflict between the Israelis and the Palestinians goes on.

# Ai

East-southeast of Bethel was a Canaanite city called Ai. It is unlikely that its original name was Ai, as this is Hebrew for "ruin," or "heap."[1] The Bible always refers to it with the definite article ("the"), calling it *ha'ai,* "the ruin." The Bible says that the city was destroyed by Joshua soon after the defeat of Jericho, and this is probably the source of its Hebrew name. Its Canaanite name is unknown. The names Aiath (Isa. 10:28) and Aija (Neh. 11:31) are variations of Ai.

The Bible has many references to Ai, but the best known is the story in Joshua 7–8. When the Israelites took Jericho, God commanded that everything in the city be destroyed, and that no loot be taken. After the defeat of Jericho the Israelites went on to attack Ai. It was a small town and ill-defended, so they sent only a few men to attack it. Even though they were by far the superior force, however, they were soundly defeated. God then revealed to Joshua that his command had been violated: someone had taken something from Jericho, and there would be no further Israelite victories until this transgression was punished. It was found that a man named Achan had stolen several treasures from the ruins of Jericho (Josh. 7:20). He was executed, the army returned to Ai, and this time they left it "a heap of ruins, as it is to this day" (Josh. 8:28).

One wonders why Joshua attacked Ai instead of the considerably more important nearby city of Bethel. Perhaps Ai was a fortress designed to protect Bethel, in which case it would have been a more important military objective. With the fall of Ai the siege of Bethel might have been much easier. It would have given the Israelites direct access to the Gibeonite plain, the Plains of Benjamin, and the Canaanite cities of that region.

The site of Ai is believed to be at an archaeological dig known as et-Tell, about two miles east-southeast of Bethel, located at a town called Haiyin.[2] There are extensive remains of a prosperous Bronze Age city that

---

1. The Yiddish and modern Hebrew pronunciation of this word is "oy," and it is a common colloquial interjection equivalent to "alas."

2. The Arabic *et-Tell* means "mound of ruins." The modern Arabic name Haiyin could well be a corruption of the Hebrew *ha'aiim,* "the ruins." Another possible site of the city is

was founded around 3000 BCE and that was destroyed by fire sometime between 2500 and 2000. Whether the fire was a disastrous accident or the result of foreign conquest is unknown. The largest building was a huge rectangular temple supported by four great pillars. The city lay in ruins until another Iron Age city arose on the site in the late thirteenth or early twelfth century BCE, but this is believed to be somewhat later than Joshua's conquest (early thirteenth century BCE). The site was unoccupied in Joshua's time.

There are four possible explanations of the time discrepancy of the biblical report of the fall of Ai. One is that the story refers to a recently discovered city that lies beneath Israelite Bethel, and that was destroyed by fire about the time of Joshua. Another is that the story is of a later destruction of the city, and the legendry eventually credited the conquest to the hero Joshua.

The third explanation seems reasonably plausible: The Bible contains several stories that are used as allegories for the sum of Israel's conquests over a long period, and the story of Ai is possibly one of these. The very fact that its name means "ruin" is indicative of this. The city's destruction is quite possibly the work of the Habiru tribe, another Semitic group that moved into Canaan at roughly the same time as the Israelites. They were eventually absorbed into the Israelites, who assimilated much of the Habiru history into their own legendry. The very name "Hebrew" is believed to be a corruption of "Habiru."[3]

The fourth is perhaps the most likely explanation. It is unusual for pure legendry to attribute a failure to a great hero, so it is probable that the story of the fall of Ai is to some degree based on historical fact. Although there was no active city there at the time of Joshua, it is entirely reasonable that the local peoples would have used the ruins and the outer walls as a fortification to impede an attacker approaching their cities. If they knew of the approach of the Hebrews and mustered an army there to defend against the Hebrew attack, the king might well have been there too.

---

the archaeological site Khirbet Nysia, but this site presents even more problems than et-Tell with respect to the timing of Joshua's conquest.

3. Many scholars believe that the Israelites and the Habiru may have been the same people. Others believe that the Habiru were eventually absorbed by the Israelites, and that their name is the origin of the name "Hebrew." Still others believe that the story of the Egyptian captivity is pure myth, and that the Hebrews/Israelites were a Canaanite tribe that underwent a period of military territorial expansion.

Joshua's slaughter of the army and the king might have evolved over time into a story of the defeat of an actual city.

Ai is referred to a number of times in the Old Testament. Long before Joshua's time, Abraham, upon first entering the Promised Land, camped between Ai and Bethel, built an altar, and "called upon the name of the Lord" (Gen. 12:8; cf. Gen. 13:3). Upon returning from Egypt he went back to the same place, which obviously had some spiritual significance to him. The city was in the land of the Ephraimites (1 Chron. 7:20-28), a troublesome and rebellious Jewish tribe. After the return from the Babylonian exile, however, it was settled by the Benjaminites, Saul's tribe (Neh. 11:31).

# Alexandria

Although Alexandria is mentioned only three times in the Bible (in the book of Acts), and then only in passing, it was nonetheless a major city in the ancient world. For much of its history it was a cultural and political mecca, for a brief period almost rivaling Rome.

About 1500 BCE there was a small fishing city on the Egyptian Mediterranean, some fifteen miles west of the mouth of the Nile at the west angle of the Nile delta. It was located on a narrow isthmus between the Mediterranean and Lake Mareotis. Off the coast was the island of Pharos, which was essentially deserted except for a few fishing huts. The city was called Rhakotis, and it had no particular significance until 332 BCE, when Alexander the Great conquered Egypt. He built a suburb to the west and called it Neapolis ("New City"), combined it with Rhakotis, and named the new complex Alexandria after himself. (Alexander founded dozens of cities, all named "Alexandria." Alexandria in Egypt, however, "the jewel of the Middle Sea," was by far the most important.) He built a mile-long mole to connect Pharos to the mainland, thus creating two well-protected harbors, with a lighthouse on the western end of the island. The western harbor and port are still active today. Soon after the completion of the city Alexander left, never to see it again. After his death, however, his body was returned to be entombed there. Almost three centuries later Julius Caesar would honor him as a god, and worship at his tomb in Alexandria.

After Alexander's death in 323 BCE, Egypt and most of northern Africa fell under the control of one of his generals, Ptolemy,[1] who soon thereafter named himself pharaoh of Egypt, establishing Alexandria as his capital.

---

1. Alexander refused to name a successor. He said that his empire should go to those who were strong enough to take and keep it. After his death, a power struggle eventually resulted in the division of the empire between three of his generals, Ptolemy, Seleucus, and Antipater. Ptolemy took Egypt, north Africa, and much of the Middle East, including Palestine. Seleucus took part of the Middle East, and Antipater became the king of Macedonia and Greece. Soon thereafter Seleucus was able to take and hold the rest of the Middle East. Alexander's prime goal was the conquest of the Persian Empire, which he accomplished. He planned eventually to move west and take Italy and Spain, but he did not live long enough to do so. In his time Rome was a growing republic, many years away from becoming an empire.

His dynasty lasted almost three centuries, ending with the death of Cleopatra in 30 BCE. The early Ptolemies were dedicated to making Alexandria the cultural center of the world, and in many respects they succeeded. They established the Museum and the Royal Library, called "Mother and Daughter," which very soon attracted scholars from all over the known world. The museum was in effect a university, and some of the greatest teachers of ancient times visited and studied there. While in modern usage the term "museum" refers to a place where items of value are collected, studied, and displayed, the term actually means "shrine of the Muses." In ancient times a museum was primarily a place of learning by discussion and dialogue, not a place to display collections of works. The collection of knowledge in the Great Library, as it was called, was never rivaled until the creation of the modern Library of Congress.[2] It is believed that it contained the original writings of most of the great ancient Hellenic and Roman historians, mathematicians, and philosophers, including those of Socrates, Plato, and Alexander's tutor, Aristotle.[3]

In 280 BCE the pharaoh Ptolemy II replaced Alexander's small lighthouse on Pharos with a 440-foot-high one. A spectacular edifice, it is considered one of the seven wonders of the ancient world. It operated for over six centuries until it was severely damaged by an earthquake in 334 CE. It was totally destroyed by another earthquake in the fourteenth century CE.

Soon after its founding Alexandria took over the maritime trade that was once controlled by the Phoenicians, and within a century it was larger than Carthage. For several centuries thereafter, the only city more powerful than Alexandria was Rome. As a free city it held its own senate until it fell under Roman power in the first century BCE, but even after that it was allowed to operate with a minimum of Roman control, almost as if it were

2. The 1800 act that established the Library of Congress was encouraged by Vice President Thomas Jefferson, who recognized the value to the ancient world of the Great Library of Alexandria. After the British burned the Library of Congress in 1814, Jefferson, taking a large financial loss, sold his personal library of about sixty-five hundred volumes to it. Today it is acknowledged as the largest and best general library in the world.

3. One of the most heinous acts of barbarism in history was the destruction of the Great Library, believed by many to have taken place in 48 BCE when Caesar was putting down a revolt in Alexandria. The burning of the library may have been an accident, but many scholars believe the library was torched by the Romans. They knew that it was so prized by the Egyptians that they would divert their attention to fight the fire rather than defend the city. Many great works of antiquity were lost, as the library held the only existing copies. None of Socrates' writings survived, and today all we know of him comes from the writings of his student Plato.

still independent. It was rich with magnificent temples and public buildings, and it had the reputation of being one of the most impressive cities on the entire Mediterranean coast.

Alexandria was not only the greatest Hellenic city but also the greatest Jewish center in the world. In fact, the Alexandrian Jews had far greater influence on worldwide Judaism than did those of Jerusalem.[4] It was in Alexandria that the Septuagint, the Greek translation of the Hebrew Bible, was made in the third century BCE by the Jewish School of Torah.[5] The reason for the translation was that the majority of Jews outside of Palestine could no longer read Hebrew. The lingua franca of the time was Greek, and every educated person anywhere in the ancient known world knew Greek. The great Jewish scholar Philo Judaeus was an Alexandrian. He proposed the concept, later also espoused by many Christians, that the one God had partially revealed himself to the pagan Greek philosophers, who often used the term "God" instead of "the gods."

Over time Alexandria began to decline in its political and economic influence, although it was nevertheless still a power to be reckoned with. It eventually came officially under Roman jurisdiction in 80 BCE, when Ptolemy XI Alexander died and left the city to Rome in his will. Although he was succeeded by his son Ptolemy XII (Cleopatra's father), from that time on Egypt's pharaohs were puppets of Rome. While Egypt was officially an independent nation, it was in effect a province of Rome.

In 51 BCE seventeen-year-old Cleopatra and her twelve-year-old brother, Ptolemy XIII, ascended the throne as co-rulers on the condition that they would marry when Ptolemy came of legal age. Three years later Ptolemy's counselors managed to wrest full power from Cleopatra and exiled her, leaving him as the sole ruler.

4. After Alexander's conquest of the Middle East in the fourth century BCE, Israel and Judah remained under foreign rule, with only a brief respite under Judas Maccabaeus, until after World War II. Although Jerusalem remained the religious center of Judaism until the destruction of the temple in 70 CE, most of the great Jewish intellectuals were to be found elsewhere, primarily in Alexandria and Antioch.

5. The translation began in the time of Ptolemy II in the third century BCE, with the translation of the Pentateuch (the first five books of the Old Testament). The translation of the remaining books has a very complicated history, probably being completed sometime near the end of the second century BCE. The translation is called the Septuagint, from the Greek for "seventy," because according to tradition it was made by seventy scholars in seventy days. In fact, it was done by hundreds of scholars over a period of more than a century. There is evidence, however, that there were seventy-two rabbis involved in the first part, the translation of the Written Torah (the "Pentateuch," the first five books of the Bible).

Ptolemy supported Pompey in the Roman civil wars, and gave him refuge when he fled to Egypt. He eventually betrayed and killed him, however, when he realized that Caesar now ruled Rome. Caesar entered Alexandria in 48 BCE in pursuit of Pompey, only to be presented with Pompey's head by Ptolemy. He was furious that his old friend and honorable enemy had met such an ignoble death. The exiled Cleopatra arranged to be secretly brought to Caesar wrapped in a rug, so that she could convince him to restore her to the throne. He did so, making her equal co-ruler with her brother. Ptolemy's followers instigated an uprising of the people against Caesar, and it may have been in this revolt that the Great Library was burned. The following year Caesar arranged to have Ptolemy killed in battle, leaving Cleopatra as undisputed pharaoh. Despite an age difference of thirty-one years, Caesar and Cleopatra had a love affair that lasted until his assassination three years later. She bore him a son, Ptolemy XV, better known as Caesarion. Octavian (later to become Augustus, the first emperor of Rome) murdered him shortly after Cleopatra's death fifteen years later.

After Caesar's assassination, Cleopatra had an affair with Caesar's friend and deputy Marc Antony, who became obsessively infatuated with her. It was a turbulent love affair, marred by Antony's notorious womanizing and his eventual marriage (for political expediency only) to Octavian's sister Octavia. As Antony's relationship with Octavian decayed, Octavian began a slander campaign against Antony, also maligning Cleopatra. He falsely accused Antony of ceding almost a third of the Roman Empire to her, precipitating a long-threatened civil war that ended in the destruction of Antony's army at the Battle of Actium in 31 BCE. Antony and Cleopatra fled back to Alexandria to try to recoup their losses, but in vain. They both committed suicide in 30 BCE, he by falling on his sword, and she by poison (according to tradition she allowed herself to be bitten by an asp). Egypt was annexed as a Roman province, and ruled by a prefect from Octavian's household. Alexandria, however, remained the capital of the province. Since Egypt was one of the richest provinces in the Roman Empire, the city prospered and flourished.

Christianity came to Alexandria very early. Because of the huge Jewish population there, the first Christians appeared in Alexandria at the time that they still considered themselves a Jewish sect. There were very likely Alexandrian Jews among those who were converted in Jerusalem on the first Christian Pentecost (Acts 2:41). There is no biblical reference to any missionary visit, although ancient tradition holds that Saint Mark preached there. The Christian catechetical school in Alexandria had strong influence on Christianity in the Mediterranean regions for centuries.

In 215 CE the Roman emperor Caracalla, in retribution for some alleged insults, massacred thousands of Alexandrians — Christian, Jewish, and pagan. In spite of this, the city recovered and was quickly restored to its former splendor, being considered second only to Rome itself.

Alexandria was not only a cultural center of the classical world but developed as a primary center of Christian theology and church government. It was also a center of many controversies. The Arian heresy[6] was founded in Alexandria, and it was also there that Arianism was quashed by St. Athanasius, the Bishop of Alexandria (328-373). Christianity in Alexandria became richly infused with many Egyptian cultural customs, producing a uniquely Egyptian form of worship known as Coptic Christianity[7] that still flourishes today. While it was not infected with Egyptian paganism, Coptic Christianity struggled for centuries with an ancient heresy known as Monophysitism.[8] This conflict, dividing Egyptian Christians, weakened the church and would help enable the Arabic Muslims to play one faction against the other and conquer Egypt in the seventh century CE.

As the Roman Empire crumbled, Alexandria declined with it. In an attempt to survive the decay of Egypt, the city tried to become an independent city-state, but without success. It fell to the Persians in 616 CE, and then to the Arabs in 646. The building of Cairo in 969 and the opening of the Cape of Good Hope as a passage to the East in 1498 fairly well destroyed what was left of Alexandria's commerce. The canal to the Nile became blocked up, and by the time Napoleon took the city in 1798 it was hardly more than a large town.

The Bible pays amazingly little attention to Alexandria, considering its huge importance throughout much of ancient history. The main reason

6. Arianism, founded by a priest named Arius, taught that Christ is not divine but was created by God as a separate creature second only to God himself, higher than the angels, but nonetheless a creature. Arianism also denies the doctrine of the Trinity (the teaching that the One God is Father, Son, and Holy Spirit). The modern extrapolation of Arianism is the Jehovah's Witnesses, who also deny the Trinity and honor the teachings of Arius.

7. From the Arabic *Qupt,* "Egyptian."

8. Monophysitism teaches that Christ had only one nature, the divine, and only appeared to be human. Orthodox Christianity teaches that he assumed total humanity, and thus has two natures, divine and human. To some extent monophysitism is still found in the Coptic Church, although recent discussions with Eastern Orthodox theologians indicate that today this is more tradition than basic belief, and that a restoration to full communion with the Orthodox churches is likely in the near future.

for this is that the rise of the city after Alexander's time coincided with the decline of Judea. Alexander's conquests marked at the same time the beginning of Alexandria and the beginning of the end of Israel. Similarly, as Christianity arose and the Christian Scriptures were being written, Alexandria was in a state of corruption and decline. The city began too late to be noted by the Jews, and declined too early to draw much attention from the early Christians.

Alexandria's renaissance to importance in modern times began in the mid-nineteenth century with the Egyptian viceroy Mohammed Ali, who wanted a deep port and powerful naval station in his domain. The western harbor that had been built by Alexander the Great two thousand years earlier had never filled in, and still protected an ideal port. Ali developed the port and expanded the city, making it almost an equal to Cairo. During both world wars Alexandria was a critical strategic center in the Mediterranean. Today it is one of the most important naval centers on the Mediterranean, and is becoming increasingly popular among Egyptians as a resort.

# Antioch

Antioch, the now insignificant city known as Antakya, Turkey, was once considered one of the most important cities in the Roman Empire, ranking behind only Rome and Alexandria. It was founded at the end of the fourth century BCE by Seleucus I Nicator, one of Alexander the Great's generals. After Alexander's death his empire was divided up among his generals, and Seleucus managed to gain control of Asia Minor and much of the Middle East, later adding a large portion of Greece and Macedonia to his realm (although he held these only briefly). He founded the city at a critical navigational point on the Orontes River, only about fifteen miles from the Mediterranean coast, in what was then the northern part of Syria. Its location was a major point on the land trade routes between Asia Minor, Syria, and Palestine, and it was centrally located in Seleucid territory. It was located on a bend of the river, assuring a plentiful water supply. The land around it was richly fertile, and it was appropriately near the luxurious resort of Daphne. It had only two disadvantages — it was subject to flooding, and it was the site of frequent earthquakes. Seleucus named the city after his father Antiochus, who had been one of Philip of Macedon's (Alexander's father's) generals. It had its own port, Seleucia Pieria, where the Orontes flowed into the Mediterranean. Seleucia was founded before Antioch, and was originally designed as the capital of Seleucus's territory. After he built Antioch, Seleucia took a very secondary place to that great city, eventually serving only as its port. Seleucus actually founded sixteen cities named Antioch, but this was by far the most glorious and most important.[1]

The city began to prosper as soon as it was founded. Seleucus established a very forward-thinking government, in that all settlers, regardless of race or religion, were given equal privileges of citizenship. Because of this and its proximity to Judah (about three hundred miles north of Jerusalem),

---

1. In classical times it was common for a country to have more than one town with the same name. They were distinguished by additional descriptive names. For example, there were two Bethlehems in Palestine, Bethlehem of Judea (where David and Jesus were born) and Bethlehem of Galilee (a town near Nazareth).

Antioch quickly attracted a large Jewish population. The city was divided into eighteen districts, each of which elected delegates to a common governing council. Seleucus's successors continued to enlarge and beautify the city, building magnificent temples and public buildings. Because of geography and surges of building programs, it was divided into three roughly equal parts. About 170 BCE the Seleucid emperor Antiochus IV Epiphanes[2] built a fourth major section of the city, and thereafter Antioch was often called "Tetrapolis," "Four-City." It was an extraordinarily prosperous trade and cultural center.

With the Roman conquest in 64 CE by Pompey the Great, Antioch became an important military center because of its strategic location on the river. Pompey immediately declared it a free city, meaning that it could have its own senate and had full legal rights to engage in international trade. He made it the capital city of the Roman province of Syria (which covered most of the Middle East), and it rapidly became the third largest and third most important city in all the Roman holdings, behind only Rome and Alexandria.[3] It was well defended, as Pompey stationed several garrisons of reserve troops in the city and surrounding areas. Over the years it enjoyed the largesse of a series of important Roman benefactors, including Julius Caesar and the emperors Augustus and Tiberius, and it was the center of operations for Rome's wars against the Persians. The Romans built public works, baths, and temples, enlarging the city even more. So many trade goods and people moved back and forth between Antioch and Rome that the Roman satirist Juvenal quipped that the Orontes had become a tributary of the Tiber.

King Herod the Great was also a benefactor of Antioch. As a puppet ruler appointed by Rome, he was anxious to show his loyalty to the ruling power. This did little to endear him to his own subjects, the Jews, although that seems to have mattered little to him. In fact he was not a Jew but an Idumean, and even though he espoused Judaism because of political necessity, he held the Jews in the same contempt with which they held him.

2. Antiochus Epiphanes was the emperor who captured Jerusalem from the dynasty of Ptolemy, and so oppressed Judea that the Jews rebelled under the leadership of Judas Maccabaeus. They gained independence and remained a free state for over one hundred years until they were conquered in 64 BCE by the Roman general Pompey the Great.

3. At the time Pompey took Antioch, Alexandria was not yet officially a part of the Roman Republic, even though it already was in effect. Not many years hence, however, Cleopatra would lose Egypt to Rome at the Battle of Actium, making Alexandria a Roman possession.

Herod's gift to Antioch was a marble-paved colonnaded avenue that served as the main street of the city. It was 2¼ miles long, lined with porticoes supported by 3,200 marble columns.

Despite its good treatment under the Seleucids and then under Rome, Antioch had a reputation for insolent independence that often expressed itself in rebellion. These rebellions were never a serious threat to Rome or the stability of the city, however. Rome generally ignored them or put them down with a mild slap on the wrist, much like an indulgent mother might treat an impertinent child. This indomitable spirit also fostered rich cultural development, however, and was thus commended by many of the great Roman intelligentsia, including Cicero.

Antioch became the center of control of the entire region from Asia Minor to Syria and Palestine. The Seleucids were a Hellenistic (Greek-cultured) dynasty, and they infused Hellenistic practices and values into all the local cultures. Most accepted this, since Hellenization raised the standard of living in the area considerably. The Romans, who had great admiration for the Greeks, supported and encouraged this influence.[4] The Jews, however, resisted strongly, although the pagan Hellenic culture was attractive to the youth, who were easily lured away from their adherence to the Judaic Law. Physicians even developed a surgical graft to undo circumcision. To the Jews, Antioch was the symbol of this threat to their faith and culture. Notwithstanding, there was a large Jewish community in Antioch, supporting many synagogues and prosperous businesses. They kept themselves separate from their Hellenistic neighbors as much as possible, although their ethics and commitment to their faith were very attractive to many Gentiles.[5] Many committed themselves to the Jewish moral law even though they did not follow the ceremonial law. They were known as "God-fearers." It is likely that Nicolas of Anti-

4. The Romans so admired the Greeks that every upper-class Roman child was expected to be educated by a Greek slave. Any Roman who did not speak fluent Attic Greek (without an accent) was considered low-class and vulgar. The patrician Gaius Marius, one of the richest men in Rome, served as Rome's head of state seven times in the first century BCE, but was considered boorish and was shunned by many patricians because he was a man "with no Greek"; his Greek was fluent, but he spoke it with a northern accent. A few years later Julius Caesar, also a patrician and fluent in Greek, was reproached by the Senate for writing his commentaries on the Gallic Wars in Latin instead of Greek.

5. The term "Gentile" is generally used today to refer to any non-Jew, even though "gentiles" originally referred to persons of the same clan or tribe. In ancient times the Jews used the term "Greek" in the same way — regardless of real race or nationality, they called any non-Jew a Greek.

och, who would later become a Christian and one of the first seven deacons, was a God-fearer.

Christianity reached Antioch very early. Many Jews were converted, as were many God-fearers. The Jews of Antioch did not have the same antipathy for the Christians as did those in Jerusalem, perhaps in part because Antioch was a well-ordered and peaceful city, unfamiliar with the constant rebellion and turmoil of Jerusalem. Also, the Antiochene Jews had little sympathy with the fanatic revolutionary Jewish fringe groups that flourished in Palestine, among whom were those who actively persecuted Christians. There were considerably fewer disturbances in Antioch than in Jerusalem centered on the Jews' rejection of the Christians. The Christian community flourished in the midst of Antioch's dissolute pagan society, and the city quickly became a major center of Christianity in the East. Antioch was world-famous for its profligate behavior, centered around its orgiastic worship of the sun god Apollo. Despite the strong presence of this decadence, the Christians managed to remain uncorrupted, and their church grew rapidly.

When the Sanhedrin's persecution of Christians in Jerusalem intensified after the martyrdom of Saint Stephen, many Christians fled to other cities, with a large number going to Antioch. There they preached primarily to the Jews, many still believing that to become a Christian one must first become a Jew. Very soon, however, many Gentile converts began preaching there, attracting more converts from among the God-fearers and the Greek intellectuals.

Antioch was a hotbed of Greek mystery and Gnostic cults. These cults taught that the gods revealed divine secrets to a select elite, who were to keep the secrets exclusively to themselves. These secrets enabled the initiates to have special divine protection and a guarantee of privilege in the afterlife.[6] Because of these cults, Antioch attracted many people with a broad intellectual and religious curiosity, and slowly the city became a center of intellectual pursuit. This offered rich fodder for the Christian preachers, who converted a large number of intellectually superior people. As a result, Antioch developed into a Christian theological center.

6. There is evidence that several centuries earlier the Greek mathematician Pythagoras was the founder of a Gnostic cult (from the Greek *gnosis*, "knowledge"). The Pythagoreans made many profound mathematical discoveries, but most were lost because the cult kept them secret. The so-called Pythagorean Theorem and other Pythagorean discoveries are known today only because later disciples "leaked" them. Gnosticism also infected Christianity during the second and third centuries. While it was a danger to orthodoxy in much of the Greek world for a while, it did not survive.

The harbor wall of Antioch would have greeted Saints Barnabas and Paul upon their arrival there to preach and minister. It was in Antioch that believers were first called "Christians."   Photo credit: Erich Lessing/Art Resource, NY

Rome improved the roads in the province and secured the seaport, making trade and transportation even faster and safer. This proved a great boon to the early Christian missionaries. Travel was difficult and perilous, but excellent roads, the *Pax Romana* ("Roman Peace"), and powerful police protection reduced the danger significantly.

The church in Jerusalem sent Saint Barnabas to Antioch, and he in turn brought Saint Paul. The two of them spent a year there, teaching and building up the church. They called their teaching "the Way." It was in Antioch at this time that the movement was first called "Christian" (*Christianous*, Acts 11:26). The term may originally have been pejorative. In Greek, *Christos* means "Messiah" or "Anointed One," but *chrestos* means "fool." It is also possible that the term "Christian" was created by the police to designate this new sect which the Jews repudiated.[7]

---

7. Rome required that religions be licensed in order to be legal. To be licensed, the members of the religion had to add the Roman gods to their own list of gods, and in return

Little is known about the size, organization, or daily practices of the Antiochene Christian community. They unquestionably did what was done in all the other cities, meeting in private homes, where they prayed and shared in "the breaking of the bread" (the Eucharist). It is likely that at first the Jewish Christians met separately from the Gentile converts, because Jewish law forbade eating with Gentiles. This separation, of course, was soon dropped. There was a controversy in the church as to whether Christians were bound by the Jewish Law. The church in Antioch sent Paul and Barnabas as delegates to a conference in Jerusalem to deal with this issue. There is evidence that Paul's letter to the Galatians was written in Antioch just before his departure for Jerusalem. The "Judaizing" controversy was later resolved when it was determined that the New Covenant replaced the Old.

One of the great theologians at the end of the first century was St. Ignatius of Antioch (d. 117 CE), who served for many years as the Bishop of Antioch. It is believed that he was old enough to remember when St. Paul was there. One of his great contributions was his affirmation of the "threefold ministry," that of bishops, priests, and deacons, which was obviously in place as early as his time. It was he who argued that without a bishop there is no church, and this teaching has been held by the Catholic churches ever since.

Antioch remained an important city in Christian circles, although as the Roman Empire declined, so did the political importance of the city. In 636 it was captured by Arab Muslim armies who were very tolerant of the Christian and Jewish populations there. It was recaptured by Byzantine Christians in 969, but then fell to the fanatical anti-Christian Seljuk Turks in 1084. They were unseated by crusaders in 1098 after a seven-month siege, but the crusaders were soon thereafter badly weakened by disease and famine. They managed to resist the Muslims, however, retaining power until 1268. In that year the Sultan of Egypt and Syria, Baybars I, descended upon the city and slaughtered or enslaved over 100,000 of its inhabitants. In 1401 the city was again scourged, this time by the Turkmen

---

their gods would be worshiped in the Roman Pantheon, a temple dedicated to every god in the world. This was no problem to most of the pagan world, but polytheism was totally offensive to the Jews. They resisted it so strongly that to keep the peace the Romans licensed Judaism and allowed the Jews to worship only God as long as they would swear political loyalty to Rome. At first the Christians were thought to be a sect of Judaism, and were therefore legal. When the Jews denied the Christians, however, and they too refused to worship the Roman gods, Rome declared Christianity an illicit religion. This later led to persecution.

Mongol Timur Lang ("Tamberlaine" or "Tamerlane"), who leveled it. In 1432 a French traveler found only three hundred houses there, all occupied by herdsmen and peasants. The city was taken by the Ottoman Empire in 1516, and remained in its hands until the empire's fall in 1918. It passed back and forth between many controlling nations until it became part of Turkey in 1939. Today it survives as Antakya, a city of little importance other than as an archaeological site. Unfortunately, most of the ruins lie beneath the present town, and the Turkish government will not permit excavation there.

# Armageddon

The name of Armageddon strikes fear into the hearts of many because it is associated with the final battle between good and evil, and bodes the end of the world. It comes from a loose Greek transliteration of the Hebrew *Har-Magedon* (translated by many, but not all, as "Hill of Megiddo"), and it plays an important role in the book of Revelation. Contrary to the common impression of its frequency, the name Armageddon appears only once in the Bible, in Revelation 16:16. It is supposedly the place where the final battle between good and evil will take place at the end of all things. A careful reading of Revelation, however, reveals that Armageddon is only where the armies of good and evil will amass and prepare. The actual battle will take place elsewhere, most likely at "the Great City," generally interpreted to mean Jerusalem or Babylon (biblical symbols of good and evil). Nonetheless, the horror, well supported by the imagery of the Revelation, is deeply planted in the fears of many, Christian and non-Christian alike. In common use, the word has come to mean a disastrous end, usually implying a cataclysm "of biblical proportions" (whatever that overworked phrase is supposed to mean). The recent movie *Armageddon,* for example, is about the potential destruction of the earth by a giant asteroid on a collision course with it.

There is strong argument among biblical scholars as to whether Armageddon refers to an allegorical concept or a real place called Megiddo; and if the latter, which of the several possible Megiddos it might be. If the term is purely symbolic, then geographical exactness is irrelevant, and no physical description can be given of it other than that of the Revelation imagery.

There are two locations that are most likely if Armageddon refers to a geographical spot. One is the Galilean city of Megiddo (on which, see p. 138). The reason that this may be likely is that the land surrounding Megiddo was used several times by Jews, Greeks, and Romans as a spot to assemble and prepare troops. Another site is Tell-Megiddo, an artificial mound in the Plains of Jezreel that was a Canaanite fortification captured by the Israelites under Joshua's command. Over two hundred important battles were fought in the immediate region surrounding Tell-Megiddo.

The name would therefore be a reference to violent warfare that every Jew would immediately recognize.

My personal preference is the allegorical interpretation, because most of the book of Revelation is allegorical, and because the name "Armageddon" appears only in that book. The Revelation was a vision given to Saint John the Divine. It was given not to reveal specific details of the future but to reveal the nature of things to come. An analysis of the Hebrew name *Har-Magedon* seems to support an allegorical interpretation of the term "Armageddon,"[1] and if such an interpretation is correct, then it lends weight to the belief that the name is purely symbolic and does not refer to any specific geographic or political location, in Palestine or anywhere else. It simply refers to the final confrontation in which God's forces defeat evil.

Many biblical references indicate that regardless of whether it is allegorical or physical, the final confrontation will be a real point in history, and will involve real persons who will encounter God's justice. Jesus stated clearly, however, that the time and place of this confrontation are not given to us to know. It is a basic Christian teaching that since the time of the confrontation is unknown, we must constantly be prepared for it by maintaining a righteous life. Many other religions have a similar teaching of a final confrontation, with the same admonition: be prepared.

1. In Hebrew, *har* means "hill" or "mountain." The noun *Magedo* can be a secondary grammatical derivation of the Hebrew verb *gadad,* "to gather as armies." In Hebrew, a verb can be converted to a noun by prefixing it with *ma-*. Thus *maged* would be "the gathering of armies." The suffix *-o* means "his." *Har-Magedo,* then, would mean "the hill of the gathering of his armies." When this is transliterated into Greek (which requires a case ending), it becomes *Armageddon.*

# Athens

Athens, the capital of modern Greece, has been at the heart of Greek society from the earliest of ancient times, and played a major role in the development of classical culture. Named after Athena (the goddess of wisdom, the practical arts, and warfare), it was the chief city of the ancient district of Attica. It is a city of art and architecture, having produced more magnificent buildings and sculpture, in both the Greek and Roman styles, than anywhere else in the ancient world. Although Saint Paul preached there, he did not found an Athenian church.

The first settlement on the site was in the late Stone Age, about 3000 BCE, on the great rock that forms the Acropolis (Greek for "High City"). This rock outcrop made the village easily defensible, and by the late Bronze Age (about 1500 BCE) there was a well-fortified citadel there. A staircase cut in the stone led to an underground reservoir that provided a generous water supply even when the city was under siege. By the end of the Bronze Age, Athens had attained significant wealth and power. It apparently survived the Dorian invasions with little damage to either its physical or its cultural structure.

The collapse of Agamemnon's Mycenaean Empire at the end of the Bronze Age (about 1150 BCE) plunged the whole Mediterranean world into a great depression and deep poverty. There is evidence, however, that by the Geometric Period in the early Iron Age, about 1000 BCE,[1] Athens was a large city with a well defined Attic culture. It returned only slowly to prosperity, and with this return, power fell into the hands of a small but very oppressive hereditary aristocracy. Their power came from an unusual source: they played on the religious superstition of the masses, claiming to have a secret system of law given to them directly by the gods. This was a corruption of the beliefs of those in the Gnostic cults, who taught that the gods imparted secret information to them to enable them to achieve great happiness and power in the next life, not this one. The power-brokers finally lost their grip on the people in a rebellion in 621 BCE. A noble named

---

1. This is about the same time that King David defeated the Philistines and unified the tribes of Israel into the United Monarchy, taking Jerusalem as his capital.

Cylon tried to usurp all power and become sole ruler, but his attempt was crushed by a popular uprising. The rebellion spread, and the nobility lost the power of secret law.

Athens's great leap forward as a cultural giant came in the sixth century BCE. In 594 Solon was made Chief Magistrate and was given practically dictatorial powers to help pull Athens out of another crushing economic depression resulting from the political upheaval. He broke the ruling power of the hereditary aristocracy and established a social and political structure that protected the rights of all citizens, regardless of class. He came to be known as Solon the Lawgiver,[2] and is generally credited with establishing the first democracy. Although it was not completely democratic, as the preponderance of power was held by the wealthy landowners, Solon did abolish privilege by birth. He established four classes based on property and ability to pay taxes. The upper three classes ruled by a democratic vote — voting was by a show of hands at meetings in the public square — and even the lowest class had a voice in all assemblies. This democratic rule ushered in the early phases of Athens's "Golden Age." The system spread throughout Attica and even beyond into other Greek districts.

The reign of Pisistratus and his sons (560?-510 BCE) launched a massive building campaign, in which the entire city was essentially rebuilt. They erected many great buildings, temples, and public works, including the Academy, a huge gymnasium[3] that would eventually become the School of Plato. In about 509 Kleisthenes reformed Solon's democratic system, making it even more egalitarian. Every free man, regardless of social class or property, had an equal vote. It would be reasonable to call Kleisthenes the true founder of Athenian democracy.

Athens flourished, enjoying great wealth and power, for only a brief

2. Solon left such a mark on the world's legislative concepts that to this day a wise legislator is known as a "solon."

3. A Greek gymnasium was much more than an athletic arena. It was also a place of learning and philosophical discussion. The Greeks placed great value on intellectual achievement, but they also valued physical and athletic ability, believing that a sound mind could exist only in a sound body. Although there were athletic competitions for women in ancient Greece, women could not compete in the Olympic games, and married women were not even permitted to attend them. Pausanius tells the story of Callipateira, who broke this rule to see her son compete at the games. She disguised herself as a trainer, but when she jumped over an enclosure, her disguise fell away, revealing her sex. From that time on trainers as well as athletes were required to strip. The word *gymnasium* is a Latin derivative of the Greek *gymnazein,* "to exercise naked."

time. In 480 BCE the Persians attacked, and after a siege of less than a year Athens was almost completely destroyed. The Persians could not take the city, however. Under the military direction of Themistocles, the Athenian navy routed and burned the Persian fleet, and the Athenians managed to rebuild their navy and drive off the Persians in the Battle of Salamis. The Athenians continued the pursuit of the Persians, and with an alliance of other Greek city-states they drove them back to the Middle East. Athens's leadership in this campaign thrust it into the presidency of the newly formed Delian League, a confederation of primarily maritime Greek city-states. This threatened the tense but relatively peaceful relationship with Athens's ancient rival Sparta (which headed the land-based Peloponnesian League).

After the defeat of the Persians, an intensive rebuilding program was begun under the rules of Themistocles (480-461) and Pericles (461-429). The jewel in the crown of this reconstruction was the Parthenon, a huge temple to the goddess Athena. This is considered the very finest example of Doric architecture, and is often lauded as the most beautiful building ever erected. Pericles also reformed the Athenian democracy even further, placing full governmental power in the hands of the common people. This was also the era of Socrates, who, along with his student Plato and Plato's student Aristotle, is ranked among the greatest philosophers of all time. Socrates did not run a formal school, but stood in the public square debating with anyone who cared to take him on. He was the ultra-liberal of his day and was finally condemned to death for "corrupting the youth of Athens." Sad to say, none of his writings survives. All we know of him comes from the writings of Plato.

Pericles also began a period of rapid expansion, in which Athens gained territory throughout the Aegean. The years 443 to 429 were the most glorious in Athenian history, with the Delian League having become in effect an Athenian empire; but Athens's glory was not to last. Fiercely militaristic Sparta had also been growing in power, and in 431 war broke out between the long-time rivals. The Peloponnesian Wars (so named for the Peloponnesus, a peninsula in southern Greece on which Sparta was located) culminated in 404 BCE with the defeat of Athens. Athens was not destroyed, and in honor of its leadership of the Delian League it was granted a very tolerable peace; but Sparta was for the next thirty-some years the paramount Greek state.

It was some years after Athens's defeat that Plato, in 387 BCE, established his school, the Academy, on the grounds of the great gymnasium. In

367 the seventeen-year-old son of a Macedonian royal physician was sent to Athens to study with Plato. This was Aristotle, who remained in Athens until Plato's death in 347 BCE. He returned to Macedonia in 345 as the tutor to King Philip's young son Alexander, who a few years later would gain the appellation "the Great."

After its defeat in the Peloponnesian Wars in 404 BCE, Athens rose again and flourished. It slowly began re-expanding its influence, avoiding the reckless expansion of Pericles. In 395 it joined the Corinthian League, and it began rebuilding its leadership of the Delian League. When Philip II of Macedon (Alexander's father) threatened Greece, Athens rose up, inspired by the fiery oratory of Demosthenes,[4] and led the rest of the Greek city-states in resisting him. One may admire the courage and patriotism of the Athenians, but considering Philip's juggernaut it was obvious from the beginning that it was a lost cause. In 338 Philip achieved a total victory at Chaeronea, but he had such respect for the city of Athens and its culture that he offered the Athenians peace with honor, and they accepted. While they were technically under Macedonian rule, they were in fact left to govern themselves. Lycurgus[5] (338-326 BCE) reformed the whole economic structure of the city, and, supported by Alexander, sponsored a considerable building program, including a stadium, the rebuilt Theater of Dionysius, and the great auditorium on the Pnyx Hill.

Philip, and later Alexander, showed obvious favor to Athens. Even so, the people chafed at being under foreign rule and looked for every opportunity to revolt. After the death of Alexander, his general Antipater became king of Macedonia. He lost patience with the Athenians and punished the city by severely restricting its privileges. In the following years, Macedonian power ebbed and flowed a number of times, and Athens's liberty waxed and waned with it. At all times, however, it seems the city was highly respected by most of the neighboring powers simply because of its past achievements. While it lost its lead in science and scholarship to Alexandria, Athens became the mecca of philosophy and the literary arts.

By 228 BCE Rome had become an important world power, and Athens established a friendly relationship with that thriving republic. (Rome

4. Demosthenes had a severe speech impediment as a young man. According to legend, to overcome it he put pebbles in his mouth and orated to the ocean for hours at a time, shouting above the roar of the surf, until he had conquered it. He became the greatest orator of ancient times.

5. This is not the same person as Lycurgus the Lawgiver, who is often credited with the foundation of the Spartan confederation several centuries earlier.

In Athens, when Saint Paul spoke at the Areopagus about the Athenians' temple dedicated "To an Unknown God," he would have seen this view of the Acropolis, the city's center of worship.    Photo credit: Erich Lessing/Art Resource, NY

would not become an empire until two centuries later.) Athens assisted Rome in its struggles against Macedonia (200-199), and thus unknowingly helped pave the way for Rome's dominance in later years. In the great unrest that was tearing apart the Hellenic world, Athens unintentionally abetted Rome's conquest of the Achaean League, thus causing Greece to fall under Roman control. Because of its previous friendship with Rome, however, Athens was granted a special treaty guaranteeing independence and protection. Unfortunately, a small but powerful segment of the population was irate at being dependent upon Rome's largesse. Their agitation was fanned by Mithridates VI Eupator of Pontus (now in Turkey), who was at war with Rome. He finally managed to convince Athens to declare war on Rome. This was a fatal error. Mithridates was vanquished, and the Roman general Lucius Cornelius Sulla sacked Athens in 86 BCE. There was no serious physical destruction, but the humiliation and rapine left the city impoverished and broken in spirit. The one positive result of this was that the city turned its attention to intellectual rather than economic pursuits. Its philosophical schools flourished, leading it to become the prime learning center of the Mediterranean world.

In the Roman civil wars, Athens again made an unwise decision and sided with Pompey against Caesar, and after Caesar's assassination it supported the position of Brutus and Cassius. Despite these dangerous alliances, however, Rome forgave the city "in consideration of her great dead." The huge number of Roman intellectuals who had been educated in Athens, and the Romans' passionate love for anything Greek, probably inclined the Roman politicians to be merciful. Marc Antony repeatedly made Athens his headquarters, and granted it rule over several surrounding regions. This rule was later revoked by Augustus, after he had become Antony's enemy and had eventually defeated him.

As a bastion of classical Greek and Roman paganism, Athens was saturated with temples dedicated to almost every Mediterranean god. This distressed Saint Paul greatly (Acts 17:16-34), and he preached so vehemently that he roused the interest of many Athenians. One of his most famous sermons, recorded in the book of Acts (17:22-30), was given in Athens. The Athenians, to be sure they did not neglect any god who might then take out his wrath against them, had built a temple dedicated "To an unknown god." Instead of condemning them for their paganism, Paul praised them for their religious devotion. He pointed out that the unknown god was God, and they had been worshiping him all along — they just had not realized it. Many scoffed, but several wanted to learn more. Paul did not stay long enough to establish a church in Athens, but he left many converts when he moved on to Corinth.

During the ensuing five centuries, Athens remained the nucleus of the ancient intellectual world, and fiercely loyal to Rome. Except for a couple of brief attacks by barbarians, the city remained peacefully prosperous, and it was a stronghold of intellectual freedom and moral paganism, even after the Christianization of Rome begun by the emperor Constantine in the early fourth century CE. The deathblow to ancient Athens, however, was dealt by the emperor Justinian I in 529 CE, when he introduced heavy penalties for pagan teachers; the famous Academy shut down and the school's head, as well as some other philosophers, fled the city. Since the philosophical schools were the backbone of ancient Athens, the city soon sank into obscurity, and remained unremarkable for the next fifteen hundred years.

In 1833, in honor of its glorious history, Athens was selected to be the capital of the newly independent Greece, and quickly rose to take its place among the major cities of the modern world.

# Babylon

To Christians and Jews alike the name of Babylon conjures up images of oppression, captivity, and corruption. Revelation 17:5 calls it "Babylon the great, the mother of prostitutes, and of the abominations of the earth." Martin Luther compared the Roman Catholic Church to Babylon, the captor of the faithful. The name literally means "Gate of the God." The capital of one of the great early empires, Babylon was one of the most famous cities of antiquity. It was located in the part of Mesopotamia that is now Iraq,[1] and its ruins lie near the modern town of Hilla, on the banks of the Euphrates River about fifty miles south of Baghdad, at the north end of the Euphrates flood plain. The region is a rich agricultural area, and was reputed to be very beautiful.

Mesopotamia is called "the Cradle of Civilization," and this epithet is probably well-deserved. Various nations in this region produced the first writing, the first societies structured on a concern for the people, the first legal systems designed to protect human rights, and a cultural framework that was one of the primary foundations on which the superstructure of the Middle Eastern and Western civilizations would be built.

There is no historical record of the origins of Babylon, although ancient oral tradition identifies its beginning with the construction of the Tower of Babel. The book of Genesis tells of the attempt of Nimrod, Noah's great-grandson, to unite all people of the world by building a great city. In the midst of the city would be a tower high enough to reach heaven. Jewish legend says that the goal was to build a tower so high that if God should send another flood, it would reach above the waters. For this arro-

---

1. Mesopotamia (Greek for "between the rivers") covered the region that is now Iraq and eastern Syria. It was to the east of Palestine and Syria; Persia (Iran) was to the east, and Arabia to the south. It consisted of three kingdoms, Babylonia, Assyria, and Chaldea (Ur), which repeatedly rose and fell as the seats of great empires. Babylonia was in the southern region between the Tigris and Euphrates rivers, extending to the Persian Gulf. Chaldea, at a different period, was in much the same region. Assyria was the region east and northeast of the Tigris. It was the Assyrians who defeated and captured the northern Jewish kingdom of Israel in the eighth century BCE, and the Babylonians who captured the southern kingdom of Judah in the sixth.

gance God caused everyone on earth to speak a different language so that they could not communicate and thus could not so conspire against his will. The place was called Babel, meaning "gate of God," but it was also a pun on the Hebrew *balel*, "to mix." This story points so obviously to Babylon that there can be little doubt that the Tower of Babel legend was based on the huge ziggurat (stepped pyramid) that stood in the middle of the city. This ziggurat was the main part of the temple of the pagan god Marduk. The Babylonian legend of the origin of the city is quite different: after Marduk defeated a number of rebel gods, he forced them to build the city and the great temple as a tribute to him.

Archaeological evidence indicates that Babylon may have existed at least as early as 3000 BCE. The site of the ruins of Babylon is extensive, but because of the city's proximity to the river, the water table is very high there. As a result, the archaeological research has concentrated on a few specialized sites and on the remains of Neo-Babylonian and later times, with the earlier levels remaining inaccessible. The earliest written reference to Babylon, dated about 2500 BCE, mentions the city in the dedication of the temple of Marduk. At that time it was a provincial capital in the first Chaldean Empire, in the third dynasty of Ur.[2] As Ur began to decline and weaken, Assyria, under Sargon I, grew to be a strong nation of united peoples, while Babylon was simply a city-state unto itself. Although it was not at that time a particularly important city politically, it was the cultural and literary center of Mesopotamia.

By the eighteenth century BCE Babylon had grown to great importance in Mesopotamia. It was a religious center, dedicated to the god Marduk, and because of this both Babylonian and Assyrian kings sought to be crowned there. It had been overrun by a wave of Semitic peoples called the Amorites, meaning "people from the west." The first Babylonian dynasty was established by the Amorites, and one of the greatest of the Amorite kings of Babylon was Hammurabi. He was a political and military genius, and established Babylon as a great and beautiful city. He united the surrounding tribes and city-states into a single strong nation that came to be called Babylonia. It was he who enacted the Code of Hammurabi, one of the first great legal codes to be concerned with the people's rights. In

2. Chaldea is a central region of Mesopotamia that was ultimately ruled by Babylonia. Ur lies about halfway between Baghdad and the head of the Persian Gulf. Its modern descendant is the Iraqi city Tell el-Muqayyar. Ur was the city in which Abraham was born and raised sometime between 2000 and 1500 BCE, when it was the ruling city of most of Mesopotamia. See Ur of the Chaldeans, pp. 243-45.

about 1595 BCE the city was sacked by the Hittites, and the statue of Marduk was taken. After twenty-four years of disasters the Hittites concluded that their troubles were because of the god's anger, and they returned the statue to the city. Soon, however, Babylon fell to the Kassites, a barbarian tribe from Anatolia (now eastern Turkey), who controlled the region for almost three centuries.

During these centuries Babylon vacillated in its status, moving back and forth from glory and power to weakness and humiliation. It had a brief period of power and prosperity under Nebuchadrezzar I about 1100 BCE, but soon thereafter it fell under the control of the Assyrians. During this period Assyria once again rose to great power, and by the eighth century the records of the Assyrian king Sargon II indicate that Babylon was in ruins, "a jungle infested with jackals." He tried to restore it, but he died shortly after beginning the project. His son Sennacherib leveled the city in 689 BCE. Seven years later he was assassinated. He had refused to go to Marduk's temple in Babylon to be crowned, and it was said that his murder was ordained by Marduk because of his arrogance and insolence. His son Essarhaddon rebuilt Babylon, and one of Esarhaddon's younger sons, who had become the king of Babylon, revolted and tried to gain independence from Assyria. He was defeated after a long and destructive siege of the city. By this time, however, Assyria was in a steep decline, and Babylon was rising in strength and prosperity, eventually becoming independent. In the late seventh and early sixth centuries BCE Nabopolasser and his son Nebuchadrezzar II rebuilt the city and once again expanded the empire, which was known as Chaldea. This is what historians call the Neo-Babylonian Empire, and this was the Babylonia that captured Judah and carried the Jews into captivity. It was in this period that Babylon achieved its greatest fame. Because of the physical difficulties mentioned earlier, this is the only stage of Babylon's history that has been intensively studied by archaeologists.

Babylon under Nebuchadrezzar II saw its true golden age. It was reputed to be a great city, immensely powerful, lavishly wealthy, and awesomely beautiful, and archaeological evidence has confirmed this reputation. Archaeology has not confirmed the existence of the Hanging Gardens, considered one of the seven wonders of the ancient world, but their existence would certainly be consistent with the splendor of the city. Babylon also has a reputation today of having been a depraved and corrupt city, but there is no documentary or archaeological evidence to support this. The reputation is probably based on the story in Daniel of Belshazzar's depravity (Dan. 5:1-30) and on the reference in Revelation quoted earlier (Rev. 17:5). There is no question, however, that in Revelation the term "Babylon" metaphorically refers to Rome, not to the Mesopotamian Babylon. As for the story in Daniel, the captivity of the Jews by the Babylonians left no love in their hearts for Babylon, and since they wrote the Bible, they presented Babylon from their point of view.

The Assyrians and Neo-Babylonians had a unique approach to conquest. The standard of the time was that when a nation was captured, the cities were leveled and the people slaughtered or carried into hard-labor slavery so that they could never rise up against their conquerors. The Mesopotamians took a different approach. They looted and destroyed the cities, but they did not massacre the people. They gathered all the potential leaders — the ruling classes, the wealthy, educators and scholars, artisans, skilled craftsmen, and so on — and carried them back to Mesopotamia. This left the ignorant and unskilled behind to produce food and services for their conquerors, but without leadership to organize or unite them. The elite were allowed to live in Mesopotamia with a reasonable amount of freedom. They were brutally punished if they rebelled or resisted the rules imposed on them by their captors, but if they behaved and cooperated they lived reasonably well (according to the standards of the time; by today's standards their treatment might be considered harsh). The Jewish captives were not allowed to worship or sacrifice to God, but they were encouraged to educate their children. They established schools in which they surreptitiously taught prayer and Jewish religion under the guise of simple education.[3] They could conduct businesses, amass wealth, and even intermarry with local people. In the meantime, their captors learned from them, adopted their arts and skills if they were superior, let their natural leaders take positions of power in the government, and absorbed the best of their culture. The result of this was a strengthening of the local cultures, and a weakening of the Jews. In time, the Jews might have all but disappeared, being slowly absorbed into Mesopotamian culture. In fact, when they were finally freed, only a handful of the faithful — what Isaiah called the "remnant" — elected to return to Judah.

The last of the Neo-Babylonian kings was Nabonidus, who was considered a heretic by the priests of Marduk. His rule was ended when the

---

3. This was the origin of the synagogue (from the Greek for "call together"), which became an important factor in Judaism after the return to Judah. The Yiddish word for synagogue is *shul,* derived from the German *Schul,* "school."

Persian king Cyrus took Babylon with almost no resistance. The Bible identifies Belshazzar as the reigning king when Cyrus entered the city (Dan. 5:30), but other than the biblical reference, there is no historical record of any Chaldean king Belshazzar. There is a cuneiform inscription, however, that identifies Belsaruzar as the son of Nabonidus. A later inscription indicates that he may have shared the rule with his father in 550 to 539 BCE, in which case the biblical story is validated.

For reasons that scholars disagree on, the Persians showed great friendship for the Jews. Cyrus not only immediately released them and allowed them to return to Judah, but he provided soldiers to travel with them to ensure their safety. He later provided money, materials, and skilled craftsmen to help them rebuild Jerusalem.

Cyrus left Babylon unharmed, but his successors Darius I and Xerxes I looted it and severely damaged it in punishment for a revolt against their rule. It was left virtually defenseless, and although there were no major attacks on it thereafter, it never fully recovered, going into a major social and economic decline. Alexander the Great took the city in 323 BCE. He made no attempt to restore it, although he lived for a time in Nebuchadrezzar's palace. It was there that he died. He had intended to institute some rebuilding there, but after his death his successors divided his empire.

Babylon was never again a very important city, particularly after Seleucia-on-the-Tigris was founded not far to the northeast in the third century BCE and became the official royal city under Antiochus I. Nevertheless, a village did exist on the site until the eleventh century CE.

# Beersheba

Beersheba was the southernmost city in the ancient kingdom of Israel, as Dan was the northernmost.[1] It lay on the borderline not only between Judah and the Egyptian and Arabian territories, but also between the arid Negev desert and the Judean hill country. The annual rainfall at Beersheba is about twelve inches, while about five miles south in the Negev it is even less — only two inches. Despite this aridity, however, Beersheba had a plentiful supply of water. The geological nature there is such that rainwater seeps quickly into the rock crevices before it can evaporate into the air, thus supplying a number of deep wells. There was also a generous amount of water fed into the underground supply from the Judean hills to the north, as well as a supply from the annual spring flooding of a wadi[2] at the edge of the city.

It is unclear whether Beersheba's name is *Be'er-sheva*[3] ("Well of Seven," Gen. 21:22-27) or *Be'er-shevua* ("Well of the Oath," Gen. 26:17-33). It is found in both forms, although many prefer the first interpretation because there are seven wells in the vicinity. The archaeological excavation is at a mound called Tell es-Seba about three miles east of the modern city of Beersheba. The location was of value not only because of the water supply but because it was on the crossroads of several major trade routes between Israel, Egypt, and Arabia.

Beersheba was an important religious center, with a sanctuary equivalent to those of Dan and Bethel in the north. This is substantiated not only in the Bible (Gen. 21:31; 46:1) but also by archaeological finds. The reason for this is its traditional importance as a holy site to Abraham and the patriarchs, even though there is no scientific evidence to substantiate their activities there. The prophecies of Amos (Amos 5:5; 8:14) indicate that by the eighth century BCE

---

1. Thus, of course, the phrase "from Dan to Beersheba," indicating the entire nation of Israel. This is used seven times in the Old Testament. Today it is still used as an expression meaning from one end to the other.

2. A wadi is a dry riverbed, equivalent to the southwestern American arroyo, that often fills up suddenly from flash floods brought on by spring rains in the desert many miles away.

3. In most languages the sounds of *b* and *v* are interchangeable from dialect to dialect and even accent to accent. Note the modern interchangeability in Spanish between *Havana* and *Habana*.

the religious practices of Beersheba (and of Dan) were considered at least very questionable, if not plainly heretical or blasphemous; it was one of the places designated for Josiah's religious reforms (2 Kings 23:8).

The plan of the city was extraordinary, even though it was typical of Israelite fortifications. Originally established in the tenth century BCE by Solomon, it remained unchanged throughout Beersheba's golden age for almost three hundred years until the city was destroyed by the Assyrians. It consisted of a street that encircled the city, lined with houses on both sides just inside the city wall. The entrance gate opened to this street as well as to two streets that led straight to the center of the city, the highest point on the city mound, where the public buildings and religious shrine were located. The massive city gate was double, with an outer gate that opened to a passageway to the inner gate, making it easily defensible. Near the gate, inside the outer street, was a series of large rectangular buildings divided by two lines of stone columns. Scholars are unsure of the purpose of these, but they may well have been a combination of stables, arsenals, and food storage warehouses. The private dwellings were in the style typical of the Middle East in the first millennium BCE. They consisted of a broad room and three long narrow rooms divided by two rows of stone pillars. Access to the water supply was available inside the city wall in an impressive, deep water system hewn out of the rock, and entered by a stone stairwell. It consisted of at least one well and several stone cisterns and was designed to provide adequate water for a long siege, even in the dry season. There was a well-engineered drainage system that passed rainwater underneath the streets and discharged it into a well outside the city wall.

The first references to Beersheba in the Bible long precede the date of the earliest archaeological find. Abraham spent a great deal of time there, and in honor of the covenant with God (Gen. 21:33-34) he planted a tamarisk tree dedicated to El-Olam ("God Everlasting"). That name for God was the one most commonly used in worship there for many centuries thereafter. It was from Beersheba that Abraham set out to sacrifice Isaac (Gen. 22); Isaac lived there (Gen. 26:23) when Jacob set out for Haran (it was on that journey that he had his dream of the ladder); and Jacob, on his way to see Joseph in Egypt, stopped at Beersheba to offer sacrifice (Gen. 46:1). There are no early Bronze Age potsherds or other artifacts at Beersheba to support an association with the early patriarchs, or even to indicate the early name of the place. On the other hand, the Jewish tradition is strong, and there is no evidence to indicate that it is not the site of these events.[4]

4. The fact that the event is unsubstantiated is no reason for those who venerate the site

The first archaeologically proven settlement at Beersheba was a simple unfortified village of the late twelfth century BCE (about the time of the conquest of Canaan), possibly settled by Israelites of the tribe of Simeon. It consisted of nothing more than a few dwellings hewn out of the rocks, and a sixty-foot-deep well. The city apparently grew rapidly, though, because by the latter part of the period of the Judges it was recognized as the chief administrative center of the southern regions, known as the Negev of Judah. Samuel appointed his sons Joel and Abijah as judges in Beersheba (1 Sam. 8:1-2). By the end of the eleventh century BCE there was a fortified city on a hill, consisting of houses and other buildings close to each other, surrounded by a wall. The city's identity as the southernmost outpost of the kingdom remained intact for centuries, long after the breakup of the United Monarchy, when Judah was the southern kingdom. The city wall was replaced by a strong double chambered wall (a "casemate" wall) by King Uzziah in the early eighth century BCE. It stood until it was destroyed about 701 BCE, probably by the Assyrians under King Sennacherib.

After the final fall of Judah to the Babylonians in 586 BCE, Beersheba remained in shambles with a small population until the return of the "remnant" from exile in 538 BCE. It then became one of the settlements that was rebuilt and re-animated as a border fortress and commercial center on the international trade routes. It fell far short of its previous importance, however, and quickly declined to a point of political and commercial irrelevance. Thereafter the city was never rebuilt. There were squatters and occasional villages there, but it would not again rise to significance. Its ramparts and walls were considered a part of a string of fortifications along the border, and they may have been used temporarily from time to time in various border skirmishes during the later occupations, including that of the Romans. The city was never again a fortification of consequence, however. At some point in history a village grew up about three miles west of the ancient city, and today that is known as the city of Be'er-sheva or Beersheba.

---

to cease doing so. The religious significance of places and objects is often subjective. Saint Thomas Aquinas said that the validity of shrines, miracles, and holy relics is *ex parte videntium,* "on the part of the viewer." If one believes, for example, that a particular fragment of wood is a piece of the True Cross, then for that person it is — while for the one who believes that it is nothing more than a piece of wood, it is no more than that even if it is in fact a piece of the cross. If its objective validity is essential, then it has been reduced to nothing more than a magic talisman rather than a focus of religious reverence and meditation.

# Bethany

Bethany is a small village in Jordan on the east foot of the Mount of Olives, about one and three-quarters miles east of Jerusalem. The village lies on the road between Jerusalem and Jericho. It is the main approach to Jerusalem from the east, and was well known to Jesus. Its modern Arabic name is Al-ʿAyzariyeh, "The Place of Lazarus." Local Muslims consider Lazarus a saint and named the town, which was his home, after him. The meaning of the Hebrew name is obscure; scholars disagree as to whether it is Beth-Anani, "House of Ananias," or Beth-Ani, "House of Destitution." The modern Hebrew name is Beit Haniyah. There is no reference to it in the Old Testament.

Jesus stayed at Bethany when he went to Jerusalem to attend temple ceremonies. While it is only conjecture, most scholars agree that he probably stayed at the home of his friend Lazarus,[1] who lived there with his sisters Mary and Martha.

For Christians, Bethany is particularly noted for four events: the meal at the home of Simon the Leper, when the woman anointed Jesus with expensive ointment (Matt. 26:6-13; Mark 14:3-9); the raising of Lazarus from the dead (John 11:1-44); the departure to Jerusalem at the "triumphal entry" on the first Palm Sunday (Mark 11:1-11); and the Ascension (Luke 24:50-51). The raising of Lazarus is also a sacred event to Muslims.[2]

There were two early Christian shrines in Bethany. The tomb traditionally considered as that of Lazarus was a venerated spot as early as 333 CE, when the Bordeaux Pilgrim made the first official record of a European

---

1. Many interpreters identify Lazarus with "the rich young man" whom Jesus told to sell all that he had and give it to the poor (Matt. 19:16-22). The man put too much priority on his wealth and, unable to bring himself to do as Jesus commanded, went away sadly. Jesus did not expect this of everyone, only those who valued their worldly wealth too much. Whoever he was, it is apparent that Lazarus was Jesus' closest friend outside the apostles.

2. Islam recognizes Jesus as a prophet, although neither the Messiah nor divine. It accepts the virgin birth and most of Jesus' miracles, including the raising of Lazarus. The Qur'an calls him *Isa bin Maryam*, "Joshua the son of Mary." Muslims teach that Jesus' followers deified him and corrupted his teachings, so God (Allah) sent Mohammed to bear the truth.

visiting it. Also sacred was the spot where some early Christians believed Martha and then Mary had met the Lord after Lazarus' death (John 11:20 and 11:29), although it is likely that this meeting was in Bethphage rather than in Bethany (where there is also a marker commemorating the meeting location; see the section on Bethphage). By 385 at the latest, churches had been erected over both places, and at least by the seventh century there was a thriving monastery at the tomb site. In the eleventh century a basilica was built just east of the tomb, at the traditional home of Simon the Leper. Except for an underground chamber that is still honored as the crypt of Lazarus, all the rest of the buildings have fallen into decay. Archaeological research has unearthed at least three successive churches at the site of the home of Simon, at least one of which is probably the one cited by medieval pilgrims.

John 1:28 says that John the Baptist baptized at Bethany, "across [i.e., east of] the Jordan." Since Bethany is several miles from the Jordan, this causes a problem. The discrepancy is possibly due to an early scrivener's error. The most likely site for the reference is the town of Bethabara, a village that was on the east bank of the Jordan. Nonetheless many scholars maintain that "Bethany" was the original reading, but that it refers to a now-forgotten village or region about thirty miles south of the Sea of Galilee. The reason for this conclusion is that if the original was Bethany, it must have been a different Bethany from that of Lazarus: John the Baptist selected his spot "because water was abundant there" (John 3:23), and the most abundant water in the Jordan is about thirty miles south of the Sea of Galilee. In ancient times it was not uncommon for more than one village to have the same name.

# Bethel

While not a major city on the international scene, Bethel is mentioned in the Bible thirty-eight times,[1] second only to the number of references to Jerusalem. It is now the Jordanian village of Beitin, about eleven miles north of Jerusalem. The name of the city was actually Beth-El, "House of El."[2]

The first mention of the city is in the story of Abraham, and the Bible tells us that its original name was Luz. Archaeological evidence indicates that it was founded about 2000 BCE, a century before the time of Abraham. Apparently it was considered holy ground even prior to that. It is surrounded by earlier tombs, although there is no evidence of an earlier settlement there. In Abraham's time it was a thriving city, well fitting the patterns of the middle Bronze Age.

The primary biblical importance of the city originates in the story of Jacob. God said to Jacob, "I am the God of Bethel, where you anointed a pillar and made a vow to me" (Gen. 31:13). The pillar may well have been dedicated to the pagan god named Bethel (see footnote 1). Jacob, who until then had dallied with paganism, ordered his household to put away all their foreign gods. Shortly thereafter he wrestled all night with a man (who turned out to be either an angel or God), and his name was changed to Israel (Gen. 32:24-30). Many theologians believe that this represents his spiritual struggle, after which he renounced all pagan ties and devoted himself solely to God. From that time on, "Bethel" and "Israel" become almost inseparable names.

There is evidence that at the time of Joshua's conquest of Canaan, the battle that the Bible says took place at Ai (Josh. 7) may actually have been fought at Bethel. Archaeological evidence does not support the existence of a settlement at et-Tell, which most archaeologists believe to be the loca-

---

1. There was a West Semitic (Canaanite) pagan deity named Bethel, and many scholars think that Genesis 31:13, Jeremiah 48:13, Amos 5:5, and Zechariah 7:2 refer to him rather than to the city.

2. The Jews would have translated this "House of God," but the city may originally have been dedicated to the Canaanite pagan god El. The Hebrew *El* is a generic name for God, whose real name they believed to be Yahweh. They more often used the plural form, *Elohim*, possibly implying that all the gods were actually embodied in the one true God, Yahweh.

tion of Ai, in the thirteenth century BCE, when the Israelite conquest occurred; but archaeological discoveries do show that Bethel was burned to the ground at the time Ai was supposed to have been destroyed by Joshua. The city that was rebuilt on the ruins was crude compared to its predecessors, which had houses that represented some of the finest pre-Greek architecture of the time. This indicates a major cultural shift in the region.

Archaeology gives us a more complete picture of Bethel's history during the period of the Judges than does the Bible. The city was destroyed and rebuilt several times: It was captured by the Canaanites early in the period of the Judges, recaptured by the tribe of Joseph (Judg. 1:22-25), then again taken by the Canaanites. This also explains the massacre of the tribe of Benjamin (Judg. 20). It was then taken by the Ephraimites (1 Chron. 7:28) and remained in their hands. The road from Jericho to Bethel marked the boundary between the territories of Benjamin and Ephraim. In the early days of the Judges the ark of the covenant resided at Bethel (Judg. 20:27), although it was later removed to Shiloh.

Many catastrophic wars took place in the region during the following centuries, but for some reason Bethel always managed to escape capture or destruction. It was never attacked by the Philistines, and it would even survive the Babylonians' destruction of nearby Jerusalem a half millennium later in 586 BCE.

By the middle of the eleventh century BCE Samuel was frequently headquartered at Bethel, thus endowing it with great prestige. When Saul became king in about 1020 BCE, however, he established his capital at Gibeah, a village about eight miles south of Bethel. In about 1000 BCE David ascended the throne and established his capital at Jerusalem, three miles further south. Bethel faded into political insignificance, although there is evidence that it flourished as an agricultural and trading center during the United Monarchy[3] in the tenth century.

After the breakup of the United Monarchy in about 922, Bethel was located in the northern kingdom, Israel. It remained insignificant for a short time, but King Jeroboam I[4] raised it to prominence again by building an altar

3. Several warring Jewish tribes were united by David into the United Monarchy. After the death of Solomon in about 922, the kingdom broke up into two monarchies, Israel in the north (with Shechem as its capital) and Judah or Judea in the south (with Jerusalem as its capital). The kingdoms were never reunited.

4. Jeroboam instigated a rebellion against Solomon, and when it failed he escaped to Egypt. After Solomon's death he returned. He successfully revolted against Solomon's son

there in competition with the temple at Jerusalem. He made a clean sweep — new clergy, rituals, calendar, and religious center. He was a Jew, but he also worshiped pagan gods, probably among them the Egyptian bull-god Apis (1 Kings 12:28-33), and his corruption of traditional Judaism called down God's wrath upon him (1 Kings 13:1-10). About fifty years later Ahab's queen, Jezebel, would make Jeroboam's corruption in the northern kingdom permanent by infecting the cult with Phoenician Baalism. Bethel remained the royal sanctuary at least well into the eighth century BCE, although the capital, Samaria, was the primary center of Phoenician Baalist worship.

In about 914 Judah's King Abijah, Solomon's grandson, captured Bethel and incorporated it unmolested into his kingdom. It was recaptured by Israel soon thereafter, although it is unknown exactly when and by whom. When Jehu overthrew Jehoram and Jezebel in 850 BCE, he left Bethel undamaged. It seems that Jezebel's main focus was on the capital, Samaria, when she introduced pagan worship into Israel, and altars to Baal (at least major ones) had not yet been built at the sanctuary at Bethel. Archaeologists have uncovered a few female figurines, probably of nature or fertility goddesses, but there is no evidence of major pagan shrines or altars there from that period.

Bethel's next great claim to fame (or notoriety) was that it was the focus of the dire warnings of the prophet Amos, who prophesied that because of its corruption, God would give Israel over to the Assyrians. While there is no historical record of the Assyrian destruction of Bethel, it is assumed that the town was destroyed along with Samaria. It was the religious center of Israel, so it is unlikely that the Assyrians would not have demolished it. On the other hand, there is no archaeological evidence of that destruction, so for some reason it may have survived.

In the late seventh century Josiah, king of Judah, took advantage of the weakening of the Assyrian Empire and moved north, capturing Bethel and a large part of the surrounding territory. He exterminated the clergy and obliterated the sanctuary, which had become thoroughly pagan by then, but he left the rest of the city unharmed.

When Nebuchadrezzar II of Babylon took Judah, he also spared Bethel, even though he destroyed Jerusalem. This may have been because the Assyrians had moved many Babylonian colonists into Bethel. Sometime thereafter, however, the city was totally destroyed, possibly by the Persians.

---

Rehoboam and gained power over the ten northern tribes (the so-called "ten lost tribes of Israel"), thus breaking up the United Monarchy.

When the Jews returned after the exile, they rebuilt Bethel. It is likely that this was not because of its previous religious importance but because the site had an extraordinarily fine water supply. It was no longer a shrine, and although it prospered, it never again became an important city. There is no mention of Bethel in the New Testament. It flourished throughout the Roman period and well into the time of the Crusades, reaching its climax in the Byzantine era. There is no evidence of its destruction, but for some unknown reason the city simply died away rather suddenly at the end of the Byzantine era in the middle of the fifteenth century CE. It lay in ruins until the beginning of the twentieth century, when it was reoccupied by Arabs from the nearby regions, who call it Beitin.

# Bethlehem

Five thousand years ago the indigenous tribes of the region we call the Holy Land began to develop a civilization. Many of them abandoned their nomadic life and established villages that soon evolved into towns and small cities. As the Canaanites began to overrun the region, the people fortified their cities with walls to defend themselves from the raiders. One of these cities was Zion (Jerusalem), and near it on what we now call the West Bank was a small city that was destined to become to Christians one of the holiest places on earth. It was dedicated to the Chaldean god of fertility, Lachmo, whom the Canaanites worshiped as Lachama. The town was Beit Lachama, "House of Lachama"; we now call it Bethlehem. About one thousand years before the Hebrews arrived, the Canaanites built a temple to Lachama on the hill that is now known as the Hill of the Nativity. Bethlehem had a good water supply and was located near fertile valleys (the "Shepherds' Fields"), and it was a strategic military location. When the Philistines moved in from Crete and the Aegean (about the same time as the Hebrews), they established a garrison there. By 1200 BCE they had military control of the whole region and called it Philistia (which has been corrupted to Palestine).

Grain grew plentifully in the fertile valleys and was an important factor in Bethlehem's economy. The Hebrews, being faithful Jews, would naturally not honor the pagan fertility god Lachama. They called the town Beth-Lechem, meaning "House of Bread" or "Granary."[1] Today it is still known as Bethlehem to the religious, but its official name is Bayt Lachm (Arabic for "House of Food"). A small village near the city, Ephrathah, eventually was absorbed into Bethlehem. Genesis tells us that Jacob's wife Rachel died giving birth to Benjamin on the way to Ephrathah and was buried there (Gen. 35:16-20). To this day there is a shrine to Rachel in Bethlehem. Benjamin eventually returned to Bethlehem and was the patriarch of the tribe of Benjamin, Saul's tribe.

The book of Ruth tells the story of Naomi, an Israelite, and her

---

1. The Hebrew and Aramaic word *lechem*, "bread," and the Chaldean *lachmo*, "fertility," which was also the name of the god of fertility, derive from the same Semitic root.

**Today, as at the time of Jesus' birth, shepherds tend their flocks in the fields near Bethlehem.**    Photo credit: Erich Lessing/Art Resource, NY

Moabite daughter-in-law Ruth, who together left Moab (now part of Jordan) and settled in Bethlehem after the death of both of their husbands. The Moabites were not Jews but descendants of Abraham's nephew Lot. Ruth embraced Judaism and married Boaz in roughly 1100 BCE. She was the great-grandmother of David, who was reared in Bethlehem. After David ascended the throne, Bethlehem was known as the City of David, a name by which it is often called in the New Testament.

In about 750 BCE the prophet Micah prophesied the punishment of Israel (the northern kingdom) at the hand of the Assyrians. He also prophesied, however, that out of Bethlehem (which was in Judah, the southern kingdom) would come a Messiah, a Savior of all the Jews (Micah 5:2-5). This was the prophecy to which the court prophets referred when the Magi asked Herod where the Messiah was to be born.

When the Romans decreed a census in about 4 BCE,[2] it was not re-

2. There is considerable disagreement among scholars about this census (which the King James translation incorrectly calls a tax). St. Luke identifies it with a census ordered by Quirinius, the governor of Syria (the Roman province that included most of Palestine). Quirinius's census was not until 6 CE, however, ten to twelve years after Jesus' birth. Despite

quired that all individuals return to their birthplace. Galilee and Judah, however, were in different jurisdictions, and Joseph, being of the tribe of Judah, was under the jurisdiction of Judah even though he lived in Galilee. For that reason he had to go back there for the census, and the logical place for him to go was Bethlehem, his hometown. Although Mary is believed to have been a Galilean, by Roman law she was automatically under the same jurisdiction as her husband, so she also had to make the journey in spite of her pregnancy (a dangerous condition in those days). This fulfilled Micah's prophecy of 750 years earlier.

Bethlehem lay just off the main travel route from Syria to the Mediterranean, and was thus a well-known stopping point. There would have been inns there, and it is entirely conceivable that at busy times they would all be full. Herod would also have been completely aware of the city, both because of its economic importance and because it was identified with David and was the seat of the Messianic prophecy. Herod likely had little love for David, who was as much venerated by the Jews as Herod was hated. When he found that he had been deceived by the Magi, he went into a rage and ordered the massacre of all males under two years old in Bethlehem in order to eliminate the prophesied Messiah (Matt. 2:16). Even though there is no Roman record of this, it is entirely possible that it happened. This type of atrocity was common among Middle Eastern despots, and Rome would not have paid much attention to it as long as it did not hurt any Romans or interfere with taxes or tributes.

In 330 CE the first Christian Roman emperor, Constantine, erected a cathedral, the Church of the Nativity, on the traditional site of Jesus' birth. Although it was rebuilt by the emperor Justinian about two hundred years later, most of the original building still stands. This shrine has been visited by Christian pilgrims for well over fifteen hundred years.

Until 1250 CE, when the fanatical Mamelukes took power, the Muslim Ayyubid Dynasty was tolerant of Christians and Jews, and attempted to safeguard the holy places in Palestine. The Mamelukes banished Christians from Bethlehem and dismantled the walls and towers, although the Church of the Nativity survived. In 1517 they were unseated by the Turkish Ottoman Empire, which restored the policy of tolerance. The Turks ruled until the fall of the Ottomans in 1918, when Palestine fell under British control. In 1922 the Balfour Declaration proposed a Jewish homeland in

---

this discrepancy, there are many credible theories about the census at Jesus' birth, although their details are beyond the scope of this book.

Palestine. The establishment of Israel in 1948 did not include Bethlehem, which was under Palestinian control. It fell into Jewish hands in the Six Days' War in 1967, and was returned to Palestine in 1995 in compliance with the Oslo Accord.

# Bethphage

Little is known about Bethphage. The name means "House of Unripe Figs," referring to a type of fig that grows only in that region and that looks unripe even when mature and edible. The town is mentioned only once in the Bible, in the story of Jesus' triumphal entry into Jerusalem on Palm Sunday (Mark 11:1-11 and parallels). The Bible tells us that Jesus went to Bethphage and Bethany, then on to Jerusalem (the two towns were very near Jerusalem on the route from Galilee). Jesus sent the disciples into "the village ahead of you" to get the donkey on which he rode into Jerusalem. The Bible is not clear as to which of the two villages it was, but most scholars believe it was Bethphage.

When Jesus went to raise Lazarus, he was probably coming from Galilee.[1] If Bethphage was located where most scholars think it was, they would have passed through it just before getting to Bethany. Since Lazarus and his sisters, Mary and Martha, lived in Bethany and the text says that "Jesus had not yet entered the village" (v. 30), we may assume that he was still in Bethphage when they heard that he was coming and went out to meet him. He was first met by Martha (John 11:20) and then later by Mary (John 11:29). There is a stone marking the place where Mary is said to have met Jesus. It is located at the edge of the Muslim village of Abu Dis at the foot of the Mount of Olives, and this is the most likely location of Bethphage. Medieval pilgrims believed that the town was between Bethany and Jerusalem, but there is no evidence to justify this belief. Other than these scanty traditions, nothing is known of the town.

1. "Then he said to his disciples, 'Let us go back to Judea'" (John 11:7). This indicates that they had gone home to Galilee when the word of Lazarus's illness came to them.

# Byblos

Byblos, or Gebal, was an important port on the northern Phoenician coast,[1] halfway between Egypt and Asia Minor. The original name of the town was Gebal, the name by which it is known in the Old Testament. By the end of the first millennium BCE, however, it came to be called Byblos, Greek for "book," because it had become a major distribution center for Egyptian papyrus. Its harbor consisted of a small but deep inlet on the Mediterranean that was very adequate for shipping but was no competition for the superb harbors of Tyre and Sidon. Its advantage was its proximity to the great cedar forests of Lebanon, and it thus became the primary port for shipping these timbers to a number of other ports all over the Mediterranean. Because of its access to the many varieties of fine wood from Lebanon and Syria, Byblos developed a large corps of extremely skilled woodworkers, carpenters, and shipbuilders. The city also attracted outstanding stonemasons, who helped make Byblos famous for its builders.

The early Israelite conquerors tried to take Byblos/Gebal (Josh. 13:1-5), but they were unsuccessful. Solomon, when building the temple, employed carpenters and stonemasons from the region (1 Kings 5:18), and the timbers used in the temple itself were undoubtedly shipped out of Byblos. Ezekiel refers to the Gebalites' extraordinary shipbuilding skills (Ezek. 27:9). Psalm 83 lists Gebal as one of the enemies of God, and calls down his curse upon them. These are the only Old Testament references to Byblos/ Gebal, and there are none in the New Testament. As a part of the Phoenician confederation of city-states, however, it was very important.

The local tradition was that the city had been founded by El, the father of all the other gods, and that it was thus the oldest city in the world. While not the very oldest, the city certainly ranks among the oldest cities, having been originally settled as early as the eighth millennium BCE. Although not much is known about the original settlers, archaeological finds indicate that they were physically very short, that they lived in small round or rect-

---

1. For more information on the Phoenician confederation, of which Byblos was a part, see the sections on Phoenicia (p. 163), Sidon, (p. 219), and Tyre (p. 239).

angular stone huts, and that they buried their dead in clay vessels. By the third millennium BCE the city had developed into a fortified urban center, in which there were several temples to various gods. It was engaged in exporting timber, leather, wine, oil, and spices on the overland trade routes throughout the northern Middle East and Mesopotamia. Because of Byblos's ready access to all kinds of wood, Egypt tried to maintain control of it. Wood was not an important building material in Egypt, but it was essential for shipbuilding, and Egypt had no forests. During the reign of Egypt over the coastal Middle East in the third millennium BCE, Byblos was in effect an Egyptian colony. The Egyptian gods were worshiped there along with the local gods, and Egyptian records indicate huge shipments of cedar to Egypt around 2500 BCE. The Palermo stone records one shipment of forty ships bearing cedar logs.

At the beginning of the second millennium BCE a new wave of people moved into the area, mainly Amorites and other Semitic groups. With the height of the late Bronze Age a new metalworking industry began to flourish. At this period, also, Egyptian influence resurged, and a huge temple to the Egyptian god Resheph, the god of destruction, was built in Byblos. In about 1800 BCE the Hyksos moved through the area on their way to conquer Egypt. The Hyksos were a Semitic people who conquered most of Palestine and ruled Egypt for about 150 years. After the Hyksos were expelled from Egypt in about 1550 BCE, Egyptian control of Phoenicia was regained, but it was considerably weaker than in the earlier periods. Egyptian records indicate that during the period that the Canaanites and later the Israelites were taking over Palestine, Phoenicia frequently sought Egyptian aid in resisting them. There were no major incursions of Canaanites or Israelites into Phoenicia, but it is unclear whether this was because of Phoenician strength, because the Egyptians sent aid, or because the mere threat of Egyptian aid was sufficient. In 1195 BCE the Philistines, a Hellenistic people probably from Crete, invaded Byblos and destroyed it. The city was rebuilt, but much of the older city remained in ruins. As the Philistines moved through Palestine, Phoenicia regained independence from Egypt, even to the point that Byblos refused to sell the Egyptians timber.

During the Philistine period the power of Byblos waned, and Tyre became the leading city of the confederation. Notwithstanding, Byblos remained a major trading and shipping center. When the Assyrians began their incursions into the northern regions of the Middle East in the ninth century BCE, Byblos gave supplies and troops to support the anti-Assyrian forces. By the eighth century, however, it had become a tribute-paying vassal of the Assyrian Empire. It was never completely free again. As successive conquerors took power over the centuries, Byblos became consecutively a vassal of the Babylonians, Persians, Greeks, Romans, and Arabs. It remained a significant port and commercial center until the Byzantine era, but was finally destroyed, never to rise again, in the twelfth century CE in a battle between the crusaders and the Muslims.

# Caesarea

Caesarea (not to be confused with Caesarea Philippi) was a seaport twenty-three miles south of Mount Carmel (Haifa) on the northern coast of what is now Israel. It was built on the site of an earlier city by Herod the Great, who named it in honor of his patron, the Roman emperor Caesar Augustus. Its proper name is Caesarea Palestinae, but the Bible calls it simply Caesarea.

The early history of the city comes to us from the Jewish historian Flavius Josephus.[1] The first recorded city on the site was Phoenician, built by a king of Sidon named Strato in the fourth century BCE. It was called Straton or Strato's Tower, and it was more of a coastal fortress than a seaport. In the second century BCE it was ruled by a Seleucid (Hellenistic Syrian) tyrant named Zoilus. In 96 BCE he was defeated by Alexander Jannaeus, the king of Judah, who freed the city and incorporated it into his kingdom.

In 63 BCE Pompey conquered Palestine, and Straton fell under Roman rule. In 47 BCE Julius Caesar defeated Pompey in the Roman civil war and secured full power over Palestine. He placed Herod (the Great) on the throne of Judea. Throughout his life Herod revered everything Roman, and he was a favorite of Rome's power brokers. Around 25 BCE the emperor Caesar Augustus gave Straton to Herod, who named it Caesarea in his honor. Herod completely rebuilt the city in the Roman style, with temples, theaters, amphitheaters, aqueducts, and a hippodrome. He enclosed the harbor with a mole, forcing the opening to the north where the prevailing winds had the least effect on the sea. The project took twelve years and was finally completed and dedicated with a huge festival in 10 BCE. The new harbor city was in every respect a magnificent achievement, and was in a prime position to communicate with every other major Palestinian city.

After Herod's death his son Archelaus was put in charge of half of his father's kingdom, including Caesarea, but the next true king appointed by the Romans was King Herod Agrippa I,[2] Herod the Great's grandson and a personal friend of the emperors Caligula and Claudius. Agrippa grew up

---

1. See his *Antiquities*, books XIII-XV.
2. He was named after Augustus's best friend Marcus Vipsanius Agrippa, the general who defeated Marc Antony at the Battle of Actium.

and was educated in Rome, but lived much of his life in Caesarea. After his death in 44 CE, the ruling power fell to the Roman procurators. His son Herod Agrippa II was titular king, but he was completely a puppet of Rome. Under the Roman procurators, Caesarea became the capital city of Palestine. The Jews considered Jerusalem their capital, but the fact was that Rome ruled, and Caesarea was the seat of Roman power in Palestine. It was a predominantly pagan city, but there was a substantial Jewish population.

The city played an active part in the early days of Christianity. Saint Philip preached there, and Peter was invited by Cornelius the centurion to preach to the Gentiles of Caesarea (Acts 10). Paul and his friends were entertained by Philip the evangelist, who lived there (Acts 21:8). Paul passed through the city several times on his missionary journeys, and he was tried in Caesarea by Felix (Acts 24) and imprisoned for two years (57-59 CE). His case was reviewed by Herod Agrippa II and Felix's successor Festus, and he sailed from Caesarea to go to Rome to be tried before the Roman emperor.

The tension between Jews and Gentiles increased, and by 66 CE riots in Caesarea brought the heavy hand of Rome down on the Jews of the city. The general Vespasian made his headquarters in Caesarea, and in 69 CE he was declared emperor there. It was his son Titus (who would become emperor ten years later) who, in 70 CE, supervised the razing of Jerusalem and the demolition of the temple. Caesarea was the home of Akiba ben-Joseph, the great Jewish sage who was the leader of the rebellion against Rome; it is fair to say that Caesarea was the origin of the revolt that spread throughout Judah and brought about the destruction of Jerusalem and eventually the end of the Jewish nation.

Caesarea remained important to Christianity for centuries. It was the home of many important Christian thinkers and leaders, including Eusebius of Caesarea and Basil the Great. By the seventh century, however, its importance as a seaport had faded, and in 640 it fell to Muslim control. It continued to shrink in size and importance until the Crusades, when Baldwin I[3] captured it in 1101 and restored the harbor and some of the buildings. It fell to the Muslims under Saladin in 1187, and was recaptured in 1191 by Richard I (the Lionheart). In 1251 Saint Louis IX of France rebuilt the fortifications. The final demise of Caesarea took place in 1265, however, when the Mameluke Baybars took the city and leveled it. Stones were taken from the ruins in the nineteenth century for building projects in 'Akko and Jaffa. Today there is nothing left of Caesarea but archaeological excavations.

---

3. The Holy Grail was allegedly discovered in Caesarea by Baldwin I.

# Caesarea Philippi

Caesarea Philippi is an ancient city located near Damascus in modern Syria. It is not the same city as either Caesarea Palestinae (usually called Caesarea) or Philippi (where Saint Paul founded a church). It lies on the lower slope of Mount Hermon, in one of the most beautiful parts of the Holy Land. It is on a terrace 1150 feet above sea level, overlooking the luxuriant northern Jordan Valley. To the north is a breathtaking view of the nine-thousand-foot peaks of Mount Hermon. Abundant waters flow from a cave in the mountainside, forming the source of the Jordan River.

There is little doubt that the original settlers chose the site because of its plentiful water, lush farmland, and militarily ideal position. It is easily defensible, and from it the whole lower valley can be protected. It is not known when the region was first settled, although it is obvious that it was very early, possibly in the late Stone Age. Baal worship was probably practiced there in Old Testament times, and there is some evidence that the city there may have been the same as Baal-gad (Josh. 11:17) or Baal-hermon (1 Chron. 5:23). Apparently there was a shrine in the main cave (the source of the Jordan River) dedicated to one or more of the baals. When Alexander the Great's army arrived in the fourth century BCE, they took the city and replaced the shrine with one dedicated to the nature god Pan and his nymphs. By New Testament times the cave and fountain were known as Paneion (the Place of Pan), and the city was called Paneas. Its first historical significance came in 198 BCE, when the Seleucid Antiochus III ("the Great") captured Palestine from the Egyptian Ptolemy V. With Pompey's conquest the city fell into Roman hands, and in 20 BCE Augustus Caesar gave it to his protegé Herod the Great, the king of Judea (37-4 BCE). Herod erected a white marble temple there[1] and dedicated it to Augustus.[2]

---

1. Herod is also known as "Herod the Builder" because of the vast building projects that he sponsored. The most magnificent of his works was the temple in Jerusalem. It is said that in comparison to it, even Solomon's temple paled. The Romans demolished it in 70 CE.

2. Augustus disliked being worshiped as a god, but he reluctantly permitted it outside of Italy because it was politically expedient. He was not officially declared a god until after his death in 14 CE, however. In 38 CE Caligula became the first emperor to make a claim to divinity during his lifetime.

Located near the source of the Jordan River, these caves were worship sites for baals and the Greek god Pan. The town Caesarea Philippi, where Peter called Jesus "the Messiah, the son of the living God," was also located at this site.

Photo credit: Erich Lessing/Art Resource, NY

With the death of Herod in 4 BCE, Paneas was ceded to his son Herod Philip as part of his tetrarchy.[3] He enlarged and beautified the city, and when the project was completed he renamed it Caesarea Philippi, in honor of the emperor Tiberius Caesar and himself. A few years later it fell into the hands of Herod Agrippa II, who renamed it Neronias in honor of Nero. It became a popular stopping point for the Roman armies during Vespasian's and Titus's expeditions to put down the Jewish revolts in 67 to 70 CE.

After the destruction of Jerusalem, Caesarea Philippi (by then called Neronias) continued to prosper. It was outside the main region of the revolts, and was more a Roman than a Jewish city. The fertility of the region, its plentiful water, and the awe-inspiring vistas surrounding it supported its continued popularity and success, right through the Roman and Byzantine periods. It was also a place of importance during the Crusades. While it was held briefly by the crusaders, it was primarily a stronghold of the Muslims during those wars. Although the ancient city now lies in ruins, there is still a village on the site. Its name is Banyas, a corruption of the ancient Greek name, Paneas.

Caesarea Philippi is mentioned in only one story in the Bible, but it is one of the most important. When Jesus was outside the city, he asked the disciples, "Who do you say that I am?" They identified him with John the Baptist, Elijah, and Isaiah, but Peter said, "You are the Messiah, the son of the living God" (Matt. 16:13-20; Mark 8:27-30). This critical turning point in Peter's relationship to Jesus marked Caesarea Philippi as a major biblical site.

---

3. A tetrarch was originally a ruler of a fourth of a kingdom, but by Herod's time it meant any ruler of a partial kingdom. Herod's kingdom was divided between three of his sons, Herod Antipas, Archlaeus, and Philip.

# Calvary

While Calvary is the heart of countless hymns, sermons, and meditations, its exact location is unknown. The Bible identifies it as the place where Jesus was crucified and buried. The name Calvary[1] never appears in most translations of the Bible, and appears only once in the King James translation (Luke 23:33). It is also found in some of the very early English translations that were rendered from the Latin Vulgate. The Aramaic name of the place was *Gulgotâ*, "Skull," from which we get Golgotha (Matt. 27:33). The Greek translation for "skull" is *kranion*, which Luke uses, and the Latin is *calvaria*, which the Vulgate used as the name of the place — thus Calvary. The name Calvary, however, has become so deeply rooted in Christian tradition that it is the common name for the site today throughout Christianity. There are three possible reasons that the site was called "Skull": it was a place where a skull was found, the promontory looked like a skull, or it was a place of execution.

The only things known about the location of Calvary are that it was outside the city, was near to and visible from the city gate, and was near a garden with a tomb. There are two sites that meet this description, Gordon's Calvary (better known as the Garden Tomb), and the Church of the Holy Sepulchre. So much emotion is involved in the discussion as to which is the true site that it is virtually impossible to be objective about it, with each side challenging the other's orthodoxy.

The Garden Tomb was first identified in 1849, and it fits perfectly with the biblical description. There is a rock outcropping that looks like a skull, and right below it is a garden in which a tomb has been hewn out of the rock. The tomb was definitely cut in the early Iron Age, however, so it does not fit with the "new tomb" of John 19:41. Also, there is no tradition, oral or written, to support its claim as the site of Calvary.

The Church of the Holy Sepulchre is the more likely site. The tradition of that location goes back at least to the fourth century CE, and possibly further. Inasmuch as the crucifixion and resurrection of Christ are the primary events of Christianity, it is reasonable to assume that the early Christians of

---

1. Although often incorrectly pronounced "Cavalry," the word is Calvary, and it has nothing to do with horse soldiers.

greater Jerusalem would not have forgotten where these pivotal incidents occurred. The site was definitely outside the Jerusalem wall until the reign of Herod Agrippa I, who in about 42 CE extended the wall so that the site believed to be Calvary was included inside the city. Sometime thereafter, probably after 70 CE when the Romans destroyed Jerusalem and built a Roman city there, a temple to Venus was erected on the site. The emperor Constantine's mother, Saint Helena, was a devout Christian, and dedicated several years to identifying the holy sites in Palestine. She identified the site of the temple of Venus as Calvary, and convinced Constantine to remove it and build the Church of the Holy Sepulchre there. The tomb was all but destroyed by the Muslim Seljuk Turks in the tenth century CE, and the garden and hill near the tomb are so altered by the basilica that it is difficult today to identify the details of the area. There are at least two tombs hewn out of the rock, both of which are definitely of the type used in Jesus' time, and which had to have been cut out of the rock before Herod extended the wall in 42 CE. Jesus was buried sometime around 27 to 29 CE.[2]

For about seven hundred years before Jesus' time there was a quarry outside the gate of Jerusalem, creating a large pit in the ground. The quarrying ceased in the first century BCE, and the pit was filled with dirt and stone and topped with arable soil, so that it could be cultivated. At the base of a vertical rock-face gardens were grown, consisting mainly of olive, carob, and fig trees. It was in this rock-face that the tombs were cut. Such tombs were very expensive, so only the rich could afford them. This is consistent with the tradition that Joseph of Arimathea, a rich merchant and a disciple of Jesus, gave his tomb for Jesus' burial (Matt. 27:57-61).

Whether or not the Church of the Holy Sepulchre is the actual site of Jesus' crucifixion, burial, and resurrection, there is no question that under the church there was a first-century garden and gravesite. Saint Thomas Aquinas taught that the validity of holy relics and sites is *ex parte videntium,* "on the part of the viewer." If a person believes that the tomb in the Church of the Holy Sepulchre is the site of Jesus' burial, then for him it is indeed that site. If he does not believe it, then even if it is the actual location, it becomes irrelevant. If the objective validity of the site truly matters, then it is not a focus of spiritual elevation; it has been relegated to nothing more than a magic talisman. Notwithstanding, pilgrims have visited the site for sixteen centuries.

---

2. Jesus was thirty-three years old when he died, but because of calendar errors the date of his birth is believed to be between 4 and 6 BCE.

# Cana of Galilee

Cana of Galilee was a small town near Nazareth, and it had no political or economic significance in ancient times. It is nonetheless of great significance to Christians, because according to the Bible, Jesus performed his first miracle there. There are actually three biblical references to the town, all in John's Gospel. It was there that Jesus turned water into wine (the first miracle; John 2:1-11) and healed the royal official's dying son from afar (John 4:46-53). It was also the home of the apostle Nathanael (John 21:2).

The actual location of Cana is not known with certainty. It is often identified with the modern archaeological site of Kefr Kenna, about three and a half miles north of Nazareth on the road to Tiberias. The site has plentiful water springs and provides many shade-figs as described in Jesus' meeting with Nathanael (John 1:48). Most scholars today, however, identify Cana with Khirbet Kana, a ruin about eight miles north of Nazareth. Local Arabs still call this place Cana of Galilee. Archaeology has unearthed an orderly, well-laid-out village with plentiful cisterns well-spaced through the town. The village seems to have been first settled in the very early period of the Roman occupation, and lasted through the Byzantine era.

# Capernaum

Capernaum was the home of Saints Peter and Andrew, and when Jesus began his ministry, he made his home there (Matt. 4:13; Mark 2:1). Capernaum thus takes its place among the most important small cities of the New Testament. It is not known why Jesus chose to leave Nazareth in favor of this city, but it may be because he found that "prophets are not without honor except in their own country and in their own house" (Matt. 13:57). Capernaum's main industry was fishing, and it was of some importance as a military garrison, administrative center, and customs station.[1]

In spite of its powerful position in Christian tradition, the city was forgotten and ultimately lost in the centuries following Jesus' ministry. It is only thanks to the dedication of the Franciscans a century ago, along with advances in modern archaeological science, that anything of Capernaum still survives. The name means "Village of Nahum," but there is no evidence that it refers to the prophet Nahum — it was more likely named after a well-known local individual. Most archaeologists and biblical scholars are convinced that it was located at the site of what is now known as Tell Hum,[2] on the north coast of the Sea of Galilee,[3] although the precise site is not positively known. Since 530 CE this has been thought to be the site of Capernaum, and recent archaeological evidence has strengthened this belief. The ruins of Tell Hum extend for over a mile along the coast, indicating that it was once a reasonably important city. It lay open to the weather and pillage for centuries until the Franciscans obtained it in 1894. Not having either the money or the expertise to excavate it, they covered it with earth to protect it. But for that, it might have been completely lost by now.

Capernaum was the stated setting of many of Jesus' teachings and miracles, and is implied in many others. It was the place where Jesus healed the slave of the Roman centurion who had built a synagogue for the people

---

1. Levi, believed to be the same person as Matthew, was a tax collector "at the seat of custom" in Capernaum until he followed Jesus.

2. "Tell" means "Hill," and "Hum" is a corruption of "Nahum," so this could very well be "Hill of Nahum."

3. The Sea of Galilee is known today as the Sea of Tiberias, and the site of Capernaum is northeast of modern Tiberias, Israel.

(Luke 7:1-10). It would have been that synagogue in which Jesus delivered his controversial Eucharistic teachings after the feeding of the five thousand (John 6:25-59). Nearby is a hill that ancient tradition identifies as the site of the Sermon on the Mount.

There is an octagonal building that is usually identified as Peter's house, although it was obviously a church. It is probably the remains of a church built on the site of Peter's house, and is mentioned in documents dated 385 CE. In the ruins of the city is one of the best-preserved ancient synagogues in Palestine. Since it can be dated no earlier than the late second century CE, it is not the one in which Jesus worshiped and taught, although there is little doubt that it is located on the same site. The remains of Jesus' synagogue may well lie below its foundations — in 1981 a synagogue was found beneath it, but there has been minimal excavation to open it, because to do so might seriously damage the present ruins. The second-century synagogue was unusual in that it was decorated with a variety of animal, mythological, and magical geometric figures, all of which are in direct violation of the Second Commandment and the law of Torah. Contemporary rabbinic writings referred to Capernaum as a seat of the Minim, a questionable Jewish sect of the time. This is an interesting commentary on the nature of the city's Jewish community in the second and third centuries. On one of the pillars is the inscription, "Alphaeus, son of Zebedee, son of John, made this column; on him be blessing."[4]

Capernaum was well-known as the center of Jesus' ministry, and while he considered it his home, he condemned it equally with all the other cities who had heard the gospel and seen his works, yet had not repented.

4. There is nothing to indicate that this man was a descendant of Alphaeus the father of Matthew, or of Zebedee the father of James and John, but it is certainly possible.

# Carchemish

One of the most battle-torn of ancient cities was Carchemish, the fortress that guarded the west side of the primary ford across the Euphrates River. The city was first settled sometime around 3500 BCE, and because of its location on the ford and at the head of a major plain it was also on the major east-west trade route in upper Mesopotamia. It guarded the river crossing, giving whoever controlled the city control over most of the trade in the area. This made it a highly desirable prize for any enemy with a taste for conquest. It was necessary, therefore, to fortify it heavily, and as a result it quickly became a major military center.

Carchemish was recognized as an important commercial hub as early as the eighteenth century BCE, and during the next three centuries it was strongly influenced by such powerful peoples as the Hittites, the Mitannians, and the Egyptians. In the seventeenth century the city allied itself with the Mitannians in the hope of holding back the advance of the Hittites from Asia Minor. The Hittites destroyed Babylon and the nearby Syrian city of Aleppo, but Carchemish, with Mitannian support, seems to have survived. In the fifteenth century the Hyksos tried to gain control of the city, but this was at the time they had lost control of Egypt and were slipping in Palestine, and the city was able to hold out against the onslaught. In about 1350 BCE the Hittite Empire had a resurgence and conquered Carchemish. It remained the primary Hittite commercial center for over 150 years, until it was taken by the Philistines sometime in the early twelfth century BCE. After the Philistine conquest of much of the Middle East in the twelfth and eleventh centuries BCE, Carchemish became the capital of the so-called Neo-Hittite culture, a Philistine-controlled culture that combined characteristics of the Hittites and the Syrians.

Carchemish was thrust into a major role in history when the Assyrian Tiglath-Pileser I moved west and attacked the whole countryside around the city. As he approached the city, the army of Carchemish met his forces on the east side of the river, and a bitter battle ensued. Even though outnumbered, they were able to hold off the Assyrians and save the city. A few years later Ashurbanipal II and Shalmaneser III were able to exert enough force to exact tribute from Carchemish, but other than paying tribute, the city was able to hold out against the Assyrians for three more centuries. It became a city-state unto itself, and controlled most of the commerce in that region of Mesopotamia. In 743 BCE the most powerful of all the Assyrian kings, Tiglath-Pileser III, finally managed to conquer Carchemish. He exacted a huge tribute, but otherwise left the city unscathed. In 717 BCE, however, Pisiris, the king of Carchemish, foolishly rebelled against Assyria. Sargon II replied by destroying the city and killing Pisiris. Isaiah mentioned this in his warning about the impending danger of Assyria to Israel (Isa. 10:9). Sargon deported the entire population to other regions and repopulated the city with Assyrians, ruled by an Assyrian governor. The Assyrians had overextended themselves, though, and by the middle of the seventh century BCE their power over Carchemish was weakening as the Neo-Babylonians under Nebuchadrezzar II were rising to power and slowly eroding the territories of the Assyrian Empire. In 609 BCE the Egyptian pharaoh Neco II, fearful of the now rapid advance of the Babylonians, moved up the Palestinian coast and eastward toward Carchemish to assist the Assyrians. Josiah, the king of Judah, fearing the Assyrians more than the Babylonians, attempted to stop Neco at Megiddo, and was killed in battle there (2 Chron. 35:20-24). The Judeans withdrew, and Neco faced the Babylonians in a fierce battle at Carchemish. He had reinforced his army with mercenaries from all over the Middle East (Jer. 46:2-28, esp. vv. 20-21), but Nebuchadrezzar's armies were too powerful for them. The Egyptians and Assyrians were defeated, and Babylonia was established as the leading power in the entire Middle East.

After the fall of Carchemish to the Babylonians, the city went into a rapid decline. It was of very little importance for three centuries, until the rise of the Seleucid Empire after Alexander the Great's death. Seleucus I built a new city at the site of Carchemish, naming it Europos. It became a valuable point on the trade route and served as a fortress to protect the river crossing, but it was never again to rise to the wealth and influence it had known in earlier times.

# Colossae

Colossae was a city in the region of Phrygia in Asia Minor, about ten miles east-southeast of Laodicea, west of what is now Turkey. It was the city to whose inhabitants Saint Paul wrote the Epistle to the Colossians. Located on a mound that was easily defensible, it had a generous water supply and was at the intersection of two major trade routes. It was a relatively important city during the Persian period, but by the third century BCE it began a significant decline following the relocation of the trade route between Sardis and Pergamum. There is no habitation in the area of Colossae today, and although its location is known, the city has not been excavated.

Colossae plays a much more important role in Christian tradition than it does in ancient history, mainly because of Saint Paul's letter to the Christians there. The letter addresses some serious theological problems of the times and sheds light on how the early church dealt with them. The letter was written while Paul was living in Ephesus (Acts 19:1-10), and it would appear that he had not visited Colossae when he wrote it, although he hoped to do so in the near future (Philem. 22). It was probably delivered to the church in Colossae by Epaphras, who was a Colossian. Paul's friend Philemon, to whom he sent back the converted slave Onesimus, was also a Colossian. The city was severely damaged by an earthquake in 60 CE, and since there is no mention of that event in either the letter to the Colossians or the letter to Philemon, we may assume that they were written before that time. Since there is practically no mention of Colossae in any records after that date, it is reasonable to assume that it was abandoned soon thereafter.

The main problem in the Colossian Christian church was the threat of the heresy of Gnosticism. This was a heresy that stressed knowledge rather than faith. It taught that the world is basically evil, and that to counter this God imparted secret knowledge to certain Christians to guarantee their salvation. The Gnostics also emphasized the worship of angels as demigods, because it was through them that this special knowledge was imparted. Paul advocated honoring and revering the angels, but bitterly opposed any idea of worshiping them as a substitute for Christ. The heresy was an outgrowth of the Greek Gnostic cults, whose members believed that the gods imparted secret knowledge to the spiritually elite in order to guarantee them special favors after death.[1]

The other Christian issue associated with Colossae is that of slavery. Onesimus was a runaway slave who came to Paul and was converted. Paul sent him back to Colossae to his owner Philemon with the admonition, but not the command, that Philemon accept him "as a brother," implying that Onesimus should be set free. Paul did not officially condemn the institution of slavery, although it is patently clear through his writings that he did not approve of it among Christians. Slavery was such a deeply ingrained institution in all cultures of the day, even including Judaism, that to advocate its abolition would have been considered so ludicrous as to border on insanity.

1. The Greek mathematician Pythagoras founded such a cult, teaching that special mathematical insights were a secret gift of the gods. The Pythagoreans would reveal none of their mathematical discoveries to anyone outside the cult. The only way we know of the Pythagorean Theorem today is that many years later someone "leaked" it.

# Corinth

Corinth is located at the isthmus that joins mainland Greece with the Peloponnesus. Located at the base of a massive nineteen-hundred-foot rock outcropping called Acrocorinthus, Corinth can trace its history back to a group of late Stone Age villages on the lower slopes of the citadel. As these villages grew and prospered, they merged and moved to the coast, where they developed the Bronze Age city of Korakou. By 1100 BCE Korakou was very prosperous and engaged in overseas trade. This was probably the "wealthy Corinth" to which Homer refers in the *Iliad*.[1] In the Iron Age (sometime after 1100) the Dorians conquered the region, settling in several towns, one of which was on the site of Corinth. They had no interest in the sea, and although they were strong, they were a minority. The non-Dorian Corinthians retained their seafaring tradition.

The Isthmus of Corinth lies between the Gulf of Corinth and the Saronic Gulf, and many ships had to be dragged across it. While this might inhibit trade in many places, it was an advantage to the Corinthians. The isthmus was by far the easiest access to the northern Peloponnesus and the southern mainland. This gave the Corinthians great leverage in controlling trade through the region. This shipping barrier remained unchanged until Nero had a canal dug in 67 CE, but even after that it was too shallow for larger ships.

As Greece moved into its golden age, Corinth played a leading role in the development of its culture, becoming a powerful and wealthy city-state. The Corinthians planted settlements all over southern Greece. One of their accomplishments, magnificent pottery, became a profitable industry. By the sixth century BCE, Corinthian pottery and bronze-work were deemed the best in the world. The city's chief source of wealth, however, was control of the isthmus. With trade control augmented by taxes and passage fees, Corinth became one of the wealthiest city-states in all of Greece.

---

1. The evidence for this is that the Corinth of classical times, though located near Korakou, yields little archaeological evidence of prosperity in Homeric times, while Korakou was thriving in that era.

During its period of expansion, Dorian Corinth was ruled by a noble family, the Bacchiadae. They were overthrown in 657 BCE by Cypselus and his son Periander, who ruled tyrannically for twenty-five years. They developed control of overland trade, selling Corinthian wares deep into the mainland. In 682 they were overthrown, and the government was taken over by an oligarchy (rule by a small number of people with equal power). They developed a constitution that protected the rights of the people, though the power remained in the hands of the wealthy upper class. The great Greek poet Pindar praised Corinth for its governmental structure, appreciation of the arts, and military skill.

By the beginning of the fifth century BCE Athens had bypassed Corinth in seamanship and commerce. Corinth, in an attempt to regain supremacy, joined the Spartan League, which required the Corinthians to engage in land warfare. While they had a fine army and fought with valor and honor, they were not a great military force. They acquitted themselves well in the Greco-Persian wars, but the Athenian Delian League was superior to the Spartan League, and it gave Athens control of the Aegean. In 460 BCE Athens attacked and defeated Corinth. Corinth tried to establish an alliance with Athens, but centuries of often bitter rivalry prevailed. In 433 Corinth fought its last battle as a great power in the Peloponnesian War (a long war between Athens and Sparta, in which Sparta was finally victorious). Athens was defeated, but Corinth never revived. It was so weakened by war that it spent the next two centuries being passed back and forth in alliances with stronger powers. It had one more moment of glory in 342 BCE, when it allied with Athens to repel an invasion by Philip of Macedon (the father of Alexander the Great).

Four years later, in 338 BCE, Philip returned, took Corinth, established Acrocorinthus as a fortress, and used the city as the center of the League of Corinth. This was a league of Greek states that were puppets of Macedonia. The city thrived under the rule of Alexander and his successors for almost two centuries.

In 146 BCE Corinth was destroyed in a war with Rome. The city was leveled,[2] all the men massacred, and the women and children sold into slavery. It lay in ruins for one hundred years until 46 BCE, when Julius Caesar, shortly before his death, decreed that a Roman colony be built on

---

2. Leveling cities was a common Roman practice, at which they were quite efficient. When they leveled Jerusalem in 70 CE, it is said that there was not one stone left upon another.

During his year and a half of ministry in Corinth, St. Paul may have walked along this city street, now in ruins.   Photo credit: Erich Lessing/Art Resource, NY

the site. It was populated primarily with freedmen from Italy, who were soon thereafter joined by Greeks, Jews, and a variety of Middle Easterners. Still called Corinth,[3] the city thrived and flourished as the capital of the Roman province of Achaea. It was damaged in an earthquake in the first century CE, but Nero funded its rebuilding. Vespasian and Hadrian also built there, and by the second century CE it may well have been the finest city in Greece. It survived until 521 CE, when it was again destroyed, this time by the barbarian Goths; the emperor Justinian, who was dedicated to restoring the Roman Empire to its past glory, then rebuilt the city again. There has been a city of sorts at the site ever since, but in spite of its success as a Roman colony, Corinth never again saw the glory that it knew in its golden age during the seventh and sixth centuries BCE. Archaeological excavation of the ancient city began in 1896, and has continued ever since.

The first recorded trip by a Christian missionary to Corinth was that of Saint Paul. His first attempt in Achaea had not been very successful: he made a few converts in Athens, but failed to establish a church there. In Corinth, however, he stayed a year and a half, and his efforts resulted in a strong Christian church. During his time there Paul wrote at least three important letters, one to the Romans and two to the Thessalonians. While the Corinthian church had many problems, it was well rooted in his teachings. He later wrote two letters to the Corinthian Christians, focusing not only on their problems and conflicts but also on many important points of Christian theology and spirituality.

Archaeological evidence has provided support for the biblical narrative of Paul's time in Corinth. An inscription indicates the same synagogue in which Paul preached. Another identifies the meat market to which Paul referred when he spoke of eating meat sacrificed to idols (1 Cor. 10:25-31). By the pavement in the theater of Corinth there is an inscription, *Erastus pro aedilitate sua pecunia stravit:* "Erastus [in thanks] for his position as magistrate laid [this pavement] at his own expense." Because of the wording, scholars believe that this is the Erastus who later became a Christian and a friend of Paul's (2 Tim. 4:20).

As archaeological technology improves, scientists are making more and more discoveries about Corinth. These discoveries continue to validate and expand upon what the Bible and historic documents tell us about this ancient city.

---

3. Its real name was *Colonia Laus Iulia Corinthiensis* ("The Corinthian Colony of Julian Praise"), but it was generally known by its ancient name of Corinth.

# Cyrene

Although Cyrene prospered as a city for about eight centuries, it never played a particularly important part in ancient history. It is important to Christians only because it was the home of Simon of Cyrene, whom the Roman soldiers compelled to carry Jesus' cross to Golgotha.

Cyrene is located in Libya on the north coast of Africa. It was founded in 690 BCE by Dorian Greeks, and soon after its founding many Peloponnesian Greeks migrated there. It served as a haven for Greeks living among the Libyans. Its prosperous economy was based mainly on agriculture. The primary crop was silphium, a plant in great demand as both a spice and a medicine. The climate was perfect for growing it, and records indicate that three crops a year were harvested.

Cyrene was ruled by kings until the end of the fifth century BCE, at which time it started moving rapidly toward becoming a democracy. By the fourth century it was a fully functioning democracy. In 331 Alexander the Great swept through the Mediterranean, and rather than fighting and being destroyed, Cyrene submitted to him. After Alexander's death it became a part of the kingdom of Ptolemy, the general who ruled Egypt and north Africa. In 96 BCE Ptolemy XI (Cleopatra's grandfather) ceded it to Rome as a free city, and soon thereafter Rome annexed the whole region as the province of Cyrenicia.

In Roman times a significant portion of the population of Cyrene was Greek-speaking Jews who had been invited as settlers by the Ptolemies, and who enjoyed equal rights of citizenship with the Greek and Egyptian population there. Simon was of this group. He was probably in Jerusalem to celebrate the Passover when he was pulled out of the crowd by the soldiers and forced to carry the cross. Another important Cyrenian was the prophet Lucius (Acts 13:1). St. Stephen may also have been a Cyrenian, as he was arrested at the synagogue where the Cyrenians and Alexandrians worshiped (Acts 6:9). Jerusalem always had a number of Cyrenian visitors, especially at Passover time. Cyrene's end, however, was on the horizon.

Jews all over the Roman Empire revolted during the reign of Vespasian, mainly because of the destruction of Jerusalem by his son Titus in 70 CE. The initial revolt in Cyrene had little effect or repercussion, but in 115 there was a major revolt in which pagan idols were smashed and temples burned all over Cyrenicia. According to the Roman historian Dio Cassius, over 200,000 inhabitants were killed in the rioting. Hadrian restored the city, but it never truly recovered. Decades earlier the supply of silphium had diminished radically because of soil depletion from over-farming the single crop. The economy was collapsing, and there was no other significant source of revenue.

There was a Christian church in Cyrene, but the Christian community there was very ordinary, and made little contribution to world Christianity.

Archaeological research has found nothing unusual in Cyrene, there being only the remains of the expected Roman temples, baths, and monuments. The most significant ruin is that of the ancient temple of Apollo, which was rebuilt several times. In the fourth century it was converted to a Christian church.

# Damascus

Damascus, the capital of modern Syria, has been an important city for thousands of years. Much of its prosperity can be attributed to its location, which is in the Ghuta oasis at the foot of Mount Qasyun. It commands two rivers and controls most of the desert trade routes of the region. According to the Jewish historian Flavius Josephus, Damascus was already a well-known city by the time of Abraham. Its ancient name was *Damasqa,* and today it is *Dimashq-as-Sham* ("Damascus of Syria"). Most Arabs call it *Al-Fayha,* "the Fragrant," because of its profusion of gardens. Its population today is quite diverse, consisting of Arabs (the majority), Druze, Kurds, Turks, and a variety of other Middle Eastern peoples; a Jewish community and a large Christian community are present.[1]

Throughout its history Damascus has vacillated between subjugation and glory. There are traces of Stone Age and Bronze Age settlements, and Damascus appears to have been the capital of Ubi, a vassal state of Egypt. It did not gain any political or economic importance, however, until the region was settled by the Arameans (a non-Hebrew Semitic people) in about 1000 BCE. By then the city was powerful enough to be a serious rival of Assyria (modern Iraq). This was about the same time that David defeated the Philistines and was solidifying the Hebrew tribes as the United Monarchy of Israel. In the ninth century BCE, Damascus led a coalition of Syrian states against Shalmaneser III of Assyria. Although the revolt failed, the city was not captured. Later, however, weak leadership left it open to Assyrian retaliation by Adadnirari, and Assyrian power was restored over the region by Tiglath-Pileser III. In 732 BCE Damascus was destroyed, the king was killed, and the people were sold into slavery. The city was slowly rebuilt, and with the rise of the Neo-Babylonians under Nebuchadrezzar II, Assyria's power dissipated. The Babylonians assumed control of Damascus until they were defeated by the Persians, at which time Damascus became a Persian garri-

---

1. A large number of the Damascene Christians are Maronites, a Uniate group based on the teachings of the fourth-century priest Maro. The Uniates are those Eastern churches that follow the doctrines of the Roman Catholic Church (and thus are a branch of the Catholic church), but that retain the Eastern Orthodox liturgy and traditions, including a married priesthood and the use of ancient liturgical languages and rites.

son site. When Alexander the Great defeated the Persian Empire in the fourth century BCE, Damascus fell under Hellenic rule. For the next two centuries it passed back and forth between Syrian (Seleucid) and Egyptian (Ptolemaic) control. In about 85 BCE, at the request of the citizens of Damascus, most of what we would now call Syria fell under the rule of King Aretas III of Nabatea, an Arab kingdom in what is now Jordan.

In 64 BCE Pompey the Great swept through the Middle East, putting most of the region under the Roman yoke. It remained in Roman hands until shortly before the death of Tiberius, when it was taken by the Arabian emir Aretas IV. He was its ruler when Paul visited there. In 105 CE Nabatea, along with Damascus and much of what is now Syria, was incorporated into the Roman Empire as the province of Syria. Damascus began exporting produce to Rome, where Damascene plums, figs, and pistachios became very popular, and the trade brought much wealth to Damascus. Under Roman rule the city was overshadowed by Antioch, although it continued to prosper richly. At some point the metalworkers of the area developed a secret method of annealing iron, producing what came to be called "Damascus steel." Damascene swords and knives quickly became world-famous.[2] At the end of the third century CE, Diocletian established arms factories there, bringing more Roman gold into the city's coffers.

The first Christians appeared in Damascus almost immediately after the movement began, when it was still known only as "The Way." Being so close to Israel, Damascus was the home of a large Jewish community, including a large sect of ascetic Jews, a branch of the Essenes, known as "The New Covenant in the Land of Damascus." Many Damascene Jews had picked up on Jesus' teachings. This was why Saul of Tarsus (later to become Saint Paul) decided to go there in his attempt to purify Judaism of what he considered the Christian blasphemy. It was on the road to Damascus that Christ appeared to him in the vision that effected his conversion (Acts 9:3-19). Later he was nearly arrested there at the behest of the Nabatean king Aretas IV, and escaped by being lowered in a basket from a window in the city wall (2 Cor. 11:32-33). Christianity thrived in Damascus for several centuries, through the age of persecution, and on through the age of Constantine. The city was the seat of one of the important eastern bishops, and in 325 CE it sent delegates to the Council of Nicaea. After the conver-

---

2. They also developed a method of etching beautiful swirled designs on the steel blades. Such designs are still in use today, and the art of creating them is known as "damascening."

sion of Saint Paul there is no evidence of any significant persecution of Damascene Christians by the Sanhedrin.

The primary religion at the time of Paul's visit was the worship of Adad (or Hadad-Rimmon), the storm god.[3] He came to be known as Jupiter Damascenus, and was included in the Roman pantheon. One of the landmarks of the city was a magnificent temple dedicated to Adad. In the late fourth century the Christian emperor Theodosius tore down the temple and erected the Church of Saint John the Baptist on the site.

In 635 CE Damascus fell to the Muslim Arabs, who swept through the Middle East in their fervor to convert the entire Arab world to Islam. The following year the city was temporarily evacuated just before the bloody battle of Yarmuk, in which Syria fell to Arabia. For almost a century Damascus was the capital of the Caliphate of Mu'awiya, and Syria was in every respect an Islamic state. The Muslims did not force their faith on Christians or Jews, although they demanded the conversion of pagans. Christians and Jews were guaranteed possession of their property, and many held public office.

In 750, rival Muslim armies overtook the region, established Baghdad as the capital, and relegated Damascus to a provincial center. For the next four centuries it changed hands frequently, being ruled at different times by rival Arab chieftains, Persians, and briefly by Turks, all representing a variety of Muslim sects and interpretations of the Qur'an. Some of these Muslim rulers were tolerant moderates, and some were brutal and bloodthirsty fanatics.

In 1174 Damascus came under the rule of Salah al-Din (called "Saladin" by the crusaders), who recaptured Jerusalem from the crusaders. He was a fierce warrior but a just and wise ruler. Under his rule Damascus enjoyed religious tolerance, rapid cultural growth, and great economic prosperity. Shortly after his death the city fell to the pagan Mongols under Genghis Khan, and soon thereafter it was retaken by the Mamelukes, extremist Muslim rulers of Syria and Egypt. In 1516 it came under the rule of the Ottoman Turks, who ruled it reasonably moderately until the fall of the Ottoman Empire at the end of World War I. It then fell under French rule under a mandate from the League of Nations until 1941, when Free French and British troops entered the city to oust the Vichy French.[4] In

---

3. Islam did not appear until the seventh century CE. The entire Arabic world was pagan until then except for a few small Jewish and Christian communities.

4. The Vichy government was a puppet French government that collaborated with the

1946 it became the capital of free Syria, and prospered despite frequent political and religious disturbances. During the time Syria was a member of the United Arab Republic (1958-61), the city was a provincial seat, but it again became the capital when Syria withdrew from the UAR.

Saladin treated Syrian Christians with tolerance, although he was understandably brutal to the crusaders, whose invasion and rule was thoroughly corrupt and barbarian. After his death, Christians were generally oppressed until the time of the Ottoman Turks, who also ruled with tolerance. Christians were still reasonably well accepted after the fall of the Ottomans, until the Middle East began to be torn apart by political and religious hatred after the partition of Palestine by the United Nations in 1946. Today, Syrian Christians live in a tense relationship with their Muslim rulers.

Nazis from 1941 to 1944 to avoid German occupation. Its capital was Vichy, a small city in central France. They were eliminated and replaced by the true French government when the Nazis were expelled from France in 1944.

# Dan

Dan was the northernmost city in the kingdom of Israel, both before and after the division of the United Monarchy. It symbolized the whole northern border of the kingdom, just as Beersheba symbolized the southern. Also like Beersheba, it was a city of great military, religious, and commercial importance.

When the Israelites first settled in Canaan, each tribe was allotted a territory. To the tribe of Dan was given a territory in the southern regions between those of Benjamin, Ephraim, and Judah (Josh. 19:40-48), just east of what today is known as the Gaza Strip. Pressed back by the Amorites and the Philistines, and feeling themselves choked off by the surrounding tribes, the Danites decided to move north and find a place for themselves. They finally settled near the source of the Jordan. Some of the Danites remained in their original territory, where Samson, a Danite hero, was a judge. After the move, however, the tribe of Dan was always associated with the northern region.[1]

The city of Dan was originally a Canaanite settlement called Laish. The Danites sent out a search team to locate a new land, and when they returned they recommended Laish and its environs as the perfect place for them (Judg. 18:2, 8-10). The Laishites were a peaceful and unsuspecting people, with virtually no defenses (18:7). The Danites swept down on them, burned their city, and slaughtered the population.

The location of Laish made it an ideal place for a settlement, and the features that made it so attractive are still there today. The archaeological site is at Tell el-Qadi, "the Mound of the Judge," also often called simply

---

1. The book of Revelation omits Dan from its list of the tribes of Israel (Rev. 7:5-8). It is unknown whether this was intentional or the result of an early scrivener's corruption in the text. Manasseh, Joseph's son, is listed as a tribe along with Joseph, although these two names are usually interchangeable to indicate a single tribe. Irenaeus postulated that the omission was because the antichrist was to come from the tribe of Dan. He based this on Jeremiah 8:16, "The snorting of the enemy's horses is heard from Dan; at the neighing of their stallions the whole land trembles. They have come to devour the land and everything in it, the city and all who live there." Dan was a hotbed of paganism from its earliest foundation, and this is another possible reason why St. John may have left Dan out of the list of tribes.

Tell Dan. The seventy-foot-high mound covers fifty acres in a fertile valley at the base of Mount Hermon, about twenty-five miles north of the Sea of Galilee. The Nahr Leddan, a major spring that serves as the source of the Jordan River, provides a plentiful water supply not only to the city but also to the fertile valley to the south. For millennia this region has been an important producer of grain, fruit, and vegetables. The site is also located at the intersection of two important highways. One, the east-west route from Phoenician Tyre to Syrian Damascus, was the primary route connecting all the lands in the Fertile Crescent. The other was the north-south route that connected the northern countries to the southern routes leading to Egypt and Arabia.

The biblical references to the area go back to the early days of Abraham. It was to Dan that Abraham pursued the kings who had captured his nephew Lot (Gen. 14:14). Although the city could not have been called Dan at that time (since Dan was Abraham's great-grandson, and the Danite tribe did not migrate to Palestine until centuries later), Genesis calls it Dan because the story was actually written centuries after the event, after the Danites had taken the territory. It is unknown what it was actually called in Abraham's day, although it had been settled by Canaanites centuries earlier. The first settlement was in the late Neolithic period, sometime between 6,000 and 8,000 BCE, as indicated by pottery shards found there. By the mid third millennium BCE it was a city with a population of around nine thousand people (a large city by the standards of that time). By the middle Bronze Age, around 1800 BCE, Laish was a Canaanite city, well fortified with a city wall and a huge twin-towered gate. There is evidence of international relations and great wealth. By the beginning of the twelfth century BCE, the Laishites apparently had few enemies and had become complacent in their prosperity. The city was destroyed by the Danites around 1150 BCE, and it would seem that the Laishites were completely unprepared for their attack. The Danites rebuilt the city and named it Dan. By the end of the tenth century it was a prosperous community with a thick, high wall and compound arched gateway, and a sanctuary and sacrificial altar at a high point on the north side of the mound. This would have been shortly after Solomon's United Monarchy had been divided into the kingdoms of Israel to the north and Judah to the south, when King Jeroboam I of Israel established Dan and Bethel as northern border sanctuaries (1 Kings 12:26-31). Jeroboam, however, also encouraged pagan worship in these places. During the following centuries the city survived, at least for the most part, the invasions of the Assyrians, the Greeks, and the Romans, and functioned as a religious sanctuary through all these periods. Its religious history was spotty, however, because its faithfulness to Levitical Judaism was often questionable at best. There were times when it was positively pagan.

The Danites who left the south and settled at Laish may have felt pressure not only from the Philistines and the neighboring tribes but possibly from the remaining faithful Danites as well. The urge to move may have been more fired by religion than by politics or a desire for *Lebensraum,* as there is indication that their religion was strongly infused with paganism. The book of Judges (18:30) tells us that as soon as the Danites had taken Laish they set up a graven image and appointed their own priesthood. In the late ninth century Jeroboam, who had perhaps lapsed into pagan worship during his sojourn in Egypt, set up idols of a calf or bull in Dan and Bethel and declared, "Here are your gods, O Israel" (1 Kings 12:28-30). Not long afterward Ahab's queen Jezebel instituted the worship of the Phoenician baals and the fertility goddess Ashtoreth, and these would surely have been worshiped at Dan and Bethel as well. The sanctuary at Dan continued to be used through the Hellenistic and Roman periods. Because of Dan's paganism it was held in the utmost contempt by the Judean Jews, who had remained faithful to the Levitical traditions. An inscription from the Hellenistic period, written in Greek and Aramaic, contains a vow from a worshiper named Zoilos, given to "the god who is in Dan." This confirms not only that the sanctuary was still in use at that time, but also that Tell al-Qadi is indeed the site of the ancient city.

An exciting discovery was made at Tell al-Qadi in 1993, when an inscription on a victory stele of an Aramean king was found referring to the "house of David." For all its importance in Judaic and Christian traditions, the archaeological proof of the stories of David is minimal, and there are some naysayers who maintain that he, like King Arthur, was a fictional king loosely based on a real person. This inscription and others found in 1994 help confirm his existence and thus validate much of the biblical tradition.

# Decapolis

As early as 200 BCE the Seleucids had occupied most of the towns in Galilee, and had thoroughly Hellenized several, including Amman (which they called Philadelphia) and Gadara. When Pompey captured Israel for the Romans in 63 BCE, he removed Hippos, Scythopolis, and Pella from Jewish power and annexed them to the authority of the Roman province of Syria, although they were granted freedom to govern themselves within certain parameters. These cities drew up a trade treaty, and allied themselves into a federation for mutual defense against their several enemies, including local marauding Semitic tribes. There were ten original members of the federation,[1] and the region containing them, a large territory mainly southeast of the Sea of Galilee, came to be known as Decapolis ("Ten-City"). By the end of the second century CE the federation consisted of eighteen cities.

Of the huge crowds that followed Jesus around, many came from Decapolis. There are two stories of the healing of madmen in Decapolis, one in the Gadarenes (the area around Gadara, Matt. 8:28-34), and the other in the Gerasenes (the area around Gerasa, Mark 5:1-13, Luke 8:26-33). Both tell the same story, of Jesus casting the demons into a huge herd of swine. It is likely that they are stories of the same event, with confusion about the city where it happened. Nonetheless, the presence of such a large herd of swine indicates that there was a considerable Gentile population in the area, because the pig is a ritually unclean animal to the Jews. Jesus also visited Decapolis when he was en route from Sidon to the eastern shore of the Sea of Galilee; he detoured into Decapolis (probably Hippos), where he healed the deaf man (Mark 7:31-37).

During the Jewish revolt of 67 to 70 CE, a large number of Jewish Christians sought refuge in Decapolis around the area of Pella.

---

1. The Roman historian Pliny the Elder listed them as Damascus, Dion, Gadara, Gerasa, Hippos, Kanatha, Pella, Philadelphia, Raphana, and Scythopolis.

# Dothan

As a city, Dothan was singularly unimportant, although the region around it played a very significant role in ancient times. It lies in a fertile plain separating the Carmel Mountains from the hills of Samaria. This provided an easy route for travelers between Egypt and the northern countries of Lebanon and Syria. The fertile fields attracted Jacob's sons to the region of Dothan (Gen. 37:17), and when the Midianite slavers bought Joseph from his brothers (Gen. 37:28), they carried him into Egypt by this route. Archaeologists have found stone cisterns outside the town that fit the biblical description of the pit into which Joseph was thrown by his brothers. When Aramean soldiers attempted to capture the prophet Elisha at Dothan, Elisha's servant had a vision of angelic forces assembled on the hills outside the town after Elisha told him, "Do not be afraid, for there are more with us than there are with them" (2 Kings 6:16).

Archaeological excavations in the mid-twentieth century unearthed a walled city at Dothan from the early Bronze Age, about 3000 to 2800 BCE. The city was apparently destroyed, and another rose on the ruins around 2000 BCE, using the walls of the earlier one. A large tomb there contained hundreds of pots and other artifacts that reveal a great deal about the culture of the time, indicating that it was quite consistent with the culture of the other cities of the region. Egyptian records of Thutmosis III, dated around 1459 BCE, list Dothan among his conquests. Judges 1:27-36 indicates that during the Israelite conquest of Canaan many cities were not conquered, but the inhabitants were enslaved and the cities taken over by the Israelites. Although Dothan is not mentioned, there is no archaeological evidence of its destruction at the time, so it was probably among those cities. Excavations have also indicated settlements at Dothan during the Assyrian and Hellenistic periods, although sometime around that time the city appears to have been abandoned and never resettled.

# Emmaus

The site of Emmaus is unknown, although Saint Luke tells us that it was about seven miles from Jerusalem (Luke 24:13). It is only referred to once in the Bible, in the story of the resurrected Jesus walking there with two of his disciples. Walking that distance in a couple of hours was not at all uncommon in those days. There are only two known sites at roughly that distance from Jerusalem. One is a first-century CE village at El-qubeibeh, where the crusaders founded a fort called Castellum Emmaus, but the name cannot be traced back to the first century. The second is mentioned in the writings of the Jewish historian Flavius Josephus, who speaks of a military colony founded by Vespasian at Ammaous, about three and a half miles west of Jerusalem. This is believed to be at the site of the modern town of Kaloniye (from the Latin *colonia*), or of Khirbet Beit Mizza (called Mozah in Joshua; see Josh. 18:26). Here Luke's distance would be wrong, unless he counted it as a round trip.

Little is known of this small Judean town, although it has great significance to Christians. Luke tells us that two of Jesus' disciples, not having heard that he was resurrected, were dejectedly walking back to their home in Emmaus when he joined them and walked along with them (Luke 24:13-27). They did not recognize him, and he explained to them the meaning of all that had happened in the past few days — of the prophecies, of his teachings, and of his death and resurrection. Finally, at Emmaus, they recognized him "when he broke the bread" (Luke 24:35). One disciple was Cleopas, and the other is unnamed, although many scholars suggest it may have been Cleopas's wife. (Jesus had many female disciples, and it was common in those days not to identify the names of women unless it was important to do so.) The concept of recognizing Jesus "in the breaking of the bread" (the Eucharist) is a basic one in Christian spirituality, and it is based on this story.

# Ephesus

By the time of St. Paul the ancient city of Ephesus was the largest trading center in Anatolia (Asia Minor).[1] St. John and the Virgin Mary lived (and possibly died) there, and the Ephesian Christians had great influence on the spread of Christianity in the area.

The history of Ephesus goes back a long way. The historians Strabo (a first-century Greek) and Pausanias (a second-century Roman) claimed truth to the ancient myth that Ephesus was founded by the Amazons, a mythical race of ferocious female warriors. This is, of course, pure fiction, as were the Amazons themselves.

The region was originally conquered in the eleventh century BCE by the Ionian Greeks under the command of Androcles, the prince of Athens. According to the legend, Androcles consulted the Delphic Oracle before sailing. The Oracle advised him to build a city where he found a fish and a boar. One day he saw some fishermen broiling fish. Their fire spread to a thicket, driving a wild boar out, and Androcles claimed the spot for his capital city. In fact, there are fourteenth-century BCE Hittite references to a city called Apasas at about the same spot, and this may well have been the city which Androcles took for his capital. He dedicated the city to Cybele, the goddess of nature, although at some point not long after it was dedicated to Artemis (Diana), the goddess of the hunt and sister of Apollo, the sun god.

The city was ruled by descendants of Androcles for several centuries, during which it became a major banking and mercantile center. In the sixth century BCE it fell to King Croesus of Lydia,[2] who built several magnificent buildings there, including the beautiful temple of Artemis.

In 546 BCE Cyrus, the emperor of Persia, conquered Lydia and all its possessions, including Ephesus. Like Croesus, Cyrus was an enlightened conqueror, and rather than destroying the city he supported its prosperity.

---

1. Asia Minor, also called Anatolia, is the southern section of what today is Turkey, and covers the almost-peninsula between the Mediterranean and the Black Sea.

2. Lydia was one of the wealthiest kingdoms in the world at the time — thus the expression, "rich as Croesus."

In the subsequent years of Persian rule, however, much of the city was neglected, but not ruined.

In 356 BCE a madman named Herostratus burned the temple of Artemis to the ground in order to immortalize his name — obviously, he succeeded. Alexander the Great was born that very same night. The historian Plutarch said that Artemis was too busy tending to the birth of the ruler of the world to protect her temple. Alexander offered to rebuild the temple in 337, but the Ephesians refused, saying that it was inappropriate for a god (i.e., Alexander) to build a temple for another god. They rebuilt it themselves, so resplendently that it came to be recognized as one of the seven wonders of the ancient world. Antipater of Sidon wrote of it, "The Sun himself has never looked upon its equal outside of Olympus."

The Persians ruled until 336 BCE, when they were conquered by Alexander. He liberated the city and guaranteed its independence. After his death in 323 BCE, the city was ruled by one of his generals, Lysimachos. During his rule a long-developing danger came to a head. Alluvial sand brought down by the Kaistros River was silting in the harbor and surrounding the city with malaria-bearing marshes. Lysimachos had the entire city moved upriver to a protected valley. He built a six-mile-long wall around the new city, and named it Arsinon after his wife Arsinoë. The name was never accepted by its citizens, however, and it reverted to Ephesus after his death.

After the death of Lysimachos, control passed back and forth between two other empires founded by Alexander's generals, those of Seleucus (Syria) and Ptolemy (Egypt). In 188 BCE the Turkish king of Pergamum gained control. In 133 BCE, in exchange for protection of his other territories, King Attalus III Philometer, in his will, left his ruling rights of all Anatolia to the Romans. They recognized the economic importance of the location of Ephesus and made it the capital of the Asian province. It rapidly became the leading trading center of Asia Minor. By the beginning of the Christian era the city had 250,000 inhabitants — an enormous population by the standards of that time.

By 129 BCE a hatred for Rome had built up because of Rome's heavy-handed rule and excessive taxation. When Mithridates IV of Pontus drove back the Romans he was enthusiastically welcomed by the Ephesians. He declared an automatic death sentence on all Romans and Roman collaborators in the city, and an estimated eighty thousand people were massacred in a single day. He made Pergamum the capital of Anatolia, and moved on to take most of Greece. The struggle between the two powers continued for almost half a century until 87 BCE, when the Roman general Sulla recaptured Greece and drove Mithridates back to Pergamum. By 63 BCE, when Mithridates was killed in battle, the Romans had gained undisputed control and Ephesus was once again a Roman city and the capital of Anatolia.

By this time the Romans had learned to be a little less oppressive of their more productive conquests, so Ephesus prospered. The upper classes had a life of luxury and wealth equal to that found in Rome. In 29 BCE the Ephesians dedicated a sector of the city to Octavian (who later became the emperor Augustus). The city became a favorite of Marc Antony, who visited frequently. In 33 BCE he came there with Cleopatra, but soon thereafter he was forced to fight Octavian, was defeated, and died in Egypt in 30 BCE.

After the apostles were driven out of Jerusalem in 37 CE, they began their intensive missionary journeys. In 53 St. Paul visited Ephesus and established a Christian church there. He left shortly thereafter, although he returned several years later and stayed for quite a long time. Many scholars believe that he wrote his letters to the Corinthians, the Colossians, and Philemon while he was in Ephesus.[3] The Ephesians considered him the head of their church.[4] After Paul's execution in Rome in 64, St. John became the leader of the Ephesian church. He lived there for at least three years, and some traditions claim that he wrote his Gospel there. It is more likely that he wrote his Gospel while he was living on the Greek island of Patmos. (He may have been there living as a hermit, or possibly as a Roman slave in the mines.) In his later life, however, there is little doubt that he lived in Ephesus and that he died and was buried there. The emperor Justinian (sixth century CE) erected the Basilica of St. John over the site where tradition places John's tomb. Tradition also maintains (substantiated by some early church records) that the Virgin Mary, whom Jesus gave into John's care at the crucifixion (John 19:26-27), accompanied him there

3. While these have been traditionally associated with Paul's imprisonment in Rome, there is much evidence that they were actually written in Ephesus. It is very unlikely that Onesimus, Philemon's escaped slave, would have fled from Colossae all the way to Rome. He more likely would have fled to a nearby large city where he could go unnoticed. This would have been Ephesus.

4. There is doubt as to whether St. Paul wrote the letter to the Ephesians. It has a strong overtone of having been written by someone who had not been to Ephesus (cf. Eph. 1:15). In those days it was not considered dishonest to write in someone else's name if the writer were a disciple of the person in whose name he wrote. On the other hand, many scholars believe that the letter was written by Paul *from* Ephesus, but was addressed to a church which he had not founded nor yet visited.

and stayed until her death. There is a shrine, the Chapel of the Virgin Mary, at the traditional site of her tomb.

Ephesus was an important city for several centuries not only as a major factor in the Roman economy but also as a key Christian site. The church thrived there, even during the period of Roman persecution. The city was ransacked in 262 CE by the barbarian Goths, who looted it and destroyed the temple of Artemis. The Ephesians vowed to rebuild the temple, but their attempt was a poor copy of the original, and it was never finished. In 401 CE St. John Chrysostom had it torn down because it was a monument to paganism and had no architectural beauty to justify its preservation. Today only a few foundation stones survive.

Ephesus became a critical Christian location in 431 CE, when the Council of Ephesus was convened. It met there because of the tradition of its being the place of Mary's death. One of the prime concerns of the council was to define and clarify Christ's divine and human natures, and Mary's role as the mother of Christ.

After the fifth century CE Ephesus went into a rapid decline. There was a threat of Arab invasion, which weakened the desirability of the city as a trade center. The harbor became increasingly filled with silt until it was virtually unnavigable, and the disease-bearing marshes spread. The people moved higher into the hills, and the city's connection with the sea was severed and its eventual doom sealed. The population decreased markedly, and the only importance of the city was as a religious center in the (by then) Christian Roman Empire. In the seventh and eighth centuries CE the Arabs, adherents of the new Muslim faith, overran the area.

In the eleventh century CE the extremist Seljuk Turks occupied the whole region, including Ephesus. Their move toward Jerusalem was a primary factor in the launching of the First Crusade. In 1390 the Seljuks were defeated by the Ottoman Turks. The Ottomans had no religious interest in Ephesus, and saw no economic value to it. It was completely abandoned and allowed to fall into ruins. Today it is preserved by the Turkish government as a major historic site.

# Galatia

Galatia was the central region of Asia Minor,[1] although scholars are unsure of its exact boundaries. In ancient times it was inhabited by an Indo-European Celtic tribe whom the Romans called *Galli* (Gauls). These were the same Celts who inhabited France, and who ranged as far west as the British Isles. Caesar's accounts of the Gallic Wars vividly describe what a formidable people the Celts were. They were as ferocious and uncontrollable as any barbarian tribe in history.

As the Gauls moved westward into Macedonia, King Nicomedes I of Bithynia invited them to serve him as mercenaries in a war against his brother (278 BCE). They accepted enthusiastically, and eventually overran all of western Asia Minor, leaving a trail of rapine and destruction behind them. They were finally defeated by the Seleucid (Hellenistic Syrian) king Antiochus I, who controlled them by agreeing to let them settle in central Asia Minor. They were intermixed with Greeks, so the region was called *Gallo-Graecia,* which eventually was elided into *Galatia.*

There were three tribes, each divided into four tetrarchies (subkingdoms). The twelve tetrarchs (quasi kings) were puppets of Antiochus and were loosely united through a council of three hundred members representing all of the tetrarchies. This council had minimal legislative power, serving primarily as a line of communication.

There were a few small cities and towns in the region, but the Galatians were for the most part belligerent nomads. They lived in open areas, and in times of military danger they retreated to mountain caves (not unlike many of the modern Afghan tribes). They constantly raided the neighboring regions, and often took hostages for ransom.

The kings of Pergamum took upon themselves the job of controlling the Galatians. While they achieved many victories over them, they found Galatia to be basically ungovernable. It was much like Yugoslavia in modern times — a man-made nation consisting of many warring tribes and subcultures. No one, including Rome, was ever completely successful in subduing them.

1. Asia Minor, also called Anatolia, is the large section of Turkey that runs between the Mediterranean and the Black Sea.

In 190 BCE the Galatians fought alongside the Seleucid Antiochus III[2] against Rome. In retribution, in 189 Rome sent its Consul Manlius Vulso to punish the Galatians. He crushed them but still could not control their continued raids on Pergamum. Rome tried a second time to subdue them, and failed. Finally, in 166 BCE, Rome granted Galatia independence on the condition that the Galatians stay out of Roman territories. Another condition of their "independence" was that they remain a Roman province with Roman puppet leaders. Otherwise, however, Rome would leave them alone. The Galatian tribes agreed.

The relationship of the Galatians with Pontus was much better than that with Pergamum. In 86 BCE, however, Mithridates V of Pontus made a fatal mistake in dealing with them. He was at war with Rome and tried to facilitate a reorganization of Galatia, which refused to support him. In order to let more friendly leaders rise to power, he massacred several of the Galatian leaders and their families. The plan backfired, though. The remaining princes were enraged and filled with a furious resolve to destroy Mithridates. They fought for Rome and defeated Mithridates. In return, Rome backed off even further, reducing the number of tetrarchs (now completely Roman puppets) from twelve to three. Galatia was established as a unified kingdom, with Deiotarus, one of the tetrarchs, as king. Large coastal tracts and a portion of Armenia were added to his kingdom. By 42 BCE all of Galatia had grudgingly accepted him as their king. He died two years later, and his secretary Amyntas became king. He was killed in battle in 25 BCE, at which time the emperor Augustus absorbed Galatia as a Roman province, incorporating many other large regions as part of it. The capital was established as the ancient Galatian city of Ancyra (now Ankara, Turkey). In the course of the next century, successive emperors continued adding regions to the province. By 79 CE it equaled the size and power of the former Hittite Empire. During the next twenty-five years, however, it was reduced again, and under the Roman emperor Trajan (d. 117 CE), it was taken back to the size it had been at the time of the death of Amyntas.

During all these changes, the original Celtic Galatians remained in the same area of central Anatolia. They were linguistically and culturally separated from most of the other peoples of the region, and had made little progress toward becoming civilized. They were probably one of the greatest challenges that Saint Paul faced in his effort to Christianize the world.

2. This is the same Antiochus who conquered Judea in 198 BCE, and whose son Antiochus IV Epiphanes was defeated by Judas Maccabaeus.

Paul established a number of churches in Galatia, although there is little surviving evidence of where they were located. His missionary journeys took place during the period in which Galatia was expanding as a Roman province. Some scholars adhere to the "South Galatia theory," according to which the Galatian churches were limited to a few major cities in the newer portion of the province, south of the region where the Celtic tribes lived. The evidence supporting this is that the book of Acts identifies churches in Antioch, Iconium, Lystra, and Derbe, all of which are in the south. Other scholars, however, accept the "North Galatia theory," which locates the churches in the region more traditionally identified as Galatia, thus including the Celtic tribes. There is nothing in history or the Bible to indicate that Paul did not also evangelize in this area. His fervor to convert Gentiles would be consistent with a desire to face such a challenge.

Wherever these Galatian churches may have been located, we can see from Paul's letter to them that they were in as much turmoil as the region had always known. Some form of false teaching had infected them, not only questioning Paul's teaching, but also challenging his authority. A critical issue was that of "Judaizing" — whether it was necessary for people to convert completely to Judaism (including circumcision for the males) in order to be Christian. The question was finally resolved in favor of the non-Judaizers (those who held that uncircumcised Gentiles could be Christian), although the issue was still a hot one at the time the letter to the Galatians was written.

One of the most turbulent parts of the ancient world, Galatia is still so to this day. Now under Turkish control, it knows only a restless peace.

# Galilee

Galilee (also often called "the Galilee") is not technically a defined region, and never has been except when it was defined by the Romans as a district of the province of Syria. Rather, it is a part of the northern region of Palestine (and thus includes a number of cities), and is important because it was the place where Jesus grew up, worked, and began his ministry. The name comes from the Hebrew *galil*, "circle" or "ring," a term frequently used in Hebrew to mean a geographical region.

When the kingdom of Israel was first forming, Galilee was part of the land assigned to the twelve tribes. The northern tribes, however, found themselves surrounded on the east, north, and west by pagan non-Jews — the "Gentiles" or "Nations." David united all the tribes in the United Monarchy, and thus these northern tribes had strong support from the south, enabling them better to resist the pagan influences. After Solomon's death in 922 BCE, the United Monarchy broke up into two kingdoms, Judah in the south and Israel in the north. The northern tribes lost the strong support of the faithful Jews of the south and again began to slip into paganism. To make matters worse, Jeroboam, the first king of the northern kingdom, encouraged the worship of a golden calf, probably the Egyptian bull-god Apis (1 Kings 12:28). The kings of the early Omride Dynasty in Israel supported and encouraged paganism, and much of Judaism became corrupted into the heresy known as Samaritanism. The corrupting influences on these northern tribes were so strong that by the time of the Maccabees in the second century BCE, the faithful Jews were actually evacuated to the south for about fifty years in order to escape the paganism of Israel. In the first century BCE Galilee had to be recolonized by faithful Jews, who by then were seen as interlopers by the people of the northern kingdom. For this reason the Jews of the region of Galilee were looked down upon as second-class by those of the south.

Ancient Galilee consisted mainly of the region surrounding the Sea of Galilee. It was bordered by the mountains of Lebanon on the north, and on all other sides by fertile plains. Most of the New Testament stories are situated in the part known as Lower Galilee, ranging east of the Sea of Galilee. It ranges in elevation from two thousand feet above sea level to six hundred feet below. It was well watered by springs from the hills, and the land was fertile, leading to dense population and considerable prosperity. The primary exports of the region were grain, olive oil, and fish. After the end of the first century BCE the region to the southeast of the lake was called Decapolis (or "the Decapolis"), and was no longer considered part of Galilee but rather a separate Roman district. (See p. 86 on Decapolis for more information.)

The Judean Jews were for the most part faithful to the Law and ancient traditions of their faith, although there were times in their history when they had allowed the incursion of paganism. They looked down on the Galileans as spiritually low-class and even heretical. The Galilean Jews, on the other hand, were innovative (even to the point that some of the faithful ones allowed pagan customs to creep into their religion). They were somewhat defensive — often oppressed by Gentiles, and offended by what they considered the rather self-righteous attitude of the Judean Jews. The Galileans accepted their unity with the Judeans only grudgingly, and the Judeans accepted their union with the Galileans rather patronizingly. It was mutual toleration rather than brotherhood, not unlike the relationship between the north and south in the United States at the turn of the twentieth century.

Modern Galilee and the Plain of Esdraelon constitute the northern part of the State of Israel, and there is considerable effort being exerted today to restore it to the prosperity it knew in ancient times. Its dense forests have been taken over by scrub, much of the fertile land has become arid, and many of its great cities are now abandoned and in ruins. With modern technology and Israeli tenacity, however, great progress is being made.

# Gaza

Gaza was at the southernmost border of Canaan, and was one of the most important Philistine cities. Even though it almost abutted Jewish territory, it was never an Israelite city except for a brief period during the early stages of Joshua's conquest. Its origins were very ancient. The book of Genesis (10:19) refers to it as the southernmost region of the territory of the clans of Canaan, Noah's grandson by Ham. The book of Joshua (15:47) says that after the conquest the region was allotted to the tribe of Judah. At some time thereafter the Israelites again lost the area, however, because in the stories of Samson it obviously belonged to the Philistines, who imprisoned and blinded Samson there after his capture. It was in Gaza that Samson destroyed the temple of Dagon and died (Judg. 16:21-31). This story is lent some credence by the fact that the Bible says that Samson was made to perform for the Philistines to entertain them (Judg. 16:25). It was a common practice in the Cretan civilization, from which the Philistines came, to torture condemned prisoners before their execution for the entertainment of the crowds. For example, they would force them to "dance" by touching their legs with hot irons.

Sometime about the end of the twelfth century, during the Philistine wars, the Philistines captured the ark of the covenant and took it to Gaza. Shortly thereafter the city was afflicted with deadly "tumors" that killed huge numbers of their people (1 Sam. 5:6-12).[1]

Gaza lay at the conjunction of a number of important coastal trade routes from Egypt into the Middle East, and is mentioned in Assyrian and

---

1. It is likely that this was an outbreak of bubonic plague. The plague causes the lymph glands in the neck, armpits, and groin to swell up, forming large tumor-like swellings called buboes (thus the name of the plague). Death follows within two to four days. The disease is contracted by ingesting the virus, which is extremely infectious, or by its being injected through a flea bite. If the same virus is inhaled, it causes pneumonic plague, in which the capillaries rupture, causing huge black bruises and rapid death from bleeding in the lungs — thus the name the "black death" or "black plague." The virus is carried by fleas, particularly those that infest rats. The fact that the Philistines made an offering of gold rats to God indicates that they may have had a sudden infestation of rats, and thus associated this with the "tumors," which they took to be God's punishment for desecrating the ark.

Babylonian commercial and military records. It was captured in 734 BCE by the Assyrians. They lost it in a rebellion, but recaptured it in 722. In the late seventh century BCE it was captured by Egypt, which seems to have held it until the conquest of Alexander the Great in 332. The city was laid waste in a five-month siege by Alexander. It was rebuilt, however, and continued as a commercial center on the trade routes right through the Seleucid, Roman, and Byzantine eras. While it was not a port city, it was close enough to the coast to enjoy some of the profits of maritime trade.

The modern city of Gaza stands on the same site, although there are small archaeological excavations at a tell in the middle of it. It is in the news today primarily because it is a hot spot in the Israeli-Palestinian conflict. The Gaza Strip, the coastal region surrounding Gaza, is still today the primary entry into the Middle East from Egypt. It is not technically a part of Israel, but Israel gained control of it in the Six Days' War in 1967 and is loath to release control because it is a critical defensive barrier to attack from Egypt and Arabia.

# Gezer

Gezer was one of the main Canaanite cities of pre-Israelite Palestine, and it retained its importance under the rule of several successive invaders. It is mentioned in the Bible in several places, and references to it are also found in many nonbiblical Middle Eastern records. The date of its origin is not known with certainty, but it was clearly a small but prosperous city by 1800 BCE. It is located on the road from Jerusalem to the seaport of Joppa, about eight miles from the main highway between Egypt and Mesopotamia. Its control of the road to the sea, along with its proximity to the great Egyptian trade route, gave it great advantages in international commerce. It had a plentiful water supply from springs outside the city, and the fertility of the region provided lush farming and grazing lands.

The first settlement at Gezer was in the mid-fourth millennium BCE. It was at first little more than a collection of campsites, and although it increased in size during the early Bronze Age, it remained unfortified. By the middle Bronze Age in the eighteenth century BCE, however, Gezer had become well fortified, and was one of the most important Canaanite military defenses.[1] It was overthrown in 1468 BCE by the Egyptian pharaoh Thutmosis III, and the population seems to have been loyal to Egypt, at least well through the fourteenth century.

In the late fourteenth century Milkilu, the king of Gezer, appealed to the pharaoh Akhenaton for help against the attacks of the Habiru.[2] Letters from the Canaanite king of Jerusalem, however, reveal that Milkilu had also made alliances with several other Canaanite kings, indicating that he was not particularly loyal to Egypt. By the time of the Israelite expansion Gezer was back in Canaanite hands, and was captured from them by the Israelites. Like many of the Israelites' later conquests, the city was not destroyed. It was turned over to the authority of the tribe of Ephraim. Appar-

---

1. This was about the same time that Babylon reached its highest point under Hammurabi.

2. The Habiru were a fierce Semitic tribe that are believed to have been later absorbed into the Israelites. It is likely that the name "Hebrew" is a corruption of "Habiru," which means "nomads."

ently the Ephraimites lost control of it,[3] however, because Egyptian records claim that Pharaoh Meren-Ptah recaptured it. During most of the period of the Judges it was in Philistine hands, and according to Egyptian records this was with Egyptian approval and oversight. When David defeated the Philistines he drove them back as far as Gezer (2 Sam. 5:25). The city itself, however, appears to have remained in Philistine hands, although by then the Egyptian control seems to have disappeared. It was not until Solomon's reign (late tenth century BCE) that Gezer finally became an Israelite city. The Egyptians attacked the city and burned it, slaughtering the Philistine inhabitants. When the pharaoh gave his daughter to Solomon to marry, he also gave her Gezer as a wedding gift (1 Kings 9:16). Solomon recognized that the city had commercial and military importance because of its location on the major trade routes. He immediately began to rebuild and fortify it along with two other equally important Galilean cities, Hazor and Megiddo. He did this at great cost to his reputation, however, because of his heavy-handed methods of financing the project and supplying it with workers.[4]

After Solomon's death, the rebel Jeroboam returned from Egypt, and after a brief civil war brought about the division of Israel into a northern kingdom that retained the name Israel, with Jeroboam as its king, and a southern kingdom with the name of Judah under Solomon's son Rehoboam. The capital of Israel was Shechem, and that of Judah was Jerusalem. Jeroboam's victory was possible mainly because the pharaoh Sheshonk I (called Shishak in the Bible) saw an opportunity to regain what Egypt had once owned and invaded the northern part of Solomon's kingdom, then briefly ruled by Rehoboam. One of Sheshonk's conquests was Gezer. He destroyed the city, and it never again rose to its previous impor-

3. The Ephraimites were among the least cooperative of the twelve tribes that were loosely confederated to make up the Israelite people. They were often as hostile to their Jewish neighbors as they were to their pagan enemies. They fought against several tribes, but when they took on Jephthah and the Gileadites they bit off more than they could chew. They lost forty-two thousand men and were militarily unimportant thereafter (Judg. 12:1-6). It was probably after this that they lost Gezer.

4. Solomon, for all his reputed wisdom, made several very unwise decisions. One was the enslavement of huge numbers of Jews to build the temple, his palace, and these three cities. He used the riches that David had amassed to strengthen and expand the kingdom, making powerful alliances and building great fortifications and public works. His oppressive taxation and the use of his own people in forced labor led to great unrest, however, and ultimately even to revolution. His apparent lack of concern for his own people undoubtedly was a major cause of the division of his kingdom shortly after his death.

tance. It was used as a military defense along the trade routes, but it was only one of many. It was destroyed again by the Assyrians in 722 when they captured Israel, and again by the Babylonians in 587 when they took Judah.

Gezer never again rose to any particular importance. It was a minor military site during the Hellenistic occupations, and it was briefly occupied by Simon and Jonathan during the period of the Maccabees. They repaired the city gate and part of the wall, but no significant military action took place there. It was little more than a walled village during the Roman occupation, and by the end of the first century CE it had been completely abandoned.

# Gibeah

The word *gibeah* (*gibh<sup>e</sup>â*) in Hebrew means "hill," and it is often used in the Bible in this sense rather than as a place name. Since Hebrew characters are not capitalized, it is often hard to tell whether the term is used to identify a place or a topographical formation. As a proper noun, Gibeah (not to be confused with nearby Gibeon) refers to two places, the first being relatively insignificant — a town in the hill country of Judah, near Bethlehem. It is listed in the towns belonging to the tribe of Judah in Joshua 15.

The other Gibeah is a place of importance because it was the birthplace of King Saul (1 Sam. 10:26). Its history, though, is one of constant building and destruction. Its ruins are at a mound called Tell el-Ful, about three miles north of Jerusalem. There is no reliable source of water near the town, so it was not settled until the Iron Age, around the middle of the twelfth century BCE. By that time the technology had developed to build rainwater cisterns sufficient to supply a small city. At the end of the twelfth century the settlement was destroyed, possibly in the war between the tribes of Judah and Benjamin recounted in Judges 19–20. It must have been rebuilt soon thereafter, because Saul was born there in the early eleventh century. A small fortress was built about 1025 BCE, roughly the time Saul became king, and it seems to have been an active fort until about 950 BCE. There is evidence that the fort was plundered around 1000 BCE, about the time of Saul's death, although its activities were restored and it was used again as a fort, possibly in David's war against Saul's son Ish-Bosheth (2 Sam. 2–4). Shortly after that, however, it was abandoned and lay unused and decaying for about two hundred years. Gibeah was rebuilt in the eighth century BCE by Hezekiah, but it was destroyed soon thereafter. It was rebuilt again in the seventh century BCE, only to be destroyed once again, this time by Nebuchadrezzar II in the sixth century BCE when the Babylonians conquered Judah. After the Babylonians withdrew there was a short-lived village there, apparently populated mainly by squatters and homesteaders, until about 500 BCE, after which it was abandoned again. These people, with no leadership, were probably unable to maintain the rainwater cisterns that were their only water supply. A new village appeared on the site during the Maccabaean period (second and first centuries BCE), and settlement was intermittent until about 70 CE, when all the Jews who lived that close to Jerusalem were either expelled or slaughtered by the Romans. After that the site was completely abandoned and never re-settled.

# Gibeon

Gibeon was already a prosperous Canaanite city at the time of the Israelite expansion in Canaan in the thirteenth and twelfth centuries BCE. It was about five miles north of Jerusalem, just north of the small city of Gibeah, although it is a different community. It was settled in the early Bronze Age, in the early fourth millennium BCE, and by the Iron Age in the thirteenth century BCE it was a thriving city. About that time a large pit was dug in the rock roughly seventy feet deep, with a stairway about halfway down carved out of the stone. It seems that this pit was originally a cistern, and that it was nearly always full. Hundreds of water-pitcher handles and shards were found at the bottom, many bearing the royal seal, indicating that it was filled by hand, perhaps with frequent accidents to the pitchers. This was undoubtedly the "pool of Gibeon" mentioned by Samuel and Jeremiah (2 Sam. 2:13; Jer. 41:12). By the end of the twelfth century BCE the Gibeonites had dug a tunnel through the rock to the springs outside the city wall. This solved two problems — the pool was now self-filling, and there was never a concern about the water supply when the city was under siege. By the seventh century BCE, wine-growing had become a major industry of Gibeon, and storage cellars were dug deep into the rocks, guaranteeing excellent cooling during the hot Palestinian summers. The city prospered and became wealthy.

When Joshua's armies reached the regions around Gibeon, the Gibeonites tried to avoid the inevitable destruction by Joshua's superior forces. They approached Joshua in rags, presented themselves as impoverished, and negotiated a treaty offering themselves as vassals. When Joshua discovered how rich Gibeon was he did not destroy it. He agreed upon a treaty of protection, but he cursed the city and in effect enslaved the population. The Amorites, furious that Gibeon had sold out to the Israelites, attacked the city. According to the Bible, Joshua, by calling down a hailstorm and extending the daylight, defended Gibeon and drove the Amorites back (Josh. 9–10). The city was then turned over to the control of the tribe of Benjamin, and dedicated as a Levitical (priestly) city. There have been no archaeological finds at Gibeon from Joshua's time, although burials indicate that there was a settlement there.

During Saul's reign Joshua's treaty was not honored, and Saul massacred many of the Gibeonites (2 Sam. 21:1-2). When David first ascended the throne of Judah, Saul's son Ish-Bosheth claimed the right to be king of Israel as Saul's heir. Rather than wage all-out civil war, both sides agreed to settle the matter by having a contest between champions. A challenge was fought at Gibeon among twelve warriors from each side; presumably the winner from among the twenty-four would determine who was to be king.[1] All twenty-four warriors immediately killed each other, however, and the battle turned into a free-for-all (2 Sam. 2:12-17). The war lasted a long time, but David was ultimately victorious. Joshua's treaty with the Gibeonites was still considered valid, and one of its terms was that they would be allowed to live. Hundreds of Gibeonites had been slaughtered during Saul's bloody reign, and after David's victory they demanded restitution. They asked of David the execution of seven of Saul's descendants, and their request was granted (2 Sam. 21:1-7).

Apparently the altar at Gibeon was considered a particularly sacred place, because it was at Gibeon that Solomon made a massive sacrifice when he became king. It was there, in a dream, that he asked God for wisdom, and God promised it in abundance (2 Chron. 1:8-13).

After Solomon's death, as the United Monarchy broke up, Sheshonk I (the Bible calls him Shishak), the Egyptian pharaoh, attempted to regain the old Egyptian control over Palestine. He was only partially successful, capturing only a few northern cities, among which was Gibeon. Gibeon also gained attention in the sixth century BCE when Gedaliah, Nebuchadrezzar's governor of Judah, was assassinated. His killers were captured by the pool of Gibeon (Jer. 41:11-14). The last mention of the city is after the exiles had returned from Babylon, when Gibeonites worked with Nehemiah to rebuild the walls of Jerusalem (Neh. 3:7).

1. This method of resolving disputes was not restricted to medieval Europe, but was very ancient. Each side would select a champion or team of champions to fight, and the winning side was considered to be in the right. The people believed that God (or the gods) would decide by controlling the victory. This resolution by champions is what happened in Saul's battle against the Philistines at Socoh. They selected the giant Goliath as their champion, and Saul finally selected David (1 Sam. 17:1-37).

# Gilead

It is difficult to define Gilead, because the name is used in the Bible to refer to many different places, although all are in roughly the same region. It is probably best, however, to identify Gilead with the whole region of Transjordan. This is primarily the entire plot of land to the east of the Jordan River between Syria and Arabia, and bounded on the east by the Arabian plateau and Mesopotamia (modern Iraq). In today's terms Gilead would be for the most part what was the pre-1967 modern state of Jordan.[1] Its ancient Israelite inhabitants were the tribes of Reuben, Gad, and half of the tribe of Manasseh.

The name Gilead occurs over one hundred times in the Old Testament, although many times metaphorically or allegorically. It is interesting that Gilead is not mentioned in the New Testament. Much of Transjordan was richly forested, well-watered, and fertile, so in Israelite eyes Gilead was a pleasant and delightful land — something of a "land of milk and honey." The phrase "balm of Gilead," used in so many Christian hymns and sermons, is found only in Jeremiah (8:22; 46:11), but the concept of Gilead as a land of peace and luxury is widely spread through the Old Testament.

Gilead was not only a symbol of paradise, it was also a place of warfare and of sanctuary for refugees. Jacob fled there from his father-in-law Laban (Gen. 31:21-25). Jephthah, a judge in Gilead, gathered an army from all the tribes there and drove the attacking Ephraimites back over the Jordan, slaughtering forty-two thousand in the process (Judg. 12:4-7). When Saul's troops were being pushed back by the Philistines, the Israelites fled to Gilead, and after Saul's death his son Ish-Bosheth declared himself king of Israel and Gilead (2 Sam. 2:9). When King David's son Absalom revolted he camped in Gilead just before his final battle (2 Sam. 17:26).

While Gilead is used as a specific place name in many Old Testament passages, the most common use is as a general reference to a huge region, and proverbially as a place of peace and plenty.

---

1. After the Six Days' War in 1967, Jordan lost a considerable amount of territory to Israel. Much of it, but not all, has since been returned.

# Goshen

When Jacob and his sons were invited by Joseph to live in Egypt, they were given the land of Goshen to live in (Gen. 47:5-6). The location of this region is not known, but it was definitely in Egypt, and probably in the Nile delta.[1] The reference to the "district of Rameses" in Genesis 47:11 supports the delta hypothesis, since the pharaoh Ramses II did a considerable amount of building in the eastern Nile delta in the thirteenth century BCE. While this was centuries later than the time the Hebrews would have settled in Egypt, the early readers of the writings that became the book of Genesis would have recognized the reference as an identification of location. (This would be rather like identifying the location of a tribe of pre-Columbian Indians by saying that they lived where Boston is.) Also, many scholars believe that Ramses II may have been the pharaoh of the Exodus. If that is the case, the Hebrew slaves who left Egypt in the Exodus would probably have worked on his building projects, and would remember this as their home. Whether that was the original location of Goshen may never be known, although several passages in Genesis indicate that the Hebrews lived in the same place throughout their time in Egypt.

The true location of Goshen remains a mystery, the solution to which is deeply hidden behind a small handful of tantalizing but arcane clues.[2]

1. Egypt in those days also included large parts of the Middle East, although most scholars accept that Goshen was located in African Egypt, somewhere along the Nile, and probably in the delta.

2. For many years scholars believed that the Egyptian name *Gsmt*, found in several Egyptian documents, might be the same as the Septuagint's *Gesem*, "Goshen." Modern scholarship has shown positively, however, that what had been transliterated *Gsmt* should have been *Šsmt*, and thus has nothing to do with *Gesem*.

# Hazor

In the time of the Israelites' conquest of Canaan, Hazor was probably the most important city in northern Palestine. The book of Joshua calls it "the head of all these kingdoms" (Josh. 11:10). It was a capital of sorts, being a city-state that controlled a loose confederation of neighboring city-states. Hazor was located about ten miles north of the Sea of Galilee, and about fifteen miles south of Dan, the northernmost city in Israel. The ruins have been partially excavated in a mound called Tell el-Qedah. They are amazingly complete and well-preserved for a city so ancient, and they provide a strikingly thorough picture of urban life in Palestine at the time of the Israelite conquest of Canaan.

Hazor's location was perfect for the achievement of great prosperity. It was situated on the intersection of major trade routes running from Egypt and Arabia to Syria, Anatolia, and Mesopotamia. Because it had access to caravans buying and selling in all the corners of the known world, it prospered as a distribution center, and it profited greatly from serving as a stopover for these merchants. It was also in an ideal military location, being high enough to have a commanding view of the landscape for a great distance in all directions. It would have been very hard to catch the city by surprise. Finally, it was located in a fertile region that provided all the inhabitants' needs for farming, water, animal husbandry, and raw materials.

In his conquest of Canaan, Joshua conquered and burned Hazor, putting the king, Jabin, and the whole population to the sword.[1] He did not destroy the tributary cities. It is unclear when Joshua's conquest took place, but it would likely have been roughly the thirteenth century BCE. It would seem that there were survivors of Hazor, including members of the royal family, perhaps men who had been away at the time the city fell. Apparently they rebuilt the city and were ruled by another King Jabin (doubtless

---

1. We must be careful not to evaluate ancient actions by the more compassionate and civilized standards of our own times. The universal military standard in ancient times was to level a conquered city and wipe out an enemy completely so that neither he nor his descendants could rise up and become a threat later. The only exception was that some stable cultures sold their healthy captives into slavery. The taking and maintenance of prisoners or slaves was logistically impossible for a nomadic people such as the early Israelites.

a descendant of the king whom Joshua killed). Judges 4 tells us that God punished the sinful Israelites by having them "given into the hand of" Jabin and the armies of Hazor. Under the command of the judge Deborah,[2] however, the Hazorites were defeated and the Israelites recaptured the city. This time they did not destroy it, but put it under the control of the tribe of Naphtali, probably around 1100-1050 BCE. In roughly 960 BCE, along with nearby Gezer and Megiddo, it was heavily fortified and made a primary royal city of King Solomon. Soon after Solomon's death in about 922 BCE, his united kingdom was broken into two Jewish kingdoms, Israel in the north, and Judah in the south. Hazor remained an important commercial and military center in the northern kingdom. In his campaigns of 733 to 732 BCE, however, the Assyrian king Tiglath-Pileser III destroyed the city and carried the population of the northern kingdom of Israel into captivity in Mesopotamia.

---

2. The image of ancient Judaism as one of a totally male-dominated society, where women were considered possessions, is quite inaccurate. Not only were there many female leaders such as Miriam and Deborah, but the mother played a very important role in the religious observances in the home and in the early education of the children.

# Hebron

Hebron is the highest town in Palestine, well over half a mile above sea level, about eighteen miles south-southwest of Jerusalem. It was once thought to be one of the oldest cities in the Middle East, founded early in the third millennium BCE, but modern archaeological evidence contradicts this. The mistake was based on Numbers 13:22b, "Hebron had been built seven years before Zoan in Egypt." Zoan, or Tanis, once thought to be the oldest town in Egypt, is now confirmed to have been founded in the eleventh century BCE. This problem in dating the city of Hebron is an ancient mistake, because the first-century CE Jewish historian Josephus in his *History of the Jewish War* stated that Hebron was built twenty-three hundred years before his time. Modern excavations, however, clearly indicate that Hebron was first settled sometime in the middle Bronze Age (about 1700 BCE), but that sometime around 1500 BCE it was destroyed or abandoned. There is a gap indicating that there was no habitation there until it was resettled in the Iron Age, sometime around 1100 BCE. It is likely that the reference to Hebron and Zoan in Numbers refers to the second settlement at Hebron, as the timing would have been about right for both cities in that case.

The first settlement was by the Hittites, an early civilization living primarily in Syria and Anatolia (southern Turkey). Abraham lived in the vicinity of Hebron for an extended period, and he purchased a family burial site, the field of Machpelah, from the Hittites (Gen. 23). He and Sarah, Isaac and Rebecca, and Jacob and Leah were all buried there. (Rachel was buried at Ephratha, just outside Bethlehem.) According to Josephus, all the sons of Jacob were also buried there except Joseph, who was buried in Shechem.[1] Centuries later, in the first century BCE, Herod the Great would

---

1. This is entirely possible, because at the time of the sons' deaths the Hebrews were living in the land of Goshen in Egypt as an honored and prosperous people (it was not until much later that they were enslaved). Most ancient Middle Easterners thought that it was very important to be buried in one's own country, so it is reasonable that their children would have brought their remains back to the ancient family burial site. Joseph held such an exalted position in Egypt that it is likely that he was given a royal burial there, although in the Exodus his body was taken out of Egypt (Exod. 13:19) and returned to Shechem, to a burial plot that Jacob had bought long before.

build a great stone mausoleum at the site, known as the "Enclosure of the Friend" (i.e., Abraham). This still stands in modern Hebron and is sacred not only to Jews but to Christians and Muslims as well.

After the Exodus, while the Hebrews were still wandering in Sinai, Moses sent twelve spies, one from each tribe, into Canaan to reconnoiter it before entering the Promised Land. They went as far as Hebron, and reported back that it was a fertile and productive place. After Moses' death, Joshua led the Hebrews into Canaan to conquer it. One of the first conflicts was with a coalition of forces led by Adoni-Zedek, the king of Zion (Jerusalem); in it, Hoham, the king of Hebron, was killed, along with Adoni-Zedek and the other three kings in the alliance (Joshua 10). Joshua later gave Caleb, one of his generals, the city as a family possession (Josh. 14:13), and Caleb drove out from Hebron the Anakim, pre-Israelite inhabitants of Canaan (Josh. 14:12; 15:14). David was anointed king of Judah in Hebron (2 Sam. 2:1-4), and two years later he was anointed king of Israel there (2 Sam. 5:3), establishing the roots of the United Monarchy. It remained his capital for over seven years until he moved the capital to Jerusalem. Hebron played another less joyful role in David's reign, as well. It was in Hebron that David's son Absalom organized his rebellion against his father (2 Sam. 15:7-12). After Solomon's death and the breakup of the United Monarchy at the end of the tenth century BCE, Rehoboam fortified Hebron against a possible attack by Jeroboam in the north (2 Chron. 11:5-12). Although not the capital of Judah (Jerusalem remained that), many archaeological finds confirm that Hebron was a major Judean administrative center right up until the time of the Babylonian captivity in the sixth century BCE.

With the fall of Judah to the Babylonians, Hebron was damaged but not completely destroyed, although many of the residents were carried off to Babylon. When the Persians took Babylon and freed the captive Jews, one of the first places they settled was Hebron. They rebuilt the city and organized its populace, and again it began to thrive. With the conquest of Alexander the Great in the fourth century BCE, Hebron came under the control of the Hellenistic Ptolemies. At first this had little effect on Hebron's commerce and daily activities, but as the Hellenistic rulers became more oppressive the city fell into the hands of the Idumeans. They were driven out by Judas Maccabaeus when he drove the Seleucids from Judah in the second century BCE. When the Romans took Palestine they strengthened the fortifications of Hebron, but it did not play a major role in their administrative or military system. In the Jewish rebellion of 66 to 70 CE, during which Jerusalem was completely destroyed, Hebron was the headquarters of the rebel Simon bar-Giora. The Romans sacked and burned the city and crucified or enslaved most of its population.

In the Christian era, tradition says that Hebron was the birthplace of John the Baptist, and the site of the Visitation. There is no biblical or other documentary evidence to support this, however. In the seventh century the city was captured by the Muslim Arabs, who consider Hebron (which they call el-Khalil) to be one of the four most sacred cities of their faith (because of the tomb of Abraham). During the Middle Ages a number of minor historical events centered around Hebron, particularly during the Crusades, but they are not within the focus of this study.

Hebron remained in Muslim hands after the defeat of the crusaders in 1187, and in the seventeenth century it became a part of the Ottoman (Turkish) Empire. With the fall of the Ottomans at the end of World War I in 1918, it came under British rule, and eventually under the League of Nations' "British Mandate" to form a homeland for the Jews. It was not included in the original partitioning of the State of Israel in 1948, but it fell into Israeli hands with the rest of the West Bank in the 1967 Six Days' War. In 1995 Israel signed a peace treaty with the Palestinian Liberation Organization according to which they were to withdraw troops from all West Bank cities except Hebron, where a garrison would be retained to protect Jewish settlers and religious sites. Otherwise, however, Hebron is now under Palestinian control. The population of the modern city is about seventy thousand, of whom only about four hundred are Jews.

# Jehoshaphat

The prophet Joel (3:2, 12) has God calling all the Gentile nations to meet in the Valley of Jehoshaphat to be judged for their abuses of the Israelites. This is reflected in the New Testament in Matthew 25:32, where we read that Christ will judge all the nations and separate "the sheep from the goats." The name *Jehoshaphat* in Hebrew means "Yahweh has judged," and this ties in well with Joel 3:14, where Joel refers to the multitudes in the "valley of decision," when the Day of the Lord (Judgment Day) is near. It is likely, then, that the Valley of Jehoshaphat is allegorical, and does not refer to a geographical location, although many scholars have tried to identify one. Their reasoning is that Joel uses the term "valley," which seems to intend a location. One site that is often suggested is the Valley of Beracha (the "Valley of Blessings") south of Bethlehem. There Jehoshaphat, the controversial ninth-century BCE king of Judah, gathered his forces after the destruction of the pagan forces of the northern kingdom of Israel (2 Chron. 20:26). His victory was deemed the victory of Yahweh over the pagan gods, thus his judgment on the Gentiles.

Another proposed location of the valley is the Valley of Hinnom, which Jeremiah prophesied would be turned into a valley of slaughter because of the sins of Jerusalem (Jer. 7:32-34). The problem with this interpretation is that it is Israelites, not the Gentile nations, who are judged there.

There is a common strong tradition in Judaism, Christianity, and Islam that the Valley of Jehoshaphat is the Kidron Valley that runs between Jerusalem and the Mount of Olives. It was a favored burial place for Jews and Muslims, and there is a Roman-Hellenic tomb there that is erroneously revered as the tomb of King Jehoshaphat. The tradition that this was Joel's valley goes back to the fourth century CE, but there is an important semantic problem here in that Joel uses a term that means "broad valley" (*'ēmeq*), yet the Kidron Valley is called a "ravine" or "gorge" (*Nahal Kidrōn*, the "Kidron Ravine").

Most interpreters today prefer the hypothesis that the Valley of Jehoshaphat is not a place but an allegory for God's judgment on all, the faithful and unfaithful alike.

# Jericho

Jericho may well have a claim to being the oldest city on earth, with reliable archaeological finds indicating a Mesolithic (middle Stone Age) settlement of hunters dated about 7800 BCE. Jericho is located about ten miles northeast of Jerusalem on what is now called the West Bank. The city is known today by its Arabic name, Aricha. The original city was built directly over the largest spring in Palestine, which still waters the region. By Jesus' time it was about a mile south of that spot. The road from Jerusalem to Jericho passes through the Wadi Qelt, the beautiful canyon that opens onto fertile plains 825 feet below sea level, on which the city is built. Jericho is particularly famous for three major biblical references: Joshua's siege (Josh. 6), Jesus' parable of the Good Samaritan (Luke 10:29-37), and Jesus' bringing the tax-collector Zacchaeus to repentance (Luke 19:1-10). In addition, it was in the mountains surrounding the Wadi Qelt that Jesus met his first temptations after his baptism.

Although there were many earlier villages, the first settlement that could be truly considered a city dates back to the Neolithic period, in about the seventh to sixth millennium BCE, as confirmed by carbon-14 dating. There are several successive cities on the site (possibly as many as twenty!), and they occupied an area of about eight acres — this is as large as any late Old Testament city. There was military construction, including a solid stone tower thirty feet thick and a twenty-five-foot moat carved out of solid rock. After that time the city declined, and it was not until the Bronze Age, about 3000 BCE, that it again regained any importance. Archaeologists have been able to trace its existence continuously from that time until its destruction by Joshua about seventeen centuries later. An interesting contribution of these studies is that Jericho's relics give solid evidence of the time of the arrival of the Amorites and Canaanites, early invaders of Palestine.

The Jericho of Joshua's day presents many archaeological problems, as so little of it still survives. From historical reconstruction and study of military strategies and actual battles of that period, however, a considerable amount can be reasonably deduced. Unfortunately, the first archaeological excavation there was done before there was any understanding of the importance of pottery, and most of the pottery shards dug up were simply set aside or discarded without a record being made of their design or relative positions.[1] Excavations from 1929 to 1936 and again from 1952 to 1958 gave evidence that Joshua's conquest was around the beginning of the thirteenth century BCE, although the evidence is too scanty to prove the date positively. According to the biblical account, Joshua completely destroyed the city.[2] This is consistent with military standards of the time, when the philosophy was that if there is no home to rebuild and no one alive to rebuild it, an enemy is no longer a threat. Joshua also cursed the land, and according to the Bible, Jericho was not rebuilt until Hiel the Bethelite did so in the ninth century BCE (1 Kings 16:34). There is little trace of Hiel's city, but there is clear evidence that by the seventh century there was a thriving community there, which remained an active city until the Babylonian exile in about 588 BCE.

Jericho came into biblical history again in 1 Maccabees, when Simon Maccabaeus was murdered there by his treacherous son-in-law Ptolemy (1 Macc. 16:14-16).

Herod the Great founded the Jericho of the New Testament, about a mile south of the old city. Excavations in 1950 and 1951 revealed significant parts of Herodian Jericho. By Herod's time the well-watered fertile valley, and a beautiful canyon that opens into a lush plain, had made the city a desirable resort town — a fashionable vacation spot for the rich and famous.[3] Herod (who had visited Rome many times) built a palace there, and its Italian design shows his fondness for things Roman. He laid out the city in exactly the same style as Pompeii. Jericho was also a favorite spot of

1. The first excavation was made by Sellin and Watzinger in 1907 to 1911. They did very fine work by the standards of their time, but those standards unfortunately caused more destruction of evidence than preservation of it.

2. For centuries biblical scholars have challenged the veracity of the falling of the city walls because they could not explain how it could have happened. Theories have ranged from the Israelites' digging out tunnels under them, to their collapse under the shock of the frightened Jerichoites trying to get off the walls when the Israelites suddenly blew their trumpets and shouted. The most likely explanation is simple: the region of Jericho is on a geological fault, and is prone to frequent earthquakes. Often God's miracles are not interventions overruling the laws of nature, but simple timing.

3. This is significant when we consider the parable of the Good Samaritan. The obvious implication is that the robbery victim and all those who ignored him were on their way to enjoy themselves, and were wealthy men. A Samaritan would have been very unwelcome in Jericho except as a laborer or to bring supplies, yet he gave of his compassion and his meager means to help the victim, proving that he, a heretic and foreigner, was the better man.

View toward the Oasis of Jericho from the Desert of Judah. Jesus took this road to Jerusalem.     Photo credit: Erich Lessing/Art Resource, NY

the Romans for rest and recreation, and they erected a number of beautiful buildings there. At some point, probably under Herod, Jericho was made the winter capital.

Jesus visited Jericho near the end of his ministry. As he left the city, he would have passed on the road through the Wadi Qelt, the very region where he had begun his ministry three years earlier when he was tempted by the Devil. The lush, rich, powerful, and decadent Jericho may well have represented "all the kingdoms of the world" which the Devil had offered him.

Near Jericho, in the Khirbet Qumran, lived an Essene community. The Essenes were a sect of puritanical ascetic Jews who lived in communities much like monasteries. The library of this community was found in a cave in the Wadi Qumran in 1947, and is known as the Dead Sea Scrolls.

There is no archaeological evidence that Jericho was destroyed when Vespasian's army leveled Jerusalem in 70 CE, in effect marking the end of a Jewish state until 1948. Jericho's popularity with the Roman elite may have saved it, and Vespasian's son, the general Titus, garrisoned his troops there in preparation for the attack on Jerusalem. He did, however, destroy the

Essene community at Khirbet Qumran, possibly at the instigation of the dissolute Herod, who hated the Essene puritanism. They may have seen this coming, which would explain why their library was so carefully packed away and hidden in the caves of the wadi.

After the fall of Jerusalem, Jericho declined rapidly. The devastation of the whole nation dealt a major blow to Jericho's economy, and by 100 CE it was nothing more than a small Roman garrison town. It saw a resurgence by 130 CE, after a major fort was built there, and it played a key role in putting down Bar Kochba's nearly successful rebellion in 135 CE.

Jericho remained a Roman city until at least 333 CE, when accounts of it were written in the records of a Christian pilgrimage that passed by there. Sometime shortly thereafter, however, it was abandoned, and a new Byzantine Jericho called Ericha (a Greek form of "Jericho") was built about a mile to the east. This is the site of the modern city.

During the Crusades, Ericha (Jericho) was passed back and forth a number of times between the Christians and the Muslims. After the Crusades it remained a Muslim city. It was held by the Ottoman Empire from the thirteenth century until the fall of that empire in 1918, when it came under British control. Under the British, it once again became a winter resort town. In the partition of Palestine in 1948, it became part of Jordan. It embraced the population of two huge Arab refugee camps, grew rapidly, and prospered. It fell into Israeli hands in the 1967 Six Days' War, but was finally returned to Palestinian control in 1994. In recent years it has been largely rebuilt, and continues to expand as surrounding fields are more and more efficiently irrigated from the bountiful underground spring which has served the city for nearly ten thousand years.

# Jerusalem

Long before it became the sacred city of three major religions, Zion, later to be called Jerusalem, was a thriving city, albeit a den of paganism that even included human sacrifice. Like many ancient cities, it was built upon a hill, Mount Zion, today the easternmost hill in the city. Tradition also identifies the hill as Mount Moriah, where Abraham prepared to offer Isaac in sacrifice.[1] The modern city (vastly larger, of course) straddles a string of hills called Har Yehuda ("Judean Hills"). It is located about thirty-five miles east of the Mediterranean and about fifteen miles west of where the Jordan flows into the Dead Sea.

By 5000 BCE the region was occupied by a Stone Age people, but the first evidence of actual settlement and building dates from about 3000 BCE. From the fourth millennium until the fifteenth century BCE it was apparently little more than a mountain fortress containing a small town. The early inhabitants were beginning to advance into the Bronze Age when they were driven out by a Semitic tribe, the Canaanites.[2] The Canaanites built a city on the hill, named it Zion, and ruled the region until they were defeated in about 1425 BCE by the Egyptian pharaoh Thutmosis III. Ancient Egyptian records refer to the capture of a city they called Urusalim-mu, but it was clearly the Canaanite Zion. It remained under Egyptian control for almost two hundred years, although the Canaanites remained the principal residents there.

In about 1250 BCE the Israelites, who had not long before escaped slavery in Egypt, began conquering the Canaanite lands. They never took Jerusalem, but the tribes of both Benjamin and Judah claimed that it was in their territory. Soon thereafter a people from Crete and the Aegean, the Philistines, began invading and driving the Israelites back from many of the places they had previously captured. They settled most of the southwestern region of what today we call Palestine (a corruption of the name

---

1. Muslims believe that it was Ishmael, not Isaac, whom Abraham offered on Mount Moriah.

2. At about the same time another Semitic tribe, the Sidonians (whom the Greeks called Phoenicians) overran the northwestern coastal regions and settled in what today is Lebanon.

Philistine), and in time expanded to the regions southwest of the heavily fortified Jebusite city of Zion or Jerusalem. (Most scholars believe "Jebusite" was the local name for the Canaanites.) For almost two centuries the Philistines ruled the region, keeping the Israelites at bay. The Jebusites maintained a laissez-faire policy toward the Philistines because they were both enemies of the Israelites, and the Jebusites apparently were not interested in expanding into the areas controlled by the Philistines. The Philistines were eventually driven back from the lowlands, but the hills remained in their control, and Jerusalem continued to be held by the Jebusites.

That same string of hills was where huge numbers of Israelites had taken refuge from Philistine oppression and continued to wage war against them. Finally, in about 1000 BCE, the newly crowned King David subdued the Philistines and Jebusites, and captured Jerusalem, either by interrupting their water supply or (as tradition claims) by entering the city through its water shafts (2 Sam. 5:8). He declared Jerusalem his new capital (2 Sam. 5:9), which was a wise move for two reasons: The city was central and easily defensible, and, what was more important, it was on the border between the tribes of Benjamin and Judah, who were constantly squabbling like two rival siblings. It was also in a neutral location relative to the ten northern and two southern tribes, who were regularly at each other's throats. He erected a palace, moved the ark of the covenant there, and built a tabernacle (a huge tent) for it, since God had forbidden him, a man of war, to build a temple. As David more firmly cemented the twelve feuding tribes of Israel into a single nation, his realm expanded and solidified into what would be called the United Monarchy of Israel. Jerusalem began to emerge as one of the very important cities in the known world; at this time Athens was only a petty city-state in its "dark age," Rome was just about to be founded, and the warring nations in Mesopotamia were bouncing back and forth in power so much that their influence constantly ebbed and flowed. Important as Jerusalem was, however, the appearance and size of the city were quite modest — it would not become glorious until the reign of Solomon.

When David's son Solomon came to power he expanded the city, erected the first temple, and built a huge and lavish palace. The temple and palace were truly magnificent, but it was a project beyond the ability of the Jewish builders of the time. Solomon enlisted the aid of the Phoenicians, who were master builders. King Hiram of Tyre (the ruling city of Phoenicia at the time) was an ally of Israel and a personal friend of both David

The Western Wall of the temple in Jerusalem is all that remains of Solomon's magnificent structure. Destroyed by the Babylonians in 587 BCE and rebuilt by Herod in the first century CE, it was leveled by the Romans in 70 CE.
Photo credit: Erich Lessing/Art Resource, NY

and Solomon. Solomon provided the labor and money,[3] and Hiram provided most of the more valuable materials and the artisans, including the best bronze-worker in the world at the time (1 Kings 5; 2 Chron. 2:13-16). Also named Hiram (also referred to as Huram-abi or Hiram-Abi), his father was a Phoenician metalworker and his mother a Jew of the tribe of Naphtali. He built a bronze foundry in the plains of Jordan in the clay fields between Succoth and the stone quarries of Zarethan. There he cast huge bronze vessels for the temple, including the two twenty-six-foot bronze pillars that were placed at the entrance of the temple. The building of the temple secured Jerusalem as not only the political center of the kingdom but also the spiritual center of Judaism.

Soon after Solomon's death the United Monarchy broke up into two kingdoms, Israel in the north and Judah in the south. Solomon's chief overseer, Jeroboam, had attempted an unsuccessful coup d'état and fled to

3. Solomon made one of his most unwise decisions in dealing with this project. He enslaved twenty thousand Jews and oppressively taxed the rest in order to obtain the labor and money needed.

Egypt. When Solomon died his son Rehoboam ascended the throne. Jeroboam returned with his rebel leaders, assisted by Egyptian forces, and gained control over the northern ten Israelite tribes. These tribes had been heavily oppressed by Solomon, and had little love for his rule. Jeroboam declared himself king of Israel and established Shechem as the capital. Rehoboam held control over the southern two tribes, Judah and Benjamin, and Jerusalem remained the capital of his kingdom, thereafter called Judah (Judea in the New Testament). While there was tension between these two kingdoms, they were not formal enemies except for a few occasional skirmishes, usually involving foreign powers. The greatest tension was religious. Much of Judaism in Jeroboam's Israel became infected with paganism, eventually producing a heretical offshoot religion, Samaritanism, that was hated by the Judean Jews.[4] There was also extreme socio-economic polarization in Israel, with almost all the wealth being in the hands of a small plutocracy, while the rest of the population lived in abject poverty.

In the mid-eighth century BCE, Israel fell to the Assyrian Empire, and about 720 BCE the emperor Sargon II exiled all the leaders of Israel into Assyria. The prophets had warned of this because of the paganism and social injustice in the northern kingdom. Judah was for the most part spared; some of its northern cities fell and Jerusalem was attacked, but the southern kingdom survived as an independent state. The prophets also warned Judah of impending disaster, however, as it too was becoming corrupt. The kings Uzziah and Hezekiah attempted to shore up the fortifications of Jerusalem in the eighth century BCE (archaeological finds confirm this). The Judeans saw Jerusalem as the impregnable House of Yahweh, even though the prophets again and again warned them that this would be true only if they were faithful to Yahweh's Law, and that he would send Babylon to strike them down if they turned from him. In 597 BCE their confidence was dashed to pieces when the Babylonians captured the Assyrian holdings in the north and then overran Judah, sacked Jerusalem, and destroyed the temple. They exiled the leaders, teachers, and upper classes to Babylonia, and then came back and deported the rest of the leadership in 586 BCE.

This exile lasted almost fifty years until 539 BCE, when the Persians defeated the Babylonians and allowed the Jews to return home. Most of them had been assimilated into the Babylonian culture by this time, but a small faithful group that Isaiah called the "Remnant" returned to Judea and rebuilt Jerusalem and the temple. The Persians supported the Jews with

4. The very name of the religion, Judaism, means the religion of Judah.

money, craftsmen, and protective troops to help them get back on their own feet again. They ruled until the late fourth century BCE, but it was a relatively benevolent rule. It is unclear why they acted in so friendly a way, but it was a blessing to the Jews. Since Jerusalem was under Persian protection, there was no real need for city walls. They remained in ruins until the middle of the fifth century BCE, when Nehemiah, the Persian-appointed Jewish governor of Jerusalem, had them rebuilt. It was also about this time that the priest Ezra instituted massive reforms of Judaism, restoring the observance of the Law and reinforcing the role of the temple and the Levitical priesthood as the focus of the faith. He also reduced the almost absolute power of the priesthood, however, by shifting most of the scholarship and scriptural interpretation into the hands of the rabbis, who previously had played a very minor role in Judaism.[5] After Ezra's time Jerusalem was more than ever the religious center of the Jewish world, and Judaism had taken on a wholly new face. This was the form of Judaism that Jesus knew.

In 333 BCE Alexander the Great defeated the Persians, took the whole region of Palestine, and sacked Jerusalem. He was succeeded in that region by one of his generals, Ptolemy, who established a Hellenistic (Greek) empire. This was doubly distressing to the Jews, not only because they were still controlled by a foreign power, but even more so because the Hellenistic culture was very attractive to the young. They enjoyed the Greek athletic games and found the religious demands of the Greeks to be considerably easier than those of the Jews. Physicians even developed a surgical procedure to undo circumcision, which the Greeks considered to be mutilation. In 198 BCE the descendants of another of Alexander's generals, Seleucus, wrested Syria and most of the Middle East from the Ptolemies. The Seleucids forbade the worship of God and required the worship of the Greek Olympian deities. Many Jews refused to submit to this indignity and were killed. In 168 BCE the Seleucid emperor Antiochus IV Epiphanes decided to teach the Jews a lesson in submission to his authority. He destroyed most of Jerusalem and desecrated what remained of the temple, dedicating it to the Olympian gods and sacrificing a pig to Zeus on the high altar. He badly miscalculated, however, as this was the final straw for the Jews. It sparked a revolt under the leader-

5. During the Babylonian exile the Jews were not allowed to worship or sacrifice to God. The Babylonians did encourage education, however. The Jews would gather together ostensibly to teach the children and the ignorant, but they used this time as well to worship secretly and to teach the traditions of the faith. The Greek word for their gathering was *Sunagoge*, "calling together," which came to be "synagogue." In Yiddish the word for synagogue is *shul*, which derives from the German *Schul*, "school."

ship of Judas Maccabaeus, and three years later the Maccabees had driven out the Seleucids. They rebuilt Jerusalem and restored the temple,[6] and once again all Jewish political and religious power rested in Jerusalem. While the Seleucids were still technically the rulers of Palestine, the Jews for all practical purposes ruled themselves as an independent nation.

In 63 BCE Palestine fell to yet another foreign power, this time Rome, which was at this point still a republic and was just beginning its world conquests. The land was ruled by various Roman officials until 37 BCE, when Marc Antony placed the Idumean Herod the Great on the throne. Herod's grandfather's family had been forced to convert to Judaism when the Maccabaeans conquered Idumea, but they did not take it seriously, and were Jews only for show. Herod called himself a Jew, but this was obviously a purely political, not a spiritual, move. He loved anything Roman and held the Jews in contempt. The Jews hated him not only because they saw him as a hypocritical foreigner but also because he was a cruel despot. He tried to buy their favor by building a new temple (the "third temple") on the site of the partially rebuilt old one, much of which was still in ruins from the days of the several previous destructions. He erected a temple whose magnificence eclipsed even that of Solomon's temple, but this pleased only the sycophantic priests and politicians who stood to be enriched or empowered by supporting him. It was Herod's temple in which Jesus as a boy talked with the rabbis (Luke 2:41ff.). This was also the temple from which he drove out the money-changers and merchants shortly before his crucifixion (Matt. 21:12), and which he prophesied would soon be destroyed (Matt. 24:2).[7] Herod also built a palace for himself inside the western wall of the city, and alongside it, also adjacent to the temple, he rebuilt an old citadel, adding four high towers. From these he could see everything that went on in the courts of the temple, and much of what was happening throughout the city. He named the citadel

6. In restoring the temple, one of the first duties was to rekindle the *ner tamid*, the eternal light that symbolized the eternal presence of God. By the Levitical Law any oil used in the temple must be ritually pure. In all of Jerusalem they could find only enough of the proper oil to burn for one day, yet it would take several days to press, refine, and ritually purify new oil. Nevertheless, they lit the light, believing that one day was better than none at all. The light miraculously continued to burn for eight days, until the new oil was ready. The temple and its new altar were then rededicated to God. This is the origin of Hanukkah, the eight-day Festival of Lights or Feast of Dedication that Jews celebrate every December (the twenty-fifth day of the Jewish month of Kislev). The rebuilt temple is known as the "second temple."

7. It was not Herod's temple which he said he would destroy and rebuild in three days (John 2:19). In that passage he was referring to his body, which Saint Paul calls the temple of the Spirit of God (1 Cor. 3:16).

the Antonia Fortress in honor of his patron, Marc Antony. Although the location of the Praetorium to which Jesus was taken during his trial (Matt. 27:27) is not known with certainty, it is likely that it was the Antonia.

In 70 CE, fed up with a series of rebellions, the emperor Vespasian, who had been the commanding general in Palestine before ascending the throne, ordered the extermination of the Jews. His son Titus built a closed wall around the city and starved hundreds of Jews to death, then crucified thousands more. His troops then marched into Jerusalem and leveled the city and the temple, as Jesus had prophesied, with "not one stone . . . left on another" (Mark 13:1-2). All that was left of Herod's beautiful temple was the west retaining wall, which still stands today.[8] Many of the survivors fled the country. The next sixty years saw a continued series of revolts, and finally in 132 CE Rome had had enough. They destroyed cities and slaughtered Jews all over Palestine, driving the majority of the Jews to seek refuge in other countries. Many fled north, and eventually migrated to Russia and Eastern Europe, and others fled across the Mediterranean to Iberia.[9] Jerusalem remained in ruins from 70 CE until the emperor Hadrian rebuilt it (not very impressively) as a Roman city, naming it Aelia Capitolina. It retained that name until the demise of the Byzantine Empire, and during the following years it was called by a variety of names according to who had control of it. To Jews and Christians, however, it was always known as Jerusalem, and during the period that the crusaders held most of Palestine it was known as the Kingdom of Jerusalem. For centuries the city was torn apart by pagans, Jews, Christians, and Muslims alike.

In 692 CE the Muslim Caliph Abd al-Malik constructed a magnificent shrine on the site of the temple, which is the second holiest point of pilgrimage in Islam. It is called the Dome of the Rock (often miscalled the Mosque of Omar), and it has stood for thirteen hundred years. Beneath the dome is the rock believed to be the place where Abraham prepared to sacrifice Isaac,[10] which is also the place from which Muslims believe that Mohammed

8. Its proper name is the Western Wall, but it has long been known as the "Wailing Wall" because it is an ancient tradition for Jews to stand facing it to pray and to weep loudly over the destruction of the temple.

9. There are to this day two different major traditions in Judaism. The Ashkenazim are the Eastern European Jews, who were mainly Yiddish-speaking. The Sephardim are the Jews who fled to Spain and Portugal, and were expelled by the Inquisition in 1492, moving north into France and western Europe, and south into North Africa.

10. Abraham had two sons, Ishmael by the Egyptian slave Hagar, and later Isaac by his wife Sarah. Muslims believe that the Bible is in error, and that it was Ishmael, not Isaac,

ascended to heaven. The shrine is considered the oldest (and perhaps the most beautiful) example of Islamic architecture. Even though today Jerusalem is in Jewish hands, the Israelis have shown full respect for this shrine, and there is no intent to remove it or convert it to another temple.[11]

In the early days of the Muslim rule the Jews, Christians, and Muslims in Jerusalem were not in great conflict. They had worked out an almost friendly, albeit cautious, relationship, even to the point that on several occasions they helped each other out of major difficulties. The real problem began in the eleventh century CE when the Seljuks, a huge pagan population in Turkey, were converted to Islam. They accepted a fundamentalist, fanatical interpretation of the faith, and started a rapid military expansion of their empire, taking Muslim as well as non-Muslim countries and forcing them to convert to their version of Islam. When the Seljuks swept through Palestine the Muslims in Jerusalem suffered as much as the Christians and Jews. The Seljuks damaged the Church of the Holy Sepulchre, and when they left, the Jerusalem Muslims gave money to help the Christians repair the damage. The Seljuks returned soon thereafter, and this time took pickaxes to the stone that had been rolled across the entry to Christ's tomb. When the news of the Seljuk desecrations reached Europe, the Christians were enraged. At about the same time, in 1094, Rodrigo Díaz de Vivar, "El Cid," conquered the Moors at Valencia, Spain, proving that the Muslim invaders were not invincible after all. The following year, 1095, the First Crusade was launched to "drive the infidel from the Holy Land." Not only did the crusaders use a "divide and conquer" tactic by teaching the Jews and Muslims to hate each other, but their own hypocrisy, immorality, and brutality taught both to hate the Christians. To this day Palestine is paying the price of this mutual hatred.

Jerusalem continued to survive through the oppression of the Crusades, the Ottoman Empire, and the British rule. In 1948 CE it was established by the United Nations as the capital of the newly partitioned State of Israel. Part of it remained in Palestinian hands until the Six Days' War of 1967, when the two parts of the city were reunited into the modern Israeli city of Jerusalem. While Rome bears the title "The Eternal City," Jerusalem, sacred to three great faiths, has at least an equal claim to that epithet.

---

whom God commanded Abraham to sacrifice. They also maintain that it was Ishmael whom God intended to be the heir to the promise. The Arabs are the descendants of Ishmael.

11. During the Crusades the military monastic Order of the Poor Knights of Christ made their headquarters in this shrine. Because it stood on the site of the temple, they came to be known as the Knights Templar.

# Joppa

Joppa, whose name means "beautiful," played a very important role in an-cient Palestine, because it was the only natural harbor between the Bay of Acco (the crusaders' capital of Acre, near Haifa) and the Egyptian frontier (somewhere around what today is called the Gaza Strip). Today the equiv-alent city, very close to the site of ancient Joppa, is Tel-Aviv. In various translations of the Bible the city is called a number of things, including Jaffe, Japho, and Yafo. The Hebrew is *Yapho,* and the Greek *Ioppe.*

Joppa is an ancient city, and references to it are found not only in the Bible but in many Egyptian documents, as well as those of the Phoenicians and Seleucids. As important a role as it played in Jewish history, it was un-der Jewish control only briefly in the eighth and second centuries BCE. Ar-chaeological research has traced Joppa's first settlement to the early eigh-teenth century BCE. By 1468 BCE it must have become an important port city, because it is included in a document found at Karnak, listing the cities captured by Thutmosis III of Egypt. By 1300 BCE it was a Canaanite city, al-though still under Egyptian control (as was much of coastal Canaan at the time of the Israelite conquests). An important archaeological find after World War II was a thirteenth-century BCE pre-Philistine temple dedicated to a god of a lion cult. Some time before the time of King David Joppa had fallen into Phoenician hands. David and King Hiram of Tyre (Phoenicia) were not only allies but personal friends, so relations were very cordial. Even though Joppa was a Phoenician port, Israel was allowed to use it as if it were one of Israel's own. In about 950, when Solomon was building the temple, Hiram was still alive, and a friend and ally of Solomon's. He pro-vided the cedar timbers for the temple from Lebanon and conveyed them on floats to Joppa, and from there they were carted by land to Jerusalem.

Joppa finally became a Jewish port when it was captured in 705 BCE, but only three years later it fell to the Assyrians when Sennacherib launched his campaign along the coastal regions. After the withdrawal of the Assyrians in the late eighth century, Joppa fell back into the hands of the Phoenicians, who held it until it was taken by Alexander in 332 BCE. Af-ter Alexander's death his generals Ptolemy and Seleucus fought for control of Joppa. During the following centuries it passed back and forth between

Ptolemaic (Egyptian) and Seleucid (Syrian) control, although its value as a port enabled it to retain its municipal rights and function almost as if it were a free city.

Around 165 BCE an anti-Jewish group of Joppans somehow managed to convince over two hundred Jewish men, women, and children to board ships. They were sailed outside the harbor, where the ships were sunk and all the Jewish passengers drowned. In 163 BCE Judas Maccabaeus, in retribution, raided the city and burned the harbor with all the ships anchored there. He was not able to take the city, but he ordered his general Jonathan to take it as soon as possible. In 147 BCE, during the Maccabaean revolt, Joppa was forced to open its gates to the Maccabaeans. By 143 the Jews had full control of it, although they lost it to the Seleucids again soon thereafter. In a twenty-two-year struggle from 126 to 104 BCE, Joppa was once again captured by the Jews, who this time were able to hold it and gain full control over its commerce. In 63 BCE, however, Pompey the Great captured all of Palestine for Rome. In 56 BCE Joppa was given semi-independence by being declared an autonomous city by the Roman proconsul of Syria. This meant that it could have its own senate and was free to engage in international commerce. In 39 BCE Herod the Great convinced Rome to give the city to him. In the Jewish Revolt of 66 to 70 CE the general Vespasian (soon to become emperor) gave the command of the region to a brutal general, Cestius Gallus. Gallus captured Joppa, and in a succession of battles between 66 and 79 CE it was almost completely destroyed, with the loss of eighty-four hundred Jews. A large number escaped, and when the Romans left Joppa they returned. Gallus brought back his troops and slaughtered forty-two hundred more, then leveled what was left of the city. Its value as a port remained, although it didn't again rise to significance as a city for many centuries. There was a mixed Jewish and Christian population there over the centuries, and they lived side by side quite amicably.

In 636 Joppa was captured by Arabic Muslims. With brief exceptions during the Crusades[1] it remained under the control of various ethnic Muslim groups until the fall of the Ottoman Empire in 1918. Although it was destroyed by an earthquake in 1838, it was rebuilt by the Ottomans, who maintained the harbor as one of their major ports in the eastern Mediterranean. At the fall of the Ottoman Empire it fell under British rule until it became part of the modern state of Israel under the U.N. partition of 1948.

---

1. Richard I ("the Lionheart") built a citadel there, the walls of which still stand in the portion of Tel-Aviv known as the "Old City."

Joppa has a rich biblical heritage. It was Joppa from which Jonah sailed sometime in the eighth century BCE when he tried to escape God's command to preach to the Ninevites (Jonah 1:3).[2] The port was used on two occasions as the receiving point for cedar timbers shipped from Lebanon — once in the tenth century BCE during the building of Solomon's temple (2 Chron. 2:16), and once in the sixth century during the rebuilding of Jerusalem after the return from Babylon (Ezra 3:7). In the New Testament, it was in Joppa that Saint Peter raised Tabitha (Dorcas) from the dead (Acts 9:36-41). He stayed in the house of Simon the Tanner there, and it was while he was praying on the roof of Simon's house that he had the vision in which God declared, "Do not call anything impure that God has made clean" (Acts 10:9-14). This convinced him that Saint Paul was right in saying that Gentiles could be Christians without having to convert to Judaism first.

2. Scholars argue whether there was an actual Jonah or whether the story is allegorical. If the story is based on a real individual, however, he would have lived sometime in the eighth century BCE, as that was the only time that Nineveh would have captured any significant attention from the Jews.

# Laodicea

Laodicea was a city in Phrygia in upper Asia Minor, in what is now eastern Turkey. It was founded around 260 BCE by the Seleucid emperor Antiochus II, who named it in honor of his wife, Laodice. It was built at a nearly ideal location, at the crossroads of the two main trade routes in Asia Minor, enabling it to become very wealthy very quickly. It was in the fertile valley of the Lycus River, and thus had a generous food supply from the rich farmlands surrounding it. One drawback was that the water supply from the Lycus was woefully inadequate. Water had to be piped in from a hot volcanic spring far to the south, and it was still lukewarm when it got to Laodicea. While this was good for washing and cooking, it was a significant problem when it came to using the water for drinking, wine-making, or watering animals. Mineral encrustation from the warm mineral-rich water can still be found in the archaeological digs at Laodicea.

Antiochus founded several other cities named Laodicea, but none were particularly important. To distinguish this one, it was often called Laocidea-on-the-Lycus.[1] The city's main industry, aside from its commercial activities resulting from the trade routes, was the production of sandals, and clothing made from a glossy black wool fabric. Laodicean robes were highly prized. It was also noted as a medical center for the treatment of eye diseases. The religion of Laodicea for most of its history was a worship primarily of the Greek Olympian gods.

By 220 BCE Laodicea had become an independent city-state, with Achaeus as its king. It very soon thereafter became part of the kingdom of Pergamum, and thus became deeply embroiled in the war between Rome and Mithridates V of Pontus. After the fall of Mithridates, however, it fell under Roman control, and immediately rose again to great prosperity. It was declared by Rome to be a free city, meaning that it had its own senate, was granted many special rights and privileges, and was free of much of

---

1. In classical times it was quite common for several places to have the same name, especially when founded by rulers who named them after themselves or after patrons or family members. (Seleucus named several cities Antioch after his father.) Usually these were distinguished from one another by an additional descriptive name, such as "-by-the-forest," "-on-the-mountain," and so on.

the heavy taxation and tribute which other cities were required to pay. The city remained prosperous and life there was relatively uneventful throughout the Roman and Byzantine periods, but it finally fell under the Muslim takeover of the seventh and eighth centuries CE. It soon thereafter decayed and was abandoned, its commercial power having slowly moved to the nearby city of Denizli. Denizli, situated by the hot springs, is still a thriving community today.

The biblical significance of Laodicea is that Christianity came into it almost as soon as it reached Asia Minor. The faith might have been brought to Laodicea by Epaphras (Col. 4:12-13) while Saint Paul was living about one hundred miles to the west in Ephesus. There is no evidence that Paul ever visited Laodicea, although he mentions it in his letter to the Colossians. Apparently the church in Laodicea was weak. The wealth and worldly temptations were great and the persecution was light, so the Christian commitment was half-hearted — thus it was condemned in Revelation 3:16 as being, like its water, "lukewarm, neither hot nor cold."

# Magdala

Not a great deal is known about the region and town commonly known as Magdala, but more correctly as Magadan. Historically it was of little importance, and is noted by Christians only because it was probably the region from which Mary Magdalene came. There is only one reference to it in the New Testament (Matt. 15:39). In the Vulgate and the King James translation it is erroneously called Magdala, while in most other translations it is called Magadan.[1] Notwithstanding, it is generally referred to today as Magdala. The name of the town and region apparently come from the Hebrew *migdal,* "tower." It is believed that the modern town of Khirbet Mejdal now stands on the site.

The region and town of Magdala was on the west shore of the Sea of Galilee, not far from the city of Tiberias. It was in a region considered by the Jews to be defiled because of the huge number of Gentiles and Samaritans who lived there. Jesus visited the region after the feeding of the four thousand (Matt. 15:39). According to the Talmud, Magdala was a very wealthy town, and was destroyed by the Romans because of its moral depravity. The Jewish historian Flavius Josephus was often in the town of Tarichaea, which exactly fits the location and character of Magdala as described in the Talmud and the Bible. He described the destruction of Tarichaea for the same reason, moral depravity, and there is little doubt that they are the same town.

The Bible tells nothing of the life of Mary Magdalene (Mary of Magdala) before she met Jesus, other than that she had been released of seven demons (Luke 8:2). In the late sixth century CE Pope Saint Gregory I identified her with the prostitute who anointed Jesus' feet (Luke 7:37-38) and with Lazarus's sister Mary, but there is nothing in the Bible to substantiate this. From early times tradition has identified her as a prostitute, possibly because of the reputation of Magdala as a depraved place. Again, this is neither affirmed nor denied in the Bible.

---

1. The King James translation, for all its literary magnificence, contains many errors because many of the Greek and Hebrew documents from which it was translated were defective. It was an extraordinary piece of scholarship for its time, but modern biblical research has been able to produce earlier and much more accurate documents.

Little more is known about Magdala. No significant archaeological excavations have been made in the area.

# Masada

The story of Masada cannot be told apart from that of Herod. Herod the Great was made king of Judea in 37 BCE, after several years of rebellion and civil strife both in Rome and in Palestine. His father, Antipater, had been made procurator of Judea by Julius Caesar after the defeat of Pompey in the Roman civil war. After Caesar's assassination Marc Antony became the primary Roman authority in Palestine, and he placed Herod on the throne. Herod was hated by the Jews at least as much as were the Romans, and perhaps even more. He was an Idumean, not a Jew, and although he allegedly practiced Judaism, the Jews knew full well that it was strictly a political commitment, not a spiritual one. Also, for all the grand building he did in Palestine (including an extraordinarily magnificent temple in Jerusalem), he was a cruel and oppressive tyrant with an evil temper and no concern for anything but his own standing with the Romans, whom he loved.[1]

Herod was paranoid because he knew that he was hated by his own subjects, and he ruled strictly at the whim of Rome, which was itself in turmoil. He even suspected his own sons of conspiring for his throne, and killed several of them. Caesar had been assassinated just a few years before, the Second Triumvirate was falling apart, and the tension between Marc Antony and Octavian was reaching a fever pitch. To protect his own interests, Herod built a string of fortresses on the borders of his realm, just in case he had to defend his throne against a revolution or against Rome's change of mind about his right to rule. One of his greatest fears was of Marc Antony himself, the man who had placed him on the throne. Antony's affair with Cleopatra had become an irrational obsession, and he was even accused of handing over to her vast sections of the Roman Em-

---

1. It was he who ordered the massacre of all the infant boys in Bethlehem in order to try to kill the prophesied Messiah (Matt. 2:16). While there is no Roman record of this, it is entirely consistent with the behavior of many Eastern potentates, and particularly with that of Herod, who did not hesitate to murder anyone who got in his way, including his own wife and sons. The Romans, who also had minimal reverence for life, would have paid little attention to such an act as long as it did not injure any Romans, and did not interfere with their control or revenue.

pire. Herod feared that Judea might be Antony's next gift to the seductive Egyptian pharaoh.

To protect himself against a long siege, Herod built a heavily fortified palace on top of a huge isolated massif that towered a quarter mile above the southwestern shore of the Dead Sea. The name of the place was Masada. The Maccabaeans had built a fortress there in the late second century BCE, but it had been abandoned for decades. Before he was king, Herod had fled there when his life was in danger. He had left his wife and family at Masada while he sought out Marc Antony to negotiate for the throne. When he returned, he discovered that his family had survived but were almost dead from thirst. After they were all safe, and Herod was in power, he determined that he would rebuild Masada in case he ever again needed a refuge, and that he would make sure thirst would never be a problem there again. He built a huge turreted casemate wall all around the summit. The wall was supported by thirty towers, mostly on the eastern and western sides, because the northern and southern faces were impossible to scale. The only access to the fortress was a narrow pathway, primarily of stairs, cut out of the rock. It was only wide enough for a single donkey or man in armor, so if an enemy force tried to use it they could easily be picked off one man at a time by a single archer or swordsman. A rush of forces on the fort would have been impossible.

Herod then had two parallel cisterns cut into the base of the rock, dammed the Bar Yair ravine, and dug channels and aqueducts into the cisterns from several water sources in the ravine. Finally, he dug a huge underground cistern at the top of the massif, estimated to be able to hold almost eleven million gallons. This is impressive by itself, but even more so when one considers that Herod kept it constantly full, and that all the water was carried in portable jars by slaves and donkeys who climbed the narrow staircases up to the top from the cisterns at the base. The water problem was solved, meaning that with sufficient food storage Masada could withstand a siege for years. As the Romans were later to discover, the fortress was virtually impregnable.

Herod realized that it was possible that he might have to live there for a long time, and he had no intention of giving up his luxurious lifestyle if he had to go there. He built two enormous and lavish palaces on Masada, even containing comfortable and beautifully decorated interior Roman-style bath rooms and toilets. Although most of the Masada complex is now in ruins, many beautiful frescoes and mosaics still can be seen there. There were several levels, connected by staircases carved out of the rock, boasting handsome patios and balconies from which one could watch beautiful sunrises and sunsets over the desert, and see across the landscape for many miles. Herod erected storage houses to hold vast quantities of food — huge stores of the very best for himself and his family, and immense amounts of simpler food to keep his soldiers strong and well-nourished. It never became necessary for him to seek refuge there, but he and his successors kept it always ready and supplied well into the first century CE.

The last use of Masada is the best known, and has marked it for all of history as a monument to courage and determination. The story was recorded by the Jewish historian Flavius Josephus, who accompanied the Roman general Titus in his final siege against the Jews in 66 to 70 CE, including the siege on Masada. There was a sect of Jews known as Zealots, who for a century had sought a military Messiah, another Judas Maccabaeus, who would raise up a holy army and drive out the Roman oppressors at any cost. One branch of the Zealots was a group of extremists who called themselves the *Sicarii* ("Daggers").[2] In 66 CE the Zealots rose up in a full-scale rebellion against Rome. One of the first events in the rebellion was when a group of Sicarii commandos scaled the wall of Masada during the night. The Romans had only a small garrison there, and unaware of any trouble and thinking that the place was impregnable, were caught completely off guard. They were massacred by the Sicarii, who held the fortress. At first the Romans did little to try to take it back. While the rebels were in Masada they could cause little trouble elsewhere, and the Romans had more important things on their minds — they thought they could come back and clean up the Masada rebels at any time. The Jewish rebellion was a major irritation to the Romans, but it was not a real threat. There was no way that any rebel group could drive out the mighty Roman army — few nations could do that, and certainly not a band of guerillas —

---

2. Judas Iscariot was almost certainly a Zealot, and possibly a *Sicarius*. In the first century CE, most men named Judas (for Judas Maccabaeus) were of Zealot background, and this Judas came from Kerioth (thus "Iscariot"), believed to have been a hotbed of the *Sicarii*. It is very unlikely that Judas betrayed Jesus for the thirty pieces of silver. He was treasurer of the apostles, so he often carried much larger amounts than that, with which he could have absconded at any time. Many scholars believe that he betrayed Jesus because it had become patently evident that Jesus had no intention of raising an army against the Romans. An increasing number of Jews began to accept him as the Messiah, and this meant decreasing support for those who looked for a military leader. If the Zealots were to succeed, Jesus had to be shown not to be the Messiah. Judas probably expected that Jesus would be only arrested, not executed.

but by 70 CE the Romans had had enough of the Zealots. They could not allow this insolence to inspire rebellion in other parts of the empire, so they launched an all-out attack, slaughtered Jews by the thousands, leveled most of the major cities including Jerusalem, and ended the uprising — once and for all, they thought. But the Sicarii fled to Masada, where about one thousand men, women, and children sought refuge. The Romans, hoping to finish off the Zealots altogether, laid siege to Masada. But Herod had accomplished what he intended. This small group of men, women, and children held off a whole Roman legion for three years without want of food or water. They were finally defeated not by hunger or thirst or the power of the Roman army but by sheer brute labor on the part of the Romans. After three years of fruitless siege, they spent the next seven months carting dirt and stone from the desert to build a huge ramp from the desert floor to the top of Masada, then paved it with stone. The Jews had no war machines to stop them, and they finally stood helplessly on the fortress walls watching the Romans approach with their weapons and war machines at the ready. Realizing that all was lost, and refusing to submit to becoming Roman slaves, they stole the victory from the Romans. Nine hundred and sixty men, women, and children committed suicide. When the Romans came over the wall and entered the fort, they found that their mighty conquest consisted of two women and five small children.

# Megiddo

In Palestine there are at least two sites identified as Megiddo, and there is evidence that there were others known by that name. All were battle sites and regions where armies assembled, and the name possibly derives from the Hebrew for "the gathering of his armies"[1] Of the two prime sites, one Megiddo is a mound in the Plains of Jezreel where more than two hundred battles were fought over the centuries. The other, a Galilean city of great importance, is the focus of our attention. Either of these sites could possibly be associated with the "Armageddon" of Revelation 16:16 (on which, see p. 29).

The city of Megiddo was located in northern Palestine, in the Carmel mountains, about twenty miles south-southeast of modern Haifa. It had a virtually limitless water supply whose source was in an easily defensible cave in the city. It was also on the edge of the Esdraelon Plain, a region of amazing fertility. It was, in fact, the most fertile part of the Fertile Crescent, and was the breadbasket of that part of the Middle East. Megiddo's location was of extraordinary strategic importance in Old Testament times. To the east it had a controlling position over the Wadi Arah, the primary pass through the Carmel mountains. To the north and west it had a commanding view of the vast Esdraelon Plain, enabling its inhabitants to see approaching danger for several miles. This junction of the Wadi Arah and the Esdraelon Plain was an essential link in the trade and military route that joined Egypt and Mesopotamia to each other through the Fertile Crescent. It was also a critical link in the northern highway that joined the Phoenicians to the Akkadians, and in two primary routes to the southern and central parts of Palestine. Megiddo therefore, simply by virtue of its location, had control over some of the most important international highways in the Middle East. While this gave the city an unimaginable advantage in military strength and commerce, it also had its drawbacks. Over the centuries it saw countless major international battles in its own backyard. Most it could simply watch from its vantage point on the Esdraelon Plain, but many involved the city itself.

1. The derivation of this is explained in the chapter on Armageddon, p. 30, n. 1.

Megiddo is in some respects an enigmatic city, because it is very difficult to develop an accurate chronology of its history, and the archaeological
site continually produces finds that raise new questions about previous
finds. Despite its historic and political importance, it is mentioned only a
few times in the Bible.[2] It is well documented, however, in other contemporary writings. It was a walled city of the Canaanites, and its first mention in
the Bible regards its capture by the Israelites during Joshua's conquest (Josh.
17:11). Unlike most of the early Israelite conquests, however, the city and its
population were not destroyed. Apparently by the time of the fall of
Megiddo there was a strong enough stable Israelite society that such ele-
mental and seemingly barbaric measures were no longer necessary. Megiddo was allotted to the tribe of Issachar, and the population was enslaved to
do menial labor. Megiddo appears next in the Bible when Solomon included it in his fifth administrative district and developed it as a citadel
(1 Kings 9:15-19). He fortified three cities outside Jerusalem — Hazor, Gezer,
and Megiddo — as sites for the preparation of armies and the storage of
military supplies and horses. Megiddo is also identified as the site of two
important deaths: King Ahaziah died there after being injured in his flight
from Jehu (2 Kings 9:27), and King Josiah died there in his attempt to keep
the Egyptian Pharaoh Neco from aiding the Assyrians (2 Kings 23:29-30).

The earliest archaeological level of Megiddo dates to the early fourth
millennium BCE, a period when writing was first developing. A primitive
village appeared at the site, soon followed by a small shrine with an altar.
Growth was obviously rapid, however, because by the early Bronze Age
Megiddo was a bustling city, well fortified and with a large temple, probably dedicated to the baals and Ashtoreth.[3] This temple appears to have
been a regional religious center, because the large number of animal bones
found there indicate that it was a primary place of sacrifice.

2. The reference in the Song of Deborah (Judg. 5:19) is unquestionably to the Megiddo
in the Plains of Jezreel. There is a variation of the name used in Zechariah 12:11 that also refers to the Jezreel Megiddo.

3. The Semitic nature gods had many names, but were collectively known as baals or
*ba'alim*, from the Hebrew *ba'al*, "lord." Most Old Testament references to them use the sin-
gular form, Baal, as if it were the proper name of a single god (we read of Elijah battling the
priests of Baal). Ashtoreth (also known as Astarte or Ishtar) was the fertility goddess. (A corruption of her name became the name of the major Christian feast, Easter, and of the female
reproductive cycle, estrus.) Worship of the baals and Ashtoreth pervaded most Middle Eastern religion. It even corrupted Judaism in the northern kingdom of Israel during the reign
of Ahab and Jezebel, producing the Jewish heresy of Samaritanism.

Sometime around 3800 BCE Megiddo was totally destroyed by fire, and for the next couple of centuries it was nothing more than a village. By the middle Bronze Age it had again risen to the status of a prosperous city, and at some point it appears to have fallen under Egyptian control. It was well fortified, and must have served as an Egyptian citadel on the highway between Egypt and Mesopotamia. By 1750 BCE the old Egyptian adobe wall had been replaced by a large stone one, with complex gates, ramps, and parapets. This was typical of the Hyksos manner of building, indicating that Megiddo may have no longer been under Egyptian rule, but was rather an early stage in the later Hyksos conquest of Egypt.[4]

The city continued to prosper greatly, and with the expulsion of the Hyksos, Egyptian rule appears to have been restored to Megiddo. During the rule of Pharaoh Thutmosis III in the early fifteenth century BCE there was a revolt in Megiddo. Thutmosis, called the Egyptian Napoleon, was a cruel and tyrannical ruler, and the residents of Megiddo apparently rose up against him. This resulted in a seven-month siege by Egypt, during which the city was destroyed. Amazingly, the destruction acted like the pruning of a shrub — the city regrew quickly and moved into one of its most prosperous times. The new city was greatly expanded, and boasted better fortifications, larger palaces, and a hoard of rich treasures of gold, jewelry, ivory, and beautiful works of art. The Egyptian influence was weakening significantly as Egypt entered into a long period of decline. Replacing it were influences of the northern Semitic cultures, particularly those of the Hittites and Mesopotamia. In the mid-nineteenth century a shepherd boy found a clay tablet of the Gilgamesh Epic (the Babylonian creation story) near the city gate, and archaeologists have dated it to this era of the city.

At the very beginning of the Iron Age (about 1150 BCE) Megiddo was violently destroyed. It is unclear who was responsible, but the evidence points to either the Philistines, the Egyptians, or the Israelites. The city that was rebuilt on the site was a mere shadow of the previous one. The buildings were poorly built, and there was obviously no planning — like Topsy, it "jest growed." Pottery finds indicate that it was probably occupied by Philistines, who may well have been responsible for the destruction of

4. The Hyksos were a warlike Semitic people who swept down from the north and conquered Egypt in the very early eighteenth century BCE. They ruled for about 150 years and were then driven out by a revolution led by Amhose I. The early Hyksos were among the first people to domesticate the horse, and it was they who introduced horses into Egypt. It must have been a terrifying sight to the foot-bound Egyptians to see the great Hyksos bronze chariots bearing down on them, drawn by huge, galloping warhorses.

1150. The city was again destroyed at the end of the eleventh century, this time probably by Saul or David. The new city that rose on the ruins was also poorly built, and indicated a decline in the material culture of the population. This would have been consistent with an Israelite occupation. The Israelite monarchy had just begun, and the people were moving out of a simple agrarian and semi-nomadic culture into a more stable and urbanized one — but they still had a long way to go before they would reach the glory of the era of Solomon.

In the tenth century BCE Solomon, appreciating the strategic location of the city, took an interest in Megiddo. He fortified the city with a new casemate[5] wall and a great six-chambered gate, similar to the fortifications he built at Hazor and Gezer. He completely reconstructed the city and established it as his royal northern administrative center. He built two palaces there, as well as several arsenals to store military supplies. There were also sacrificial altars, and archaeologists have found a number of ritual items that indicate that Megiddo had again become an important religious center, although this time of Judaism rather than paganism. The city remained a key city in Israel until after the division of the United Monarchy after the death of Solomon.

With the breakup of the United Monarchy, Jeroboam became king of the northern kingdom, Israel, which consisted of the ten northern tribes. Megiddo, being in Galilee, was part of this. Because it was one of Solomon's royal cities and citadels, it was partially destroyed during the war between Jeroboam and Solomon's son Rehoboam, who retained control of the two southern tribes and thus became king of Judah, the southern kingdom. The destruction was probably at the hand of the Egyptian pharaoh Shesonk I (whom the Bible calls Shishak). After Omri (a later king of Israel) established his dynasty in the early ninth century BCE, he moved his capital to Samaria, and rebuilt Megiddo. He improved the city wall by giving it an offset/inset design that makes it look from the air like a string of rectangular beads, making it even harder to attack and breach. He also built huge warehouses[6] and a grain silo and greatly improved the city's wa-

5. A casemate wall is a double wall surrounding a chain of small rooms. It is very hard to breach, yet it requires much less material than a standard thick wall, and also provides storage and muster rooms for men and supplies during a siege. This was new technology at the time, but the design is so superior that it has been used in fortifications up to modern times.

6. These were originally called "Solomon's Stables," but more recent research has affirmed that they were Omride, not Solomonic, and that they were not stables.

ter system. The city prospered until it was demolished during the destruction of Israel by the Assyrians in 732 BCE. It nonetheless survived as a provincial commercial center under Assyrian rule until its destruction by Pharaoh Neco's attack in 609 BCE. It finally fell into the hands of the Persians, and was abandoned in 350 BCE.

# Nabatea

Nabatea is never mentioned by name in the Bible,[1] but there are several indirect references to it in the New Testament.[2] It was located in a barren region east of the Jordan River, between Israel and Mesopotamia. In the centuries immediately preceding and following the time of Christ, it had a significant degree of political and economic intercourse with Palestine. There are indications in the Apocrypha that King Aretas II of Nabatea was a supporter of the Maccabees, and the Jewish historian Flavius Josephus reports that Aretas fought for Hyrcanus in opposition to Herod the Great's father Antipater. According to Josephus, Herod Antipas's first wife, Areta, was the daughter of Aretas III. When he divorced her to marry his sister-in-law and niece Herodias, it precipitated a border war with Nabatea that cost him large territories in the eastern part of his kingdom.

Until the middle of the twentieth century CE little was known of this Arabian kingdom. The only accounts of it were in very questionable and conflicting works of ancient Roman writers and in the record of various war notices in the writings of Josephus. The ruins of the capital, Petra, were discovered in 1812, but most of the culture and history of the city and country remained unknown until just before World War II, when the discovery and deciphering of several inscriptions began to reveal the mysteries of the place. Since then, through the discovery of other inscriptions and documents, the story of Nabatea has continued to unfold.

In about the sixth century BCE a tribe from northwest Arabia moved into the land of the Edomites, pushing those inhabitants into southern Judah. There is no evidence to tell whether this was simply a slow infiltrating migration or a military assault. By the fourth century BCE they were the

---

1. It used to be thought that the Nabateans were descendants of Ishmael's son Nebaioth (Gen. 25:13; 1 Chron. 1:29), as is claimed by Flavius Josephus. Most biblical scholars now reject this hypothesis, however, because of differences in the Hebrew spellings.

2. Paul barely escaped arrest in Damascus at the behest of Aretas IV, the king of Nabatea (Acts 9:23-25; 2 Cor. 11:32). He also speaks of journeying into Arabia (Gal. 1:17), and it is generally accepted that this meant Nabatea. The Nabatean capital, Petra (on which, see p. 157), may have been an important stop on the journey of the Magi to visit Jesus at his birth.

primary inhabitants of Edom and Moab as far south as the Negev. Some of this must have been a military incursion, because by that time they had control of several Edomite and Moabite fortresses, and they built a string of forts in the Negev. At first they were technically in Persian territory and therefore under the rule of the Persian Empire, but they were in effect independent. They retained that independence after Alexander's defeat of the Persians. This was probably because the region they inhabited was arid and undesirable, so neither the Persians nor Alexander were particularly interested in fighting very hard to control it. The first official record of the Nabateans is in 169 BCE, when Jason, a contender for the office of High Priest in Jerusalem, was being pursued and sought sanctuary from Aretas II "the Tyrant" of Nabatea (he was refused). There are fairly thorough records from then on, but they are conflicting and their accuracy is questioned by modern scholars. It is reasonably sure, however, that in the border wars with Aretas III Herod lost most of the region of Transjordan as far north as east of Decapolis. This was a significant expansion of the Nabatean kingdom. In 85 BCE the citizens of Damascus asked Aretas III to rule over them, and apparently he remained their king until 63 BCE, when Pompey the Great captured Syria for Rome. Nabatea, however, was apparently as uninteresting to Pompey as it had been to previous conquerors, and thus retained its independence.

In 106 CE the Roman emperor Trajan annexed all of Nabatea, probably as an outpost defense in his war with Parthia. Rome interfered very little with the kingdom's activities, however, and it continued to prosper. It is likely that the Roman emperor Philip the Arab (who reigned from 244 to 249 CE) was a Nabatean, as he was born in that region. With the decay of the Roman Empire and the resultant weakening of the Middle Eastern economy, Nabatea finally faded into obscurity. The kingdom and its people simply faded away and eventually disappeared from history.

The first Nabateans were Arabic nomads who lived very much as the desert nomads still do today. After they moved into Edom and Moab, however, they gained control over a number of major trade routes, and in time they became the primary merchants of goods from the Arabian peninsula, mainly spices and perfumes. Their capital, Petra, was a beautiful city located at the intersection of several major north-south and east-west trade routes. Despite the aridity and barrenness of most of the country, Nabatea, and particularly Petra, became very prosperous. It is possible (and even likely) that Petra was the source of the frankincense and myrrh that the Magi brought to Jesus (see the section on Petra, p. 157).

# Nazareth

Were it not for the fact that Jesus grew up in Nazareth, it is unlikely that anyone today other than a handful of scholars of antiquities would have ever heard of it. It was never mentioned in the Old Testament or Apocrypha, and in New Testament times it was held in scorn by pious Jews. When Nathanael asked about Jesus and heard that he was from Nazareth, he said, "Nazareth! Can anything good come from there?" (John 1:45-46). It is located in lower Galilee, an area that for the most part was a turbulent region outside the mainstream of Jewish life. It had been part of the northern kingdom of Israel, an idolatrous and troublesome kingdom ever since it broke away from Solomon's United Monarchy in the late tenth century BCE. Sepphoris, the only important city in the area, was just a few miles to the north of it. Nazareth was close enough to Sepphoris and the trade routes that it had ready access to the mainstream culture of the times, but far enough in the "boondocks," on steep hills at the edge of the fertile agrarian Esdraelon Plain, that it remained relatively unnoticed and that its inhabitants could live pretty much unto themselves. After the Romans took Palestine they secured Galilee and made it a considerably safer region, bringing it a bit more into the mainstream of Judean culture. The name of the place may have come from its high location in the Esdraelon hills, being a corruption of the Aramaic *naserat,* "watch-tower."

Archaeological evidence indicates that Jesus' Nazareth was higher up in the hills than the present town. It appears to have been settled sometime during the third century BCE during the Hellenistic era when the Ptolemaic Empire ruled Palestine. The town was of absolutely no importance in classical times, its modern importance resulting strictly from its having been Jesus' home.[1] There are several sites of pilgrimage there, including the Church of the Annunciation, the Church of Saint Joseph, and Mary's Well. The churches were partially destroyed by Muslims in the late Middle Ages, but they have since been restored. Mary's Well, one of the main sources of

1. Jesus was rejected by the townspeople of Nazareth when he began his ministry in about 30 CE (Matt. 13:57), so he moved to Capernaum where he made his home until his crucifixion three years later.

water for the town, has been associated with Mary only since about 1100 CE, when the crusaders identified it as such. There is no archaeological evidence of any first-century dwellings nearby, so there is no reason to think that this was anything other than a general water source for the whole region. There is a small fountain in a cleft of the rocks that is much nearer the town, and probably served as the main town water supply.

The Nazareth of Jesus' time was an unimportant and insignificant village, and it is likely that many of the people who lived there worked in the fields in the Esdraelon Plain, herded sheep, and eked out a living plying trades. Many of the tradesmen probably worked at least part-time in the building projects of nearby Sepphoris, a large and important city that long served as Herod Antipas's capital. The Nazareth of today is alongside the site of the ancient town and is under Israeli control. It is a prosperous town because of the hordes of tourists and pilgrims who visit there, although its tourist business has been severely hurt by the recent Israeli-Palestinian conflicts.

# Nineveh

Nineveh in its day of glory was the oldest and greatest city in Mesopotamia (modern-day Turkey, Iraq, and Syria), and was the capital of Assyria until the city's fall in 612 BCE. Thereafter it became a universal symbol of the collapse of oppressive might. Nineveh was located on the east bank of the Tigris River, across from the site of the modern city of Mosul in Iraq. It is about twelve hundred miles northeast of Jerusalem, and about six hundred miles north-northwest of Babylon. The city was on two great mounds separated by a small river, the lesser of the two being called Tell Nebi Yunus, "The Mound of the Prophet Jonah." The ruins of the city cover about eighteen hundred acres and are surrounded by a wall nearly eight miles long. Nineveh was therefore an immense city by ancient standards, and it is not surprising that by the time stories of it had spread to Israel the city's size had become grossly exaggerated. The stories said that it took three days to walk across the city (Jonah 3:3), which would indicate a perimeter of thirty to fifty miles. The name apparently comes from the Assyrian word *nina* or *ninuwa,* and the cuneiform symbol for it consists of a fish in an enclosure. Nina was the river goddess. This is interesting in consideration that Jonah was swallowed by "a great fish" (Jonah 1:17).

The first settlement of the site was no later than 5000 BCE. A stone axeblade indicates that there was trade with Armenian settlements from the beginning of the first village. Archaeological digs have unearthed countless valuable relics from the site, but by far the most remarkable is a realistic life-sized bronze head of a bearded monarch. It is considered the finest example of metal sculpture ever found in Mesopotamia and is believed to represent Sargon I of Agade, about 2350 BCE. He was the first to unite all the warring city-states in Mesopotamia, laying the foundations for the Assyrian Empire.

After Sargon united the region, little of importance seems to have happened at Nineveh for several centuries. The prologue of the Code of Hammurabi (early eighteenth century BCE) mentions a magnificent temple of Ishtar there, but tells nothing else of the city. (Ishtar was the Mesopotamian goddess of fertility, and the chief deity of the region.) The Assyrian monarchs apparently did little building at Nineveh. During the second millennium BCE Assyria was of little importance, being over-shadowed by the great empires of the Hittites, Kassites, and Mitannians. Nevertheless Nineveh seems to have gained some fame, since a Ninevite statue of Ishtar was sent by the Mitannians as a gift to the pharaoh of Egypt in order to effect his healing from some disease.

By the end of the second millennium, Assyrian kings Shalmaneser I and Tiglath-Pileser I had both done some building in Nineveh, and in the ninth century BCE Shalmaneser III erected an obelisk, now in the British Museum, showing Jehu, the king of Israel, kissing his feet.

The Assyrians defeated Israel, the northern Jewish kingdom, in 722 BCE. They destroyed the kingdom, devastated the capital city of Samaria, and carried off most of the leaders into exile. While this event was critical in the history of the Jews, from the Assyrian point of view it was just an-other of many conquests, and had little significant effect on the empire. A century later, after the fall of Assyria, the southern Jewish kingdom, Judah, would suffer the same fate at the hands of the Neo-Babylonians under Nebuchadrezzar II.

Significant expansion did not take place until the beginning of the seventh century, when Sennacherib made Nineveh the capital of the rap-idly expanding Assyrian Empire. He rebuilt it into a magnificent city, building streets and public edifices, and his magnificent "Palace Without a Rival." After Assyria gained control over Egypt in the seventh century BCE, Nineveh was the most powerful city in the world. It covered about eighteen hundred acres, with eighteen great gates in its defensive walls. There were eighteen canals bringing water to the city from the outlying hills,[1] and the system of aqueducts exceeded that of Jerwan, also built by Sennacherib, which until then had been the finest in the world. Sen-nacherib was murdered in Nineveh in 681 BCE, but his son Esarhaddon kept the capital there. He continued building, including a massive arse-nal adorned with a statue of Pharaoh Tarku in honor of the defeat of Egypt.

Nineveh's glory was short-lived. In 612 it fell to the combined armies of the Medes (Iranians) and Babylonians, who destroyed most of the city, leaving the rest to crumble and decay. Fortunately, the great library of Ashurbanipal did not perish and was rebuilt twenty-five years later. Some

1. That there were eighteen hundred acres and eighteen gates is pure coincidence, as the acre is a much later unit of measure. There may be a connection between there being eigh-teen gates and eighteen canals, however.

twenty thousand tablets and fragments have survived, providing extensive knowledge of the history, customs, and legendry of Mesopotamia.

Nineveh never again rose to importance. There is some evidence of Greek and Seleucid (Syrian) activity, but it appears to have been insignificant. The city continued, however, and seems to have enjoyed moderate prosperity under Muslim rule in the thirteenth century CE. There were houses there as late as the sixteenth century, but after that it appears that for some unknown reason the city was totally abandoned, with all activity having moved across the river to Mosul.

With any consideration of Nineveh, the question of the prophet Jonah cannot be ignored or easily explained. There are some who maintain that the book of Jonah must be a historical document, else the very resurrection of Jesus comes into question. (Jonah's three days and nights in the belly of the fish have long been considered an allegory for Jesus' time in the tomb.) This seems a bit extreme, and most scholars regard the story as a parable. Among other things, there are too many inconsistencies for most scholars to take the story literally.

Jesus referred to Jonah and to the Ninevites' repentance after hearing Jonah preach to them, as well as implying the connection between the great fish[2] and the tomb (Matt. 12:38-42). Jesus loved parables, however, and there is no reason to believe that he took the story literally. He simply implied that God would be more pleased by pagan Ninevites who repented than by Jewish hypocrites who would not see their own need for repentance. There was a prophet Jonah bar-Amittai recorded in 2 Kings 14:25 who lived in 785 BCE and prophesied the expansion of Israel under King Jeroboam II. Although the name is the same, there is every reason to believe that the writer of the Jonah parable simply picked up that name to lend a note of historicity to his tale. It was undoubtedly written after the exile, probably between 400 and 200 BCE. If the Jonah story is history, then we have to deal with a number of problems: a cowardly, petulant, and disobedient prophet, whom God forces into service, and who is angry with God for being merciful; a fish large enough to swallow a man, yet mild enough that three days in its belly do not harm him; and a Nineveh that was of importance for only a very brief time at the end of the sixth century

---

2. The Bible makes no reference to a whale in the book of Jonah — it is "a great fish." The ancient Hebrews did not consider whales to be fish — they thought they were sea monsters, and called them *leviathan*. If the writer of the book of Jonah had meant a whale, he would have called it a leviathan.

BCE, and otherwise merited little notice on the international scene. If, on the other hand, the story is a parable, then we have a commanding allegory of God's forgiveness, the power of repentance, and man's resistance to serving him.

Nineveh basked in spectacular splendor for less than seventy-five years, yet long after its glory had crumbled it was remembered not only for its majesty but also for its fragility. It serves as a humbling reminder that despite any worldly majesty, "dust thou art, and unto dust shalt thou return."

# Nob

The exact location of Nob is not known, although biblical references indicate that it was probably just north of Jerusalem. After the destruction of Shiloh by the Philistines in the early eleventh century BCE, the priestly center was moved to Nob, and this became the primary religious center of the Israelites, at least until late in Saul's reign.

The most famous event at Nob took place during Saul's last days as king. When David was fleeing from Saul he visited Nob, where the priest Ahimelech sheltered and fed him. When Saul found out about this, he raided the shrine and massacred Ahimelech, all eighty-five priests there, and the entire population of the town including the women, children, and animals (1 Sam. 22:9-23). Only Abiathar, son of Ahimelech, escaped.

The only other references to Nob are a prophecy of Isaiah (10:32) that the Assyrians would reach there when they conquered the northern kingdom, and a mention in Nehemiah (11:32) that it was reinhabited after the return from the exile. Other than this, nothing is known of the place.

# Palestine

Palestine, also known as "the Holy Land" to Christians and Jews,[1] is a region whose boundaries have never been clearly defined.[2] It is generally considered to be the land in the Fertile Crescent bounded by Phoenicia and the Lebanese mountains in the north and Egypt and the Sinai Peninsula in the south, and ranging from the Mediterranean in the west to the Arabian desert in the east and southeast. In the Bible and in contemporary writings the land is often also called Canaan, from the original inhabitants, the Canaanites, and Israel because it was known as the land of the Jews. In the twelfth century BCE it was invaded by a highly civilized Hellenistic people from Crete and the Aegean, the Philistines.[3] The name "Palestine" is simply a corruption of "Philistine."[4] They settled in the region they called Philistia, known today as the West Bank, and controlled much of Palestine until the beginning of the tenth century BCE. The name "Palestine" ap-

1. Much of the region, particularly Jerusalem, is also sacred to Muslims, although the holiest of places to them are in Arabia (Mecca and Medina). The term "Holy Land" first appeared in the Middle Ages in the writings of the crusaders, so most Muslims find it offensive.

2. Modern Palestine should not be confused with ancient Palestine, even though they lie in essentially the same geographical location. In ancient times the term "Palestine" referred to a loosely defined region, much as we today use the terms "Middle East" or "Orient." In modern times many desire to hammer out specific borders and establish Palestine as a defined political entity, distinct from Israel and the surrounding nations. The name is sensitive to many, because it is a reminder of Hadrian's attempt, after the second Jewish revolt, to remove from the land any indication that it was a land of Jews by renaming the former *Provincia Judaea* as *Provincia Syria Palaestina*. The modern people who call themselves Palestinians are mainly of Arabic origin.

3. It is ironic that the term "Philistine" is used today to describe a boorish barbarian. In fact, the Philistines were highly civilized. Despite the fact that their religion and culture also had a strong streak of cruelty, they demonstrated a genuine appreciation of the arts. Unfortunately for their reputation, however, they lost, and history is written by the winners.

4. In ancient times the entire region we now call the Middle East was called by the generic name "Syria." In the fifth century BCE the Greek historian Herodotus referred to Philistia as *Palaistine Suria* (Philistine Syria), and later writers used the term to refer to all of what we now call Palestine. In 135 CE the emperor Hadrian changed the name of the region to *Provincia Syria Palaestina*, "the Province of Philistine Syria," and thereafter it was usually called simply *Palaestina*. By the time this worked its way into English it had become "Palestine."

pears nowhere in the Bible except in the King James translation of Joel 3:4; here the Hebrew reads *Pelesheth,* which is translated in many versions of the Bible as "Philistia." There are only a few references to Philistia in the Scriptures, but a huge number to the Philistines.

The early settlements in Palestine played a key role in the Old Testament stories. The Bible records 622 place names west of the Jordan River, many of which are mentioned only once, and many of which are now unidentifiable. Archaeological research has only begun to reveal what we hope will eventually be known about the region, but it appears that the earliest human habitation was in the Jordan Valley. The oldest city in the valley, and possibly the oldest in the world, was Jericho, settled about 8000 BCE. There were few settlements in the central mountains until the thirteenth century BCE, probably because of the thick forestation there. The Israelites were among the first to settle there in any numbers, although the Canaanite cities of Bethel and Jerusalem (then called Zion) were already established by that time, and Hebron was originally settled by the Hittites shortly before the Israelite conquests. The southern coastal plain was ideal for habitation, and was populated very early, but the northern coastal regions were densely forested and made settlement difficult. As settlements spread throughout Palestine, their locations were usually determined by water supply, defensibility, availability of pastures and agriculture, and proximity to trade routes.

Palestine has been the homeland of a huge number of peoples and tribes, mostly Semitic. The most important of these were (chronologically) the Canaanites, Amorites, Hittites, Jebusites, Horites, Philistines, and Israelites. While Egyptians, Assyrians, Babylonians, Greeks, Romans, and European crusaders at different times ruled the land and influenced the culture, their numbers were not such that they made a significant impact on the racial or ethnic mixture of the inhabitants. After the destruction of the Jewish nation and the massacre of the Jews by the Romans in 132 CE, vast numbers of Jewish survivors left Palestine and eventually migrated into Europe and Spain. Peoples from all over the Middle East slowly moved in to fill the void. With the Arab Muslim invasions in the seventh century CE, the majority of the population was soon Arab, and as they intermarried with other Semitic peoples from Mesopotamia and Syria, the predominant religion became Islam. Their descendants are the people who today identify themselves as Palestinians.

For a more detailed survey of the region, see "A Brief History of the Holy Land" on pages 1-11.

# Patmos

Patmos is a small island off the Dodecanese in the Aegean Sea, southwest of Asia Minor. It has little historic or political significance, but it is of great importance in Christian tradition. It was to Patmos that the aged apostle John ("the Divine") was exiled from Ephesus in about 95 CE. It was there that he had his apocalyptic vision, after which he wrote the book of Revelation while living in a cave in the mountainside of the island (Rev. 1:9). The rugged volcanic terrain of the island was unquestionably an influence on the imagery in the apocalyptic portions of Revelation.

Patmos is a volcanic island (the volcano is extinct) about six by ten miles in size, with a rugged coastline about thirty-seven miles long. The highest point (now called *Hagios Elias,* Mount Saint Elias) is a volcanic cone about 1050 feet in elevation, with caves in its sides. It was in one of those caves that John lived. In John's day the island was covered with a huge palm grove, earning it the alternative name of Palmosa. Today all that is left of the grove is a small clump in the valley now known as "the Saint's Garden."

The modern town of Patmos is nestled at the base of the mountain, looking up to the battlements of Saint John's Monastery, which was built in 1088 during the Crusades by Saint Christobulus.

# Peniel

The city of Peniel (or Penuel), whose name means "Face of God," was built in the late tenth century BCE by Jeroboam, the first king of the northern kingdom of Israel. After his successful revolt against Solomon's successor Rehoboam, he became the king of the ten northern tribes and established his capital at Shechem. Soon thereafter he built Peniel to the west of Shechem as a fortification against invasion from the coastal highways. The site of Peniel was a sacred place to the Jews, although it is unlikely that Jeroboam selected it for that reason — he was hardly noted for his piety. The exact site of the city is unknown, although some scholars believe that its ruins lie at a mound about four miles east of Succoth called Tulul ed-Dahab. Tradition says that Jeroboam later moved his capital to Peniel, but there is no biblical or archaeological information to confirm this.

Peniel's importance to the Jews springs from its role in the story of Jacob. Several years after having cheated his brother Esau out of his birthright and Isaac's blessing, Jacob returned to Canaan. He finally screwed up his courage and crossed the Jabbok River to meet his brother. He expected Esau's rage, but was willing to face it to try to effect a reconciliation. That night he wrestled until dawn with "a man" who is typically identified as an angel or God. This is symbolic of Jacob's wrestling with his own conscience, and at daybreak God told him, "Your name will no longer be Jacob, but Israel, because you have struggled with God and with men and have overcome" (Gen. 32:28). Jacob named the place *Peniel*, Hebrew for "The Face of God," because he said he had looked on the face of God and survived. The site was a holy place to the Jews, although there is no record of any major shrine being built there.

Peniel was probably located in a strategic pass in the hills, as is indicated by there being a fortress there that Gideon destroyed when he defeated the Midianites in about the twelfth century BCE (Judg. 8:8-17). There is no further biblical reference to any settlement at Peniel until the tenth century BCE, when Jeroboam built his fortress city on the site, and after telling of the building of it (1 Kings 12:25), the Bible never again refers to the place. Beyond this, nothing is known of Peniel.

# Pergamum

Pergamum has great historic importance, but its religious significance is based primarily on its listing as the location of one of the "seven churches in Asia" in the book of Revelation (1:4, 11); there it is identified as "the place where Satan's throne is" (Rev. 2:13). It was situated on the banks of the Selinus River in the west of what today is Asiatic Turkey. Although little is known of its early settlement, the site was undoubtedly occupied at a very early date. The first literary reference to it is in the annals of Xenophon, a Greek soldier and student of Socrates in the fifth century BCE, who fought in the Greco-Persian wars. He records the capture of Pergamum by the Greeks, and then its immediate recapture by the Persians. In 362 BCE it was severely punished by the Persians for a revolt.

Pergamum did not actually become particularly important until 301 BCE, when Lysimachus, king of Thrace, took the city. He founded a new kingdom and made Pergamum its capital. One of his successors as king was Attalus I (241-197 BCE), and the realm came to be known as the Attalid Kingdom. In 133 BCE Attalus III, in his will, left the entire kingdom to Rome, which formed the Roman province of Asia from it. It became a center of Roman pagan religion, and was the first Asian city to have a temple to the imperial cult (worshiping the Roman emperor as a god). The rampant and often immoral pagan worship in the city, which negatively influenced much of the Christian practice there, is undoubtedly what caused John to list it as the seat of Satan. Pergamum survived through the time of the eastern Roman Empire, and eventually fell into Muslim hands. Today the small Turkish town of Bergama is located at the base of the hill on which Pergamum once stood.

As an interesting side note, it could be mentioned that the great Greek physician Galen was a native of the city, and that Pergamum was the place where parchment was invented. The word "parchment" is a corruption of the Latin name for the material, *pergamentum.*

# Petra

Petra was the capital city of Nabatea, an Arab nation east of Judea. The Nabateans were originally from the northwest portion of Arabia, but after a series of migrations they settled in the region that is now part of Jordan. Petra was built sometime in the sixth century BCE when the nomadic Nabateans finally settled down to build a permanent home. In time they built a vast commercial empire that extended from Arabia to Syria. Because of the defensibility of the terrain, the Nabateans survived attempts of the Seleucid Antigonus, the Roman Pompey, and Herod the Great to control them. While their commercial ventures gave them great economic power, the Nabateans were not otherwise a particularly valuable conquest, so these foreign powers never levied their utmost strength to conquer them. They may have had the same value in ancient times that Switzerland has in modern Europe — being more useful as a neutral economic force than as a territorial conquest.

In 100 CE Nabatea did finally come under Roman control. Petra retained its economic value, however, until the decay of the Roman Empire, although it declined slowly but continuously after Rome lost its influence and Constantinople became the focus of the empire. The crusaders built a fort in Petra in the twelfth century, but soon thereafter lost it to the Arabs. It was inhabited by local people thereafter.

Neither Nabatea nor Petra is mentioned in the Bible, although when Saint Paul was in Damascus he was ordered to be arrested at the behest of King Aretas (2 Cor. 11:32). This would have been Aretas IV of Nabatea. Paul escaped by being lowered in a basket outside the city wall. In Galatians 1:17 he speaks of going into Arabia, and this surely would not have been the Arabian Peninsula, but Nabatea.

Petra may have played an important part in the story of the birth of Jesus. This is only conjecture, but the circumstantial evidence is very compelling. There can be no doubt that the "wise men from the east" were magi, Zoroastrian priest-astrologers from Persia. Their astrological divinations led them to believe that a great king was born in Herod's household, so they came to Jerusalem to honor him and present him with gifts. Frankincense and myrrh were very precious, but extremely hard to get outside of the southern portion of the Arabian Peninsula, where they were grown and refined. It is highly unlikely that they would have been readily available in either Persia or Palestine. This means that the magi would have had to detour to southern Arabia to get them, which would have added months to their trip. This posed a great problem to biblical scholars until the late 1930s, when the Nabatean inscriptions were finally deciphered, revealing a trove of knowledge about their culture. Because of the Nabateans' Arabian origins and the Nabatean commercial structure, Petra was a major market for Arabian goods, including frankincense and myrrh. The city was directly on the travel route the magi would have taken from Persia to Jerusalem, so they could have easily purchased their gifts in Petra.

# Philadelphia

Philadelphia was a city in the west of what is now the Asian part of Turkey. Its origins are not known with certainty, but it is believed to have been founded in the second century BCE by Eumenes, the king of Pergamum, in honor of his brother Attalus II. Attalus had been noted for his fidelity to Eumenes, and had earned the epithet *Philadelphos,* Greek for "Brotherly Love" or "Loving Brother." As Rome expanded its empire into Asia, Philadelphia fell under Roman control only a few years after its founding. The city was located in a valley leading to the sea, in which Sardis and Smyrna were also situated. It also abutted a large and extremely fertile plateau that contributed generously to the prosperity of the city. Unfortunately, the region around Philadelphia was subject to violent earthquakes, one of which destroyed it in 17 CE. A series of tremors during the following few weeks caused most of its populace to move out into the nearby country, but a grant from the Roman emperor Tiberius enabled them to rebuild the city, and they renamed it Neocaesarea. As the memory of the quake faded the people returned, and the city again became prosperous. When Flavius Vespasian became emperor in 69 CE, the town voluntarily renamed itself Flavia. Its particular claim to fame was its extraordinary number of temples and religious festivals. The city thrived through the Byzantine and Ottoman Empires, and survives today as the Turkish city of Alasehir.

To Christians, Philidalphia is noted because it was the location of one of the "seven churches in Asia" (Rev. 1:4, 11). Apparently the Christians in Philadelphia, as in Smyrna, underwent persecution, particularly from the Jews. Philadelphia and Smyrna are the only two of the seven churches that were not chastised in Revelation 2 and 3, but were praised for their faithfulness and encouraged to keep strong during the persecutions.

# Philippi

The city of Philippi lay on a plain in eastern Macedonia, at the foot of a spur of the Orbelos massif, a huge rock outcrop. Running through the city and across the plain was the main overland trade route from Asia to the West, known by the Romans as the *Via Egnatia.* This route passes by Thessalonica (the home of the Thessalonians). The plain was about ten miles inland from the port of Neapolis on the Aegean Sea and was enclosed by mountains.

The region was probably originally inhabited by Thracians. It was called Datos, and there was a village named Krenides, probably with reference to the springs (Greek *krenai*) in the vicinity. The first major settlement there was in the fourth century BCE. The Greek orator Callistratus was forced to flee Athens in 361 BCE, and it is believed that he brought with him a group of people from the offshore island of Thasos, and with them established a city. Gold mines were discovered in the vicinity, so it quickly rose to a position of importance. It also, however, fell into danger when its value was discovered. A threat from the Thracians caused the city to appeal for help to Philip II, the king of Macedonia (and father of Alexander the Great). He secured the city, sent a large number of new inhabitants, enlarged its facilities, erected a theater, and built a defensive city wall. He renamed it Philippi after himself, and established a military base there to defend the gold mines. Alexander passed by there when he marched against Thrace. Tradition has it that he stopped in Philippi to feed his horse Bucephalus.

Little of importance happened for the next three centuries. The city thrived under Macedonian protection, although other than being near some moderately productive gold mines, it was of little importance. In 42 BCE it was suddenly thrust into the pages of history. After Julius Caesar was assassinated in 44 BCE, his grand-nephew and adopted son Octavian, and his closest friend Marc Antony, pursued the conspirators Brutus and Cassius onto the plains in Macedonia. At the Battle of Philippi in 42 BCE they defeated the assassins' armies, thus gaining more power in Rome than even Caesar had enjoyed.

After the battle, Antony assigned a garrison of Roman soldiers to

Philippi, and his legate Quintus Paquius Rufus established the region including Philippi as a Roman colony. He named it *Colonia Victrix Philippensium* ("Victorious Philippine Colony"), but the city continued to be called Philippi. After Marc Antony's defeat and death in 30 BCE,[1] Octavian rounded up all the families throughout Italy who had sided with Antony. Recognizing that killing them would be a dangerous political move, he exiled them, allowing many to settle in Philippi. He renamed the colony *Colonia Iulia Philippensis* ("Julian[2] Philippine Colony") in honor of Julius Caesar. Three years later the Roman Senate named Octavian emperor and gave him the title *Augustus* ("Majestic One"), and he once again renamed the colony, this time as *Colonia Augusta Iulia Philippensis.*

Philippi remained an unimportant town in Roman eyes, but it gained immortality among Christians when in the first century CE Saint Paul was called in a dream to preach in Macedonia. He visited Philippi at least twice and established a Christian church there.

Roman colonies were usually surrounded by a protective space in which no building was allowed, and in which no "strange cults" were permitted. The Philippians may have regarded Jews as a "strange cult," thus requiring them to meet outside the city. This may be why Paul had to go "outside the gate to the riverside" to the "place of prayer" (Acts 16:13) to preach to the Jewish women. It was there that he made his first Gentile convert in Europe, the lady Lydia, who was a "seller of purple cloth."[3] An

1. Octavian and Antony, along with an ally Lepidus, formed the Second Triumvirate, sharing power equally. In 36 BCE Lepidus vainly attempted to usurp Octavian's power and was forced to retire to private life. Octavian incited the Romans against Antony, using Antony's affair with Cleopatra as leverage against him. In 30 BCE he defeated Antony in the Battle of Actium, and having gained full power, went on to become the first emperor of Rome, calling himself Augustus.

2. After Caesar's death the adjective "Julian" in Roman writing almost always referred exclusively to him or to his family, the Julii. The Julii were one of the most exalted patrician families in Rome, claiming direct descent from Aeneas, the legendary Trojan War hero and founder of Roman culture, who was believed to be the son of Venus.

3. The purple referred to was probably "Turkey red," a relatively inexpensive and very popular substitute for Tyrian purple. It was extracted from the madder root and was manufactured in Thyatira. Since Lydia was a Thyatiran (Acts 16:13), it is likely that she was a representative of a Thyatiran turkey red merchant. Tyrian purple is a very rare and expensive dye imported from Tyre. It is extracted from a mollusk that grows only off the Tyrian coast. Its color is a rich magenta, not to be confused with the deep purple (from grapes and berries) that symbolized penitence or mourning. Because Tyrian purple was so valuable it eventually became illegal for anyone but royalty to wear it. Today it is the color traditionally worn by bishops.

inscription in the city indicates that commerce in purple was one of the city's industries. Although a Gentile, Lydia worshiped as a Jew.[4]

During the reign of Marcus Aurelius (161-180) the city was renovated and expanded. He rebuilt the forum and theater and erected baths and several new buildings. In subsequent years the baths were expanded and adorned with beautiful mosaics. Two Christian basilicas were built there in the fifth and sixth centuries.

Although the Philippian church survived to modern times, Philippi itself was never important politically or ecclesiastically, and today the city is in ruins. Its only real importance is as an archaeological site which has yielded a great deal of knowledge about Roman colonial life. Ecclesiastically it was no more than a subsidiary of Thessalonica, and by the eighteenth century CE it had no ecclesiastical importance whatsoever except as the site of Saint Paul's efforts. As such, however, it is of great importance, because it was the location of the first Christian community in Europe, and therefore had a special place in Paul's heart as well. After Paul's death the city faded from importance, because by then the main Christian centers had become Antioch, Ephesus, Alexandria, and Rome.

4. Many Gentiles followed Judaism without actually converting to the faith. They were called "God-fearers," and although not Jews, were highly respected by the Jews. Many scholars believe that Saint Luke, a Greek physician, came to Judea as a physician with the Roman army, and became a God-fearer before becoming a Christian.

# Phoenicia

Phoenicia (also called Sidonia) was not really a nation but a federation of independent city-states of which Tyre, Sidon, and Byblos were the most important members. The region today is largely in Lebanon, on the northeast coast of the Mediterranean. The Bible refers to the people as Sidonians, but Homer called them Phoenicians;[1] the latter is now the almost universal term for these people. The primary cities in the Phoenician alliance were Acco ('Akko, known as Acre during the Crusades), Arwad (Rouad), Berytus (Beirut), Byblos, Jubeil, Sidon (Saïda), Simyra (Sarafand), Tripolis (Tripoli), Tyre (Sur), and Zarephath. Over the centuries the controlling power of this alliance passed back and forth between Sidon and Tyre, a city about twenty-five miles south of Sidon. Byblos was never an important part of the political structure of Phoenicia, but it was a major contributor to its economic prosperity.

The Phoenicians were a Semitic people, related to the Canaanites of ancient Palestine, and archaeology indicates that they settled along the northwest coast at about the same time the Canaanites settled further south and inland. Some scholars believe that they were once the same people, and that their cultures and political systems slowly diverged. The Phoenician and Canaanite languages were very similar, and both are quite similar to ancient Hebrew. The first evidence of the Phoenicians' settlement in the region dates to about 2500 BCE. As their culture developed they were strongly influenced by the Akkadian and Sumerian cultures of early Babylonia, although it is unclear whether they were actually under Babylonian control. By the eighteenth century BCE the Egyptian empire, under the control of the Semitic Hyksos invaders, acquired large holdings in the Middle East and invaded and held Phoenicia. Egypt ruled for about three hundred years, but by 1400 BCE the expulsion of the Hyksos and the constant raids of the Hittites weakened the Egyptian hold sufficiently that

---

1. "Phoenician" is the adjectival form of "phoenix," the mythical desert bird that consumed itself by fire every five hundred years, then rose again from its own ashes. It is unclear why Homer used this name for these people, but it was possibly an allusion to their phenomenal rise from ignominy to prosperity after gaining independence from Egypt.

the Phoenician cities began to revolt. By 1100 they had achieved complete independence.

The Phoenicians developed a high level of civilization, and in time came to be known throughout the Mediterranean world as the finest seafarers and the best architects and builders in the world. This reputation was well-earned, and they maintained these skills for centuries. Through most of history, the Phoenicians had an amicable relationship with the Jews. Their religion was polytheistic, their main god being Melkart. The Jews referred to the Phoenician gods as *ba'alim* ("lords"), and in the Bible this term is most often translated as "Baal" and used as if it referred to a single god. When we read of Baal in the Old Testament the reference may be just to Melkart or to the whole pantheon of Phoenician gods.

For more detail on Phoenician culture and history, see the sections on Byblos (p. 56), Sidon (p. 219), and Tyre (p. 239).

# Qumran

In Jesus' time there were four major sects or schools among the Jews, which were the Pharisees, Essenes, Sadducees, and Zealots.[1] The Pharisees and Essenes were formed in the second century BCE, the Sadducees in the first, and the Zealots during Jesus' lifetime. The Pharisees were dedicated to strict observance of the Law, both as it was written and as it was interpreted;[2] the Sadducees were the aristocratic priestly party and acknowledged only the written Torah (Law) to be binding; the Essenes were ascetics who had effectually removed themselves from Jewish society; and the Zealots were a fanatic political movement, dedicated to seeking a military Messiah like Judas Maccabaeus, who would expel the Romans, reunite Israel and Judah, and restore it as an independent world power. It was the Zealots who would eventually revolt twice against the Romans and bring about the total destruction of Israel.

The Essenes were an ascetic brotherhood, in effect a Jewish monastic movement. They were founded in the second century BCE and disappeared by the time of the destruction of Israel in 132 CE. They withdrew from the mainstream of Jewish life and lived in isolated communities in the desert, mainly around the shores of the Dead Sea. Because they were totally apart from the rest of the Jews, they are not mentioned in the Bible. They had little or no effect on Jewish culture, politics, or religious life. There are many contemporary documents that tell of their way of life, however, including writings of the Alexandrian Jewish scholar Philo Judaeus, the Roman historian Pliny the Elder, the Jewish historian Flavius Josephus, and the writings of the Essenes themselves. There were several Essene communities, al-

---

1. The Scribes against whom Jesus so often spoke were actually lawyers and interpreters of Scripture from both the Pharisee and Sadducee schools.

2. We tend to think of the Pharisees as hypocrites, because Jesus railed so vehemently against them. They were, in fact, along with the monastic Essenes, the most righteous of all the Jews, truly dedicated to living by God's Law. Unfortunately, they had missed the point — they were so intent on obeying the letter of the Law that they had completely forgotten about its spirit and true meaning. The reason Jesus was so hard on them is that they did want to be righteous but were on the wrong path. He saw in them the greatest hope for Judaism if he could only wake them up.

though the best known is the one located at Khirbet Qumran on the banks of the Wadi Qumran on the northwest coast of the Dead Sea. It was their preserved library that was discovered in 1947 and came to be known as the Dead Sea Scrolls.

The Essenes focused on strict observance of Torah (the Jewish Law) and the Sabbath, scholarship, and prayer. They were scrupulously clean, bathing daily in cold water and wearing only white clothing. Because of their religious requirements the Jews were a clean people, but the Essenes went well beyond the basic standards. They would not take oaths other than the oath of membership, and they did not engage in trade or commerce other than to sell their agricultural surplus and pottery, which contemporary writings report was exquisite. They were totally nonviolent, refusing even to touch weapons. They were opposed to slavery and would often buy slaves in order to free them. They did not practice animal sacrifice, and were strict in observing the law that required that animals for meat be killed as quickly and mercifully as possible. They did not, of course, eat anything that was ritually unclean according to the Law. They recruited from Jews who had decided to renounce material possessions, and from orphans and unwanted children given to them to raise (but if at adulthood the children chose to leave the community, they were free to do so). Membership required a three-year novitiate, during which any novice was free to leave the community at will. After three years the novice took a lifetime oath of obedience and secrecy, and violation of the oath could be punished by expulsion. To a dedicated Essene, expulsion was tantamount to a sentence of death, because he had also committed himself to separation from the rest of society, and this meant that he was left to wander in the desert to die of starvation or thirst. In most respects, the Essene communities were very like the early Christian monastic communities before the time that they became wealthy and corrupt.

Khirbet Qumran appears to have been first settled sometime during the Maccabaean period, but by whom is unknown. The settlers built a round cistern, which seems to have been abandoned and left untended for many years. The first Essenes moved in around 120 BCE, cleaned out the old round cistern, and built two new rectangular ones. Their water supply was from an aqueduct that brought water from generous springs in the northwestern hills. They also constructed a few small buildings and a potter's kiln. By 40 BCE the site had expanded considerably, apparently to accommodate a large increase in the number of brothers. A burial ground has been found between the community and the Dead Sea. Only a very small portion has been excavated, and already over one thousand bodies have been found, buried with their heads to the south. The site seems to have been abandoned in 40 BCE, probably because of an invasion by the Parthians, a Mesopotamian people who were rivals of Rome. The monks may have found refuge in another of the Essene communities elsewhere around the Dead Sea. The buildings remained unoccupied and were seriously damaged in 31 BCE by an earthquake. About 4 BCE either the community returned or a new one took up residence at the site. The buildings were repaired and strengthened, and new flour mills, storage bins, and a smelting furnace were added.

The archaeological record indicates that about 68 CE the community came to a violent end, and the site was thereafter occupied by a Roman garrison. The date is not consistent with the Romans' retribution for the revolt of 70 CE or the revolt of 132 CE. The first revolt did begin in Jerusalem in 67 CE, but the Romans surely would have known that the Essenes were not involved. It is possible that the Romans simply decided that the site would be a good spot to place a garrison, and destroyed the community in order to do so. They were not wont to negotiate for property that they wanted and could easily just take by force. The Essenes, being nonviolent, would have offered no resistance, which would have made it an easy conquest.

Khirbet Qumran was thrust into world news in 1947. A local Bedouin shepherd boy, looking for a lost sheep, stumbled across a small cave opening in the Wadi Qumran, a dry riverbed that runs past the site of the monastery. As boys will do, he threw a rock into it, and when he heard the sound of breaking pottery he climbed down into it. In the cave he found a number of pottery jars containing ancient leather scrolls. He brought one back to his camp, and after a few weeks it fell into the hands of a Bethlehem cobbler named Kando, who dealt in antiquities on the side. Because of Kando's efforts the scrolls eventually came into the possession of Professor Sukenik of the Hebrew University and Archbishop Samuel of Saint Mark's Monastery. Both men immediately recognized the importance of the find, and the world was soon made aware of what came to be called the Dead Sea Scrolls. After the Six Days' War in 1967, all the scrolls were moved for safety to the Shrine of the Book at the Israel Museum in Jerusalem. There scholars from all over the world are working to preserve and translate them. They are in effect the entire library of the Qumran Essene community. The scrolls revealed a great deal about life in the communities and theological thought of the times, and they contained fragments of several

In the caves of Qumran in 1947, a shepherd boy discovered what turned out to be the preserved library of a monastic Essene community that had lived near the Dead Sea from the second century BCE to the third century CE.

Photo credit: Erich Lessing/Art Resource, NY

of the Hebrew Scriptures, as well as commentaries on others. It is unknown why they were placed in jars and hidden, although the most likely explanation is that the community realized that the Roman destruction was looming and hid their library for safety. Although no others have been found, it is hoped that other Essene communities might have done the same as the destruction of Israel approached.

# Rome

## I. The Republican Era

Rome, the "Eternal City," began as a crude and tiny village that was destined to become the seat of one of the most powerful empires the world has ever known. The city had little effect on Jewish history until 63 BCE, when Pompey the Great swept east and captured Palestine. Consequently, there are no references to Rome in the Old Testament, and all but three in the New Testament are in the book of Acts, the first history of the Christian church.[1] Notwithstanding, the influence of Rome on the life and culture of New Testament Palestine, as on the future development of Western civilization, was greater than that of any other city in the world, even including Jerusalem. It is therefore impossible to gain a clear understanding of Western culture, including Christianity, without an understanding of the history of Rome and the events that shaped its culture. It would be rather like trying to understand colonial America with no knowledge of Britain.

The *Campagna di Roma* ("Roman Country") is a large area of lowlands in central Italy, and it was the last region on the Italian peninsula to be settled. The Tiber River runs through it, and during high-water periods some areas flood, producing mosquito-bearing marshes. Despite this, it was a popular residential area in classical times.

In the late Stone and Bronze Ages there were a few settlements along the coast and on the shores of the Tiber, but none penetrated the lush inland forests until about 1000 BCE.[2] At that time movements of several dif-

---

1. The three references are in Romans 1:7 and 1:15, which address the Christians who are in Rome, and 2 Timothy 1:17, in which Paul states that Onesiphorus searched for him while he was in Rome. Some translations render *oikoumene* ("the whole world") in Luke 2:1 as "the Roman world" and *praitorion* ("praetorium") in John 18:28 as "the palace of the Roman governor." These, however, are liberal interpretations rather than accurate translations. The word "Roman" *(Hromaios)* occurs only in the book of Acts in reference to Roman citizenship.

2. This is about the same time that King David was unifying the Jewish tribes into the United Monarchy of Israel. A few years later, when Solomon's Israel was one of the wealthi-

ferent peoples resulted in settlements that eventually became two historic peoples: Etruria (Clusium, now Tuscany) was on the north of the Tiber, and Latium on the south. The people of Etruria developed the Etruscan civilization, one of the great cultures of early European history. The inhabitants of Latium, a simple and uncultured people, were completely different, even in language. They lived in crude huts, burned their dead rather than burying them (which was the usual custom), and spoke a rare Indo-European language, Latin. By the eighth century BCE (the Iron Age) they had been thoroughly mixed with immigrant shepherd peoples from the Alban hills (Alba Longa). The Albans adopted the Latin language, but they infused a higher level of civilization into the Latians. They improved their villages and developed a simple governmental system. One of the villages, Rome, eventually evolved into a small city. The Romans considered the Alba Longans to be their ancestors, but scholars long rejected this as a myth. Recent archaeology, however, has shown that it is probably true.

There is, on the other hand, no historical evidence to support the legends of the founding of Roman culture and the city itself; the stories of Romulus, Remus, and Aeneas may well have germinated in the feats of real men, but they stretch so far back into the mists of history that it is impossible to separate truth from myth. Nevertheless, one cannot consider Rome without noting them. The story of Aeneas was immortalized in the *Aeneid*, the Latin epic of the great Roman poet Virgil. According to legend, Aeneas was the son of the goddess Venus and a Trojan prince. He fought bravely in the Trojan War, and Virgil writes that after the sack of the city he escaped with his father on his back and his household gods in hand; Aeneas thus was seen as exemplifying the Roman virtue of *pietas*, a sense of duty and devotion to one's parents, the gods, and the fatherland. Eventually he and his army of brave heroes were cast up on the shores of Latium, where he married a Latin princess. He became the king of Latium, and thus became the ancestor of the Romans by uniting the Trojan and Latin peoples.

The legend of Romulus and Remus tells of the founding several centuries later of the city of Rome itself, and of the creation of the Romans, who considered themselves apart from all other Italians. According to the legend, Rhea Silvia, a royal descendant of Aeneas, was the daughter of Numitor, king of Alba Longa. Amulius, the brother of King Numitor, overthrew his sibling, and forced Rhea Silvia to become a Vestal Virgin (in ef-

---

est and most powerful nations in the known world, Rome was nothing more than an insignificant Italian agrarian community.

fect a nun)[3] so that she could not have any children who could overthrow him. Amulius's plan was foiled when Rhea Silvia was raped by the war god Mars and bore him twin sons, Romulus and Remus. The new king ordered that she be killed and the babies abandoned to drown in the flooding Tiber, but they were rescued by a she-wolf, who suckled them and nursed them back to health.[4] They were then found by a shepherd and raised by his wife.

As adults, Romulus and Remus restored their father to the throne and then returned to the place where they had been rescued from the Tiber, determining to build a city there. They decided on a point at the top of the hill that eventually would be known as the Palatine. While quarreling over the city's location and fortification, Remus jumped over Romulus's wall to show how inadequate it was, and Romulus killed him. Romulus thus became the sole ruler of Rome, naming the city after himself. He next sought to expand the population (which was then only a few local tribesmen). Next to the Palatine Hill is the Quirinal Hill, on which the tribe of the Sabines lived. Between them is a depression, somewhat like a camel's hump (this depression would eventually be the location of the Roman Forum). Romulus declared the depression an asylum — any criminal could move there and be able to start his life all over again, no questions asked. So many men came, however, that there were not enough women for them. To solve the problem Romulus planned a great feast and invited the Sabines. During the festivities Romulus's men killed the Sabine men and abducted the women and forced them into marriage. This was the foundation of the Roman people. It was also the inspiration for Girolamo del Pacchia's *The Rape of the Sabines,* as well as a number of other famous Renaissance paintings on the subject.

Romulus was of course made king, and reigned for some time. One day he went on a trip up the Tiber and never returned. The Romans were convinced that he had been taken by the gods to live with them. The fact

3. Vestals were women who were cloistered in the temple of Vesta, the goddess of the hearth and the protectress of Roman families. The Vestals served fifteen to thirty years as priestesses of Vesta. They entered the service at puberty and remained chaste throughout their service. If a Vestal violated her chastity, even as the victim of rape, she was buried alive. At the conclusion of their contract of service they were free to marry. Since they came from patrician and often very wealthy families, ex-Vestals were much desired as wives.

4. The wolf remains a symbol for Rome to this day. One of Rome's prized works of art is a great statue of the two infants being suckled by the she-wolf. The crest of the dictator Lucius Cornelius Sulla was the wolf suckling the babies.

that the Romans revered Romulus even more than Aeneas, and honored this story as their founding, says a great deal about the moral basis of Roman society. Honor was more a matter of being the shrewdest and strongest than of being the most ethical as we would use the term. It was only among the later Romans that the story of Aeneas was revered over that of Romulus. Patricians claimed descendancy from Romulus, although the highest families took this back even further, claiming to be descendants of Aeneas himself, and thus direct descendants of Venus. One of these families was the Julii, the family of Caesar.

By the sixth century BCE, Rome and the surrounding villages were prosperous, having established trade relations with several other cities. They developed a friendly relationship with Carthage, a colony that had been founded in north Africa by the Phoenicians three hundred years earlier. (The modern city of Tunis is on the site where Carthage once stood.) Political stress abounded in Rome, however. Much of the history of the period is shrouded in legend, but historians can glean a reasonably accurate account of it. Although Rome was a monarchy, the names of most of its kings suggest that the Etruscan civilization to the north of Rome dominated the city. About 510 BCE, the Romans, angered by the despotism of their ruler (and, according to legend, outraged by the rape of the chaste Lucretia by the king's son), rose up and overthrew their seventh and last king, the tyrant Tarquinius Superbus; he was of Etruscan descent, and the Romans exiled him to Etruria. According to Roman legend, when Tarquinius retreated in defeat, Castor and Pollux, the brothers of Helen of Troy, rode down from the sky to tell the Romans that Tarquinius was deposed and they were free.[5]

Tarquinius had appealed for help to the Etruscan king, Lars (Lord) Porsena, who attacked Rome. Porsena's army was met at the bridge over the Tiber, where Horatius Cocles and a handful of men held them back while the Romans dismantled the bridge.[6] Porsena was unable to cross the Tiber and take the city, and a treaty was drawn up between the Romans and the Etruscans. Many scholars believe that Porsena actually did take the

5. Zeus turned Castor and Pollux into stars, the constellation Gemini. The Romans worshiped them among the gods, and believed them to be the protectors of Roman freedom. Two mild expletives were derived from the names Castor and Pollux: *"Ecastor!"* (used only by women) and *"Edepol!"* (used only by men). They were roughly equivalent to "Gee!"

6. This story is the source of Macaulay's poem "Horatius at the Bridge." According to the legend, after the bridge was dismantled Horatius and his men leapt into the river and made it safely back to the Roman side.

city, and that after he was later driven out, the Romans concocted the bridge story to cover the embarrassment of defeat. The Romans admitted to very few defeats in their accounts of history.

After the expulsion of Tarquinius, Rome instituted a republican form of government in 508 CE, in which a hereditary senatorial body ruled the people. The Senate was obliged to consider, but not obey, the desires of the people. (The word "republic" comes from the Latin *res publica,* "affair of the people.") Hatred of monarchy became deeply ingrained into Roman culture, and the Romans fiercely defended their republican system. The Romans also delineated the city limits by a circle of stones known as the *Pomerium,* and in later years this boundary came to be seen as sacred and protected by the gods. Anything inside the *Pomerium* was Rome, and anything outside it was Italy. They established that no king of any nation would ever be allowed to cross the *Pomerium* and enter Rome, and that proscription lasted almost to the end of the Republic. The Romans had already begun to develop a feeling of superiority that eventually would build a social barrier between them and the rest of Italy.

After the Etruscan attack the Romans developed a superbly disciplined militia to keep watch over and defend their territories. Many of the local Latian tribes, also harassed by the Etruscans, were brought under the aegis of Rome and contributed to the support of the militia. While some tribes joined in happily, the majority were annexed by force. This militia was the origin of the Roman army, which would in time become the most fearsome war machine in the ancient world.

In order to understand the Roman army one needs to understand the Roman class system. Members of the Roman upper class were called *Patricianes,* "Conscript Fathers." They saw themselves as the paternal caretakers of Rome, and considered themselves "conscript" because *noblesse oblige* required them to serve. It was not a difficult service, however, considering the enormous wealth, honor, and privilege that their hereditary position afforded them. Technically, under the patronage system that Rome espoused, there was no Roman army. The militias that were in effect the Roman army were usually paid for by individual patricians, who more than recovered their expenses from the spoils of war. Generals were appointed by the Senate, and oftentimes the head of a campaign was one of the consuls (heads of state, of which there were two each year). It was rare that a military venture was paid for from the common treasury, and that was usually only in an emergency or when the venture would greatly fatten the treasury.

In the early years of the Republic the city prospered and expanded well outside the *Pomerium,* eventually encompassing the seven hills in the *Campagna.* Officially, only the portion inside the *Pomerium* was considered Rome; the rest was land belonging to Rome. The center of the city was the Capitoline, Quirinal, and Palatine hills (although the Capitoline was outside the *Pomerium*). These three hills were the location of the major temples, the forum, and most of the governmental and public buildings. Although the common image of Rome, probably as a result of Hollywood and the tourist industry, is that of a magnificent city rich with marble temples and palaces, the fact is that throughout the republican era it was attractive only in a few small areas. It was for the most part a sprawling, stinking, noisy, squalid, overcrowded slum of adobe and wood buildings. It was not until after Rome burned in 64 CE (allegedly by Nero's command) that a stone city was built, including many beautiful public works, an expanded marble forum, and the famed Colosseum.

Already by the fifth century BCE, Rome was actually going into a decline. Class struggles were tearing the Republic apart, and as a result the Latin League, a confederation of Latin states that had been subordinate to Rome, was able to free itself of Roman domination. In 494 CE, only fifteen years after the founding of the Republic, the plebeians — the common, though not necessarily poor, class of Romans, distinct from the hereditary aristocratic families — rebelled and formed their own tribal assembly. This led to the creation of a new office, that of tribune. Although usually members of the senatorial class, the tribunes represented the plebeians. They soon developed controlling power over magistrates and all governmental officials except senators. From then on the tribunes were an important factor in Roman government, and the rights and interests of the common people were defended. Rome's motto was *Senatus Populusque Romae,* "The Senate and People of Rome."

The heads of state were two consuls — one senior and one junior — who were elected each year. They had the power to negotiate treaties, conduct war, and in general exercise what would be considered royal powers, although they were clearly not kings, and to imply that one was a *rex* (king) would be a supreme insult. After their terms they were known as *Consulares* and were afforded great honor and respect, much as we treat our ex-presidents. At first the consuls could come only from the patrician class, but after a senatorial law (the *Lex Licini*) passed in 367 BCE, at least one consul each year had to be from the plebeian class. In times of dire emergency the Senate could declare a consul to be dictator. Dictatorship gave him absolute power, including the power of life and death, and was intended to last only until the crisis had passed, but never for longer than six months. Generally a consul could not succeed himself in office, and it was even considered somewhat extreme for one ever to run again in later years. Gaius Marius (155?-86 BCE) would become the first to hold successive consulships. He was elected for seven terms, several times in absentia while he was conducting the wars against the Germans. Marius also instituted an important reform in the Roman military. Until the end of the second century BCE, no man could serve in the army unless he owned property. The idea was that a landowner would be more interested in seeing his property protected, and thus would fight harder for a Roman victory. Marius proved that even the "rabble" were loyal enough to Rome to make fine soldiers.

The Roman class structure and the government were closely intertwined. The government consisted, as has been noted, of two classes, patricians (the aristocracy) and plebeians (the bourgeoisie). There was a third class, the *proletarii* (laboring class), who had no representation, although the higher classes recognized their economic importance and looked out for them. In the early days of the Republic it was found that a regular census needed to be taken to keep the tax records up-to-date. Because of the importance of this job and the ease with which corruption could enter into it, the men appointed to take the census were selected from those whose reputations and morality were above reproach — most, in fact, were nothing less than puritanical. They were called censors. In time, because of their recognized morality, they were given the authority to ban books, supervise the general morality, and even appoint senators. Although members of the Senate were still patricians, membership rules were changed so that it was no longer a hereditary institution. It was made up of three hundred life members who were selected by the censors, usually from former magistrates. Despite the changes, most senators still had ancestors who were senators. Those who did not were generally looked down upon and called *homines novi*, "new men," or "upstarts." Even though they were patricians they were treated like social climbers, and had difficulty breaking into the aristocratic levels of society. The tribunes, the representatives of the plebeians, controlled the magistrates, and usually came from the patrician senatorial class even though they represented the plebeians. Tribunes were given the right to veto Senate legislation. The veto could then be overridden by a two-thirds majority of the Senate, which was the inspiration for the American Constitutional provisions for veto and override.

Those who had a consul in their ancestry were called *nobiles,* "nobles." Intermarriage between the classes was common. The *proletarii,* of course, had no say in governmental affairs and often did not even possess citizenship. For the most part, however, the tribunes felt a *noblesse oblige* to watch out for their interests. Citizenship was a privilege of the upper classes and property owners, although it would occasionally be granted by the Senate to others for heroic deeds or great acts of loyalty. One of the great conflicts toward the end of the Republic was a movement to grant Roman citizenship to any Italian property owner (Italy being defined as any part of the peninsula south of the Rubicon River). This finally resulted in a revolt by the Italian tribes and a terribly bloody war.

Rome's governmental system was one of patronage rather than bureaucracy. Leaders developed large numbers of *clientes,* "clients," people responsible and answerable to them. A man obtained clients by giving favors, bartering and juggling positions of power or state, and often by simply purchasing their support. A freed slave was legally bound to be the client of the man who freed him. A man became a senator, governor, or consul by the support of his clients and by buying enough votes. This was the way the Roman system worked, and was not considered corruption.[7] Only the very wealthy could achieve high positions of power. Money alone was not enough, however, as one also had to have the proper bloodlines to be considered for high office. One had to be at least thirty years old to be a senator, and anyone much older than that just entering the Senate was considered a "slow starter" and was of questionable value. The position of a man's seat in the Senate hall depended as much on his bloodlines as on his seniority or importance. The senior consul sat on an ivory throne, the *Sella Curulis* ("Curile Chair"), on the Senate floor.

Land was the basis of all wealth in the Roman world, and as in many early agrarian cultures, slavery was a basic element of Roman society and the economy was based on it. For the most part, slaves were held only by the patricians and the upper plebeian strata. Any citizen could own slaves, however, and many among the lower classes owned one or two. The wealthy sometimes owned many hundreds of slaves.[8] By the first century

---

7. While this sounds incredibly corrupt to those of us who live in a bureaucratic republic, patronage did have one great advantage — in patronage, every official is answerable to his patron for his actions and decisions, whereas in bureaucracy an official can hide in the system if he just follows the rules blindly and makes decisions only "by the book."

8. Slaves were very expensive to purchase and maintain. In modern terms, a slave with an education or with special talents or skills could cost many thousands of dollars. That

BCE there were more slaves in Rome than there were free men. The main source of slaves was conquered territories. The better classes of conquered people would become household slaves, the best educated being used as teachers or stewards. Slaves with exceptional administrative, artistic, or musical talents were highly prized, and were very well treated. Barbarians and lower-class victims were used as laborers in the fields, as mine and quarry workers, and as oarsmen on ships. Oftentimes skilled military prisoners of war were trained as gladiators for the entertainment of the masses. If a gladiator were particularly good, he could earn his freedom and even Roman citizenship.

Ancestry and the family were essential constructs in Roman society, and the patricians claimed to be able to trace their families directly back to Romulus, Aeneas, and even to the gods. The head of the household was the father, whose title was *paterfamilias* ("family father"). The paterfamilias had absolute authority over all family property and over every member of his family, even to the point that (at least until well into the first century CE) he had the right to kill any of his children up to the time they were of marriageable age (about thirteen).[9] He arranged their education, careers, and marriages. He could kill his wife for adultery, and all he had to do was provide sufficient evidence of her crime, either before or after he killed her. Surprisingly, given that family structure and bloodlines were critical to the Romans, either a man or woman could obtain a divorce simply by requesting it. The minor children of a divorced couple always remained with the father unless he voluntarily gave them into the care of their mother.

Marriages were arranged to unite families for either bloodline or financial reasons. Many of the finest families in Rome had relatively little money (Caesar's was one), while many without such pedigrees had amassed enormous wealth in wars or business. Many marriages were arranged so that one side could elevate its bloodlines in exchange for the other side's financial gain.[10] In all patrician and plebeian families, a woman was given a

---

there were many Roman households with several hundred slaves is an indication of the kind of wealth some Romans possessed.

9. Sometime in the late second century BCE a law was passed requiring a paterfamilias to give eight days' notice to a magistrate if he intended to kill his child. This was not to protect the child, but to protect the man from doing something in a fit of anger that he might regret after he had cooled off.

10. Julius Caesar's aunt Julia came from one of the finest bloodlines in Rome (the Julii), but the family had relatively little money. She married the patrician Gaius Marius, who was of an acceptable but unimpressive bloodline but was one of the richest men in Rome. This

dowry — if the family were rich enough, it could be a huge fortune. This did not become the property of her husband, but was held in trust in case she were widowed or divorced. This would provide her enough income to live on until she could marry again, or, in many cases, for the rest of her life. Women could not own property, and if a man died his property went to his sons or to the nearest male relatives. A good dowry trust, however, enabled a woman to live as if she were a property owner.

Adoption was a common practice in Rome, especially among the patricians. Often a rich man who had no sons would pay a poorer patrician family for the right to adopt one of their sons. In this way the boy (or young man) attained a large inheritance with which he could eventually help his own family, and he became part of an important family whose wealth and status could help him gain an otherwise impossible political position. Frequently poorer patrician families would give all but one or two of their sons for adoption. This not only enhanced their wealth but reduced the number of divisions of the estate when the remaining sons inherited it. An adopted son was legally considered a full part of his adoptive family, even to the right to claim the bloodlines and ancestry. If he were already of high lineage he could also claim that ancestry. It was not at all unusual for a man to adopt an adult as his son (as was done in the fictional novel *Ben-Hur*). This was often done in order to replace a dead heir, or simply to honor and enhance the career of the adoptee. Octavian, Julius Caesar's grand-nephew, was an adult when Caesar adopted him posthumously by a codicil in his will.

Ancestral lineage was essential to Roman social status, and the family line to which one belonged was of the utmost importance. One's name was extremely important, as it announced one's status and lineage. Every patrician and plebeian Roman had at least two names, the second (the *nomen*) declaring the ancestral family (the *gens*). The first name *(praenomen)* was given, although most families used no more than four or five.[11] To distin-

---

gave Marius the social credentials to become consul (seven times), and it later gave Caesar the money to be able to start up the political ladder that eventually led to his dictatorship.

11. The *praenomen* was a mark of the authenticity of the family membership. There were very few *praenomina* used — in Gaius Julius Caesar's time there were no more than twenty or so used at all among patricians, and only about ten common ones. The Julii, for example, used only three, Gaius, Sextus, and Lucius. Anyone named Publius Julius would, by his name, have declared that he was not a true Julian. He might be a freedman from a Julian owner, or at best a member of a splinter side branch of the Julians. For any such Julian to have used a true Julian *praenomen* would have been an effrontery that would have cut him totally out of Roman society.

guish one from another, most Romans had at least one descriptive name (*cognomen*) as well, which was placed after the *nomen* and *praenomen*. This name might be traditional in the family, given by associates, or even assigned to oneself. Often these would be passed down for several generations, even if the descriptions no longer applied: There were at least five successive generations of men named Gaius Julius Caesar, the last being the famous general and dictator. "Caesar" means "fine head of hair," but from descriptions of the time that did not seem to be appropriate for Julius Caesar, who was very upset over his semi-baldness. Some *cognomina* were humorous, but were used by famous Romans and were passed on for generations. Some examples are Cicero ("chick-pea"), Flaccus ("big-eared"), Galba ("potbellied"), Porcellus ("piglet"), Silanus ("pug-faced"), and Catullus ("puppydog"). Until the imperial era it was considered rude and forward for anyone but an intimate friend to address any man by his cognomen, and even then never in public. No one, unless he intended to insult, would have addressed Julius Caesar as Caesar in public — Caesar would have been addressed only by both his names, Gaius Julius.[12] Some Romans bore several *cognomina*, some hereditary and some earned or applied. The emperor Nero's full name was Nero Claudius Caesar Drusus Germanicus Lucius Domitius Ahenobarbus!

Around the same time that the Roman sociopolitical structure was stabilized, the Roman religion shifted from local cults worshiping the agrarian nature spirits to the worship of the state-sponsored Olympian gods (primarily Jupiter, Juno, Vesta, and Mars), which were actually rather unimaginative copies of the much older Greek pantheon. Mediterranean society at the time was highly superstitious. Even those who did not believe directly in the gods believed in powerful occult and supernatural forces that controlled mankind. As Roman influence in the world expanded, the Romans were exposed to more and more religions. They were very tolerant of most of these, and often accepted foreign gods into their own worship. Most Romans believed that their family was watched over by a particular god, and many accepted foreign gods such as the Egyptian Isis or the Persian Mithra as their patron. In later years, as the Roman conquest of Europe and the Middle East expanded, Rome only had one religious requirement of the nations it conquered — accept and worship our gods

---

12. Cicero, in his oration at the conspiracy trial of Lucius Sergius Catilina, began, "How long, O Catiline, will you abuse our patience?" This was an intentional sign of contempt for the conspirator. To be polite, he would have asked, "How long, O Lucius Sergius . . . ?"

along with your own, and we will accept and worship yours in a special temple in Rome. The only people who would not accept this were the Jews. The Romans were harsh, but they were not foolish. Seeing how Antiochus Epiphanes's desecration of the temple enraged the Jews and ultimately caused his defeat, they decided to make an exception of their religious policy for the Jews. They agreed that if the Jews would not make trouble, they would be allowed to worship just their own God, and that the image of this Jewish God would not be placed in the Roman temples. The Jews conceded to this, and a tense submission was achieved. The Romans also agreed not to bring their pagan military symbols into Jerusalem, and not to place the Roman eagle, a graven image offensive to the Jews, on the palace.

But we get ahead of ourselves, and must return to where we left off our historical account. The history of Rome from the mid fifth to third centuries BCE is ambiguous, because the writings of the Roman historians of that period conflict on a huge number of events. About 400 BCE the Galli, ferocious barbarian Celtic tribes, were moving down the Italian peninsula.[13] In 390 they conquered and ravaged Etruria, and at the Battle of Allia they wiped out the Roman legions. Without the legions, the city walls were insufficient to keep them out. They came only for booty, however, and after a rampage of vandalism and looting they left. The Romans immediately rebuilt their city and their armies. The Etruscans, recognizing the importance of an alliance with Rome, helped. There is some evidence that Rome also received aid from Carthage.

During the middle of the fourth century BCE the Galli rose up again. Many of the surrounding states, seeing an opportunity to achieve independence, declared war on Rome. Rome sought help from the Samnites, a ferocious people who inhabited a huge region in central Italy. With their help Rome defeated their enemies, subduing not only the rebellious states but also the Galli. There are no surviving records to indicate why, but at some point soon thereafter the Samnites became enemies of Rome; then later they appear as allies again. Many historians believe that it was rather like siblings who fight each other but join together if an outside bully threatens one of them. The Samnites were Italians, but were as proud not to be Roman as the Romans were proud not to be Samnites. The result of all this, however, was a weakening of the states that were hostile to Rome, the dissolution of the Latin League, and Rome's emergence as the dominant power in Italy.

13. These were the same Celts who inhabited central and northern Galatia, Gaul (France), and later Britain.

Another rebellion arose at the end of the fourth century, again led by the Samnites. After several years of conflict, however, Rome again emerged victorious and dominant, and by 290 the Samnites, Etruscans, and Latin states had been reduced to minimal power. They would not rise up against Rome again until the Italian wars in the beginning of the first century BCE. Rome expanded its colonization efforts, and, unlike its neighbors, was extraordinarily efficient and well-organized in military and governmental control.[14]

In 289 a mint was established. This is the first certain evidence of Roman coinage, which consisted of rectangular bronze bars and cast round bronze coins. Silver and gold issues would not come until much later. Rome's treasury contained much gold, but it was in the form of ingots, and was used when necessary to purchase baser metals for coinage.

In 282 the Greek colonies in Italy, who were at war with Rome, sought help from King Pyrrhus of Epirus (a Hellenistic kingdom in northwestern Greece). Rome responded by reaffirming its old friendship with Carthage, using Punic[15] ships to transport soldiers. Pyrrhus defeated the Romans in two great battles, but at a terrible cost to his armies. He brought the battle to Sicily but accomplished little, and upon returning to Italy he found Rome stronger than ever. Although victorious at first, the great losses his armies suffered eventually led to his defeat and death (and to the term "Pyrrhic victory," meaning a victory obtained at too great a cost). His defeat led to the expansion of Roman colonization and commercial influence, including an alliance with Egypt under Ptolemy II.

It became painfully apparent to all the civilizations around the Mediterranean that Rome was a new rising power that would soon inject itself forcibly into their affairs. In addition, great tensions developed among the Roman and Punic colonies in southern Italy, Sicily, and north Africa, all of whom were in competition with each other for resources and trade. A series of unfortunate alliances eventually brought the old friendship between Rome and Carthage to an end. Neither wanted war, but neither was willing to allow control of the sea passages to fall into the hands of the other. Finally, the First Punic War erupted in 264 BCE; it lasted twenty-

14. The fourth century BCE was the era of the conquests of Alexander the Great. While he took the Adriatic, the Middle East, Persia, and Egypt, he did not live long enough to move west against Europe and Italy. In the following centuries, much of his empire fell under the control of Rome.

15. "Punic" is the adjective for Carthage. It is a corruption of "Phoenix" or "Phoenician," as Carthage was originally a Phoenician colony.

three years. Near victory passed back and forth between Carthage and Rome several times. In the course of time Rome ended up with full control of Sicily, which it made into a Roman province. By 241 Carthage, having lost Sardinia, Corsica, and its Sicilian holdings, withdrew from the conflict. Rome chose not to pursue its victory further but continued its expansion northward into southern Gaul (France) and the Balkans, and eastward into Greece and the Adriatic.

During the period of Roman expansion, Carthage, under the leadership of Hamilcar Barca, had been strengthening its army and navy, and had developed extensive holdings in Spain. In 237 Hamilcar took his nine-year-old son Hannibal to Spain, having sworn him to eternal hatred of everything Roman. In 229 Hamilcar died, and his son-in-law Hasdrubal became king. He immediately made a peace treaty with Rome, enraging the young Hannibal. When Hasdrubal died in 221, Hannibal ascended the throne with the full support of the army, who were devoted to him. At once he drew up plans for a war against Rome, launching a two-year campaign in which he took all of non-Roman southern Spain. In 219 he attacked Saguntum, a Roman seaport on the southern coast of Spain, thus launching the Second Punic War, an eighteen-year conflict. After the fall of Saguntum, Hannibal undertook the foray for which he is best remembered by every schoolchild: with a fully equipped army of forty thousand men and a cavalry of African elephants (the military tanks of his day) he crossed the Alps and launched a surprise attack on Italy from the north. After a series of impressive victories, however, he was finally defeated in 201 BCE by one of Rome's greatest generals, Publius Cornelius Scipio Africanus. Rome chose not to destroy Carthage, but rather to allow it to remain an independent state. It was trimmed to a size no larger than modern Tunisia, however, and was rendered virtually powerless.

During the following half-century Carthage again grew stronger, making many Romans fearful of their old enemy. Carthage was no economic threat and posed little military menace, but old prejudices and fears were stirred up by the censor Cato the Elder and his followers.[16] Eventually the

16. Cato the Elder was one of the few Romans who hated everything Greek, claiming that the Romans' love of the Greeks had made them soft and effete. As censor, he purged the Senate of all whom he thought unworthy or who disagreed with his puritanical views of Roman morality. When he was sent to Carthage in 157 BCE to arbitrate a dispute between Carthage and Numidia, he became equally appalled by Carthaginian wealth, luxury, and "softness." After he returned to Rome he concluded every speech he gave to the Senate with the phrase, *"Carthago delenda est"* ("Carthage must be destroyed").

war party gained sway over the moderates, and in 149 BCE Rome declared the Third Punic War on Carthage. Carthage immediately offered to surrender, but upon hearing Rome's terms they decided to fight. Rome had demanded that the city be leveled and that no Carthaginian could live closer than ten miles from the coast. The war lasted three years, and in 146 the city fell. Rome destroyed it completely and sold all its surviving inhabitants into slavery. This war cast a blight on Rome's honor, and many Romans looked on it with the same shame as many Americans look on the Indian wars.

Rome's strength, which gave it victory in the Punic wars, was the willingness of the Roman people to sacrifice anything for Rome's sake. After the fall of Carthage, Rome had no serious enemies to fear, and that strength of will quickly decayed into greed and corruption. On the other hand, the lack of danger allowed the might of the Roman army to unify the Mediterranean world and spread the so-called *Pax Romana,* the Roman Peace, throughout the known world. It was, however, a peace that was brutally enforced with an iron hand and the dreaded Roman short sword.

It can be said that the fall of the Roman Republic began in 133 BCE. Corruption and greed in high places had eventually allowed the Senate to usurp most of the governmental power. In 133 a tribune, Tiberius Gracchus, proposed agrarian reforms that would have restored many of the rights of the common people. He so alienated the Senate that he and three hundred of his followers were murdered. His brother Gaius, a much more able politician, took up the cause, and after getting himself elected tribune of the people he managed to bring about significant reforms. Foremost among them was the reduction of the power of the Senate, with significantly more power going to the wealthy commoners. This brought about the fury of the aristocracy, however, and a series of assassinations followed, including that of Gaius Gracchus himself. Rome moved to the brink of civil war; ironically, in an attempt to protect the rights of the common people, the Gracchi unintentionally had set in motion a process that eventually brought about the end of the Republic and the enthronement of an emperor.

The turmoil in Rome was increased by a series of defeats the army had suffered on the northern frontier. Gaius Marius, with the help of his friend, the general Lucius Cornelius Sulla, cleaned up a military mess in north Africa, and as a result of that (and a politically very profitable marriage to Julius Caesar's aunt) Marius managed to get himself elected consul. He then achieved the aforementioned feat of being re-elected six more times, five of them consecutive and some *in absentia* (an unimaginable feat to most Romans). During his consulship he took command of the armies in the field, and with Sulla's help he was able to hold back the Germans, who were migrating south and presented a threat to Italy. Unfortunately for their friendship, Sulla claimed all the credit for both achievements, which eventually resulted in their becoming bitter enemies.[17]

In 91 BCE a movement arose to grant Roman citizenship to all male property holders in Italy. The Italians had supplied the majority of Roman soldiers for at least a century, and their labors were what enriched Rome. They felt they had earned the right to citizenship, but the patricians were jealous of their own privilege and refused. It looked like a major war would break out until Marcus Livius Drusus garnered enough support among the senators that it appeared the law might pass. Just before the vote Drusus was assassinated, and the movement collapsed. Enraged, the Italians, under the leadership of the Samnites, revolted in what is called the Social War. Marius finally managed to subdue the Italians, but at a terrible cost to Rome of lives and money.

Increasing tension and occasional rioting broke out between Sulla's and Marius's followers. Marius tried to deprive Sulla of his military command, and a civil war broke out. Marius was defeated and was forced to flee. Sulla, a highly successful general in his own right, managed to put down most of the provincial revolts, and in 88 BCE marched against the armies of Mithridates VI, king of Pontus, who had been a serious threat to Rome. While he was away Marius returned to Rome with Sulla's old enemy, the general Lucius Cornelius Cinna. The spineless Senate capitulated to them, naming Marius and Cinna consuls in 86 BCE. Marius then launched a vicious vendetta against all his old aristocratic enemies in an orgy of murder. Fortunately for Rome, this once great but now bitter old man died a few days into his consulship.

Cinna led Rome as consul for the next few years, but Sulla was not idle during this time; after defeating Mithridates he returned to Rome in triumph in 83 BCE. He was the first to violate an ancient Roman law that no general could enter Italy without first disbanding his army. Sulla not only

17. Sulla was a member of the Cornelii, one of Rome's proudest families, but one with little money. Marius, on the other hand, was from a much lower patrician family, but he was one of the wealthiest men in Rome. It galled Sulla to be a military and political subordinate to Marius simply because Marius could afford the expense of high political office and Sulla could not. Eventually Sulla's early admiration of Marius turned into an irrational hatred.

brought his army into Italy, he marched it right into Rome. He was so popular that he was welcomed by the common people, but the leaders were horrified. They could do nothing, however — he had effectively captured the city. The Senate (at Sulla's order) declared him consul, and after a series of political maneuvers, he managed to have himself declared dictator. While the dictatorship was supposed to be a temporary position lasting no more than six months, Sulla persuaded the Senate to make him dictator for five years, from 83 through 79 CE. His dictatorship was in some respects temporarily beneficial, but it was also violent and brutal. He effected several reforms designed to return control of the city to aristocratic hands and restabilized the Roman government, but he also murdered all his old enemies, particularly those of the Marian party. (One of his intended victims was Marius's nephew, the young Julius Caesar, who temporarily fled Rome.) In 79 BCE he resigned and retired to private life, dying soon thereafter. In 63 BCE one of Sulla's old friends and partisans, Lucius Sergius Catalina, having lost several elections to the consulate, led a conspiracy to take power in Rome by force. The statesman and jurist Marcus Tullius Cicero, who had defeated him in one of those elections, found out about the plot and exposed it in a series of orations before the Senate. Catalina and his co-conspirators were declared enemies of the state and banished from Rome.

It was not long before three men undid all of Sulla's reforms. They were Gaius Julius Caesar and the generals Gnaeus Pompeius Magnus (Pompey the Great) and Marcus Licinius Crassus, an opportunist who, by a lifetime of unscrupulous and immoral dealings, had become the richest man in Rome (and possibly the richest in the world). Pompey had been Sulla's right-hand man, and had won great power and popularity with the masses through his extensive military victories, through which he vastly expanded Rome's holdings in the Middle East. (It was Pompey who captured Jerusalem during his campaigns of 66 to 61 BCE.) He had become consul for the first time in 70 BCE, along with Crassus, who had great influence in the Senate because of his status and great wealth. Crassus had also overseen the defeat of the slave revolt of Spartacus in 71 BCE (though Pompey played a role in Spartacus's defeat as well).

During Pompey's absence fighting in the East, Caesar had become a rising star, and in 59 BCE he was elected consul. Caesar desperately needed Crassus's wealth and Pompey's influence, while Crassus and Pompey needed someone to push through the laws they desired. The three men thus formed an informal alliance known as the First Triumvirate, and together they ruled all Italy. Each man was playing a dangerous game, however, as all three had vast ambitions. Pompey tried to grasp full power by pushing Caesar and Crassus out of the central activities in Rome. He sent Caesar to subdue the Gauls at the northern border of Italy, and Crassus to put down a revolt in Syria. Crassus was killed in Syria in 53 BCE, leaving just Pompey and Caesar with power. Though Pompey himself had loaned Caesar legions to help him start his military campaign against the Gauls, he became increasingly fearful of Caesar's growing power. After passing laws intended to diminish Caesar's power, including one that would have allowed Caesar to be prosecuted for electoral bribing if he returned to Rome, Pompey ordered Caesar to disband his legions and return to Rome. Caesar, fearing treachery, refused. Instead, Caesar defied the Senate and Pompey by crossing the Rubicon River with his army, thus invading Italy (and thus following the precedent of Sulla, whose dictatorship also foreshadowed the coming reign of Caesar). Pompey sent his troops against Caesar, but after nearly defeating him at Pharsalus Pompey was forced to flee to Egypt in 48 BCE. He sought refuge from King Ptolemy XIII, Cleopatra's younger brother and husband, but was betrayed and murdered. This left Caesar with virtually full power. The Senate was corrupt and torn apart by internal conflicts, so it had little ability to hold him in check. Caesar was the leader of the *Populares* ("people's") party that claimed to protect the interests of the common people. This gave him powerful influence over, and thus control of, the tribunes. He finally managed to have himself declared Sole Consul and Dictator for Life.

In Caesar's first years of dictatorship he did much good for Rome, but by his fourth year he had become increasingly autocratic. He was accused of wanting to become a king (a much hated concept to Romans). He was even accused of claiming divinity — he had appointed Marc Antony as the priest of a temple erected to honor him — but it is more likely that he was using this as a device to secure the obedience of the superstitious common people. Finally, by 44 BCE, he had so alienated the old republican Roman nobility that Gaius Longinus Cassius and Marcus Junius Brutus, along with sixty others, conspired to assassinate him and restore the Republic. On the Ides of March (the fifteenth), 44 BCE, he fell at the foot of Pompey's statue at the entrance to the Senate.

After Caesar's death, Rome was plunged into thirteen years of civil war. Cicero proposed amnesty for the assassins and the full restoration of the Republic, but while the Senate hesitated, Marcus Antonius (Marc Antony) and Marcus Aemilius Lepidus seized power. They were challenged by Caesar's grand-nephew and adopted son Gaius Octavius Caesar, better known as Octavian. Realizing that only by working together could they hold onto power, the three formed the Second Triumvirate. In one of their first acts, in 43 BCE, they punished the assassins and leading republicans, forcing many into exile; Cicero was killed, and his hands and feet were then displayed on the speaker's podium in the Senate as a warning to others.

This triumvirate was ill-fated from the start, as it was made up of Lepidus, who was weak; Antony, who was a barely competent general and obsessed with the Egyptian pharaoh Cleopatra; and Octavian, who was ruthlessly ambitious and power hungry. The death rattle of the Roman Republic had sounded.


## II. The Imperial Era

The last years of Gaius Julius Caesar's life thus marked the end of the Roman Republic, a fact that was clear to most by the time that Lepidus, Antony, and Octavian formed the Second Triumvirate. Under the triumvirate the three allegedly ruled with equal power. Lepidus, who had been a general under Marc Antony and fought beside him in the civil war, was weak, however, and in 36 BCE he was expelled and forced to retire to private life. Octavian had gained great victories in the civil war, had restored order, and thus had effectively become the master of Rome. In the meantime, Marc Antony had become obsessed with Cleopatra, the last Egyptian pharaoh. She had earlier been the lover of Julius Caesar; now she and Antony carried on a torrid love affair while he was married to Octavia, the sister of Octavian. Octavian, in a successful attempt to wrest power from Antony, started a smear campaign against him and Cleopatra. He accused Antony of ceding to Egyptian control a third of the Roman Empire. This seeming treachery turned the Romans against both Antony and Cleopatra.

The power struggle between Octavian and Antony finally came to a head in 31 BCE, when Octavian's armies defeated Antony's legions and the Egyptian forces under Antony's command at the Battle of Actium. Antony and Cleopatra fled back to Egypt, where, surrounded by Octavian's troops, they committed suicide. Cleopatra had sent Caesarion, her son by Julius Caesar, into hiding under Egyptian protection, but Octavian found him and had him murdered. By 27 BCE Octavian was seen as the undisputed ruler of Rome, and the Senate gave him the title *Imperator*, "Commander" (although the common translation of *Imperator* is "Emperor").[18] In Roman usage *Imperator* had no constitutional significance. It simply meant "commander," in the sense of "general," but implying an exceptional authority or *imperium*.

Octavian was careful never to claim the title *Rex*, "king," but although not technically a king, he had extraordinary power as a ruler. Legally he was First Consul, but instead of being consul for a year he was considered Consul for Life. His role was similar to that of dictator, so he had almost limitless power. The Senate gave him the title *Augustus*, "majestic one," which carried overtones of reverence and sacredness. From that time on he took it as a cognomen and used it as his name. He then resigned all his posts, renounced all power, and turned himself over to the Senate for an appointment as governor of a province. This was all lip service, of course. The Senate immediately recognized him as governor of all Roman lands, thus effectively making him undisputed ruler of all Rome. He always thereafter claimed that he ruled at the will of the Senate and people of Rome, and that Rome was still a republic. While this may have been technically true, the weak Senate rarely got in his way, and since he had absolute authority over the Roman army, he controlled the source of Roman power.

In the overall picture, Augustus was not a bad ruler, despite the ruthlessness that brought him to power. He did not abuse his authority or live in opulent and excessive luxury, and he strengthened and solidified a Rome that had been rent asunder by civil wars for almost a century. It is unlikely that the healthy days of the old Republic would ever have returned, and if he had not taken power, Rome would probably have fallen into the hands of someone more unscrupulous. Unfortunately, some of Augustus's successors were the vilest sort of rulers.

Augustus's wife was Livia Drusilla. She was the granddaughter of Marcus Livius Drusus, whose assassination precipitated the Social War in 91 BCE. He had adopted a Claudian, Livia's father, and Livia was thus also a Claudian, one of Rome's oldest and most honored ruling families. She had two sons, Drusus and Tiberius, by a previous marriage to her cousin Marcus Claudius Tiberius. Augustus adopted Tiberius, thus making him a Julian as well as a Claudian. Drusus had died as a result of an equestrian accident, and Livia allegedly poisoned Augustus's other heirs so that her

---

18. *Imperator* is in fact difficult to translate. A general in the field was called an *imperator*, but only after he had merited the title by significant victories. Anyone with authority was said to have *imperium*, and the range and degree of his *imperium* could be clearly defined by the Senate. When they named Octavian *Imperator* they effectively granted him an *imperium* of absolute power.

son Tiberius would be that only one remaining. When Augustus died in 14 CE Livia was accused of having poisoned him as well, but most scholars doubt that she perpetrated these crimes. Augustus's successful reign of forty-one years was the longest of any Roman emperor.

The Senate declared Tiberius emperor at the age of fifty-five, despite his protestations (whether feigned or genuine is debated) that he would rather not have sole power. Tiberius had spent much of his life as a successful general, and was well liked by his men, although he lacked Augustus's affability and skill at managing people, and was a rather suspicious man, afraid of plots against him. In his old age Tiberius left Rome to live on Capri, delegating increasing power to Lucius Aelius Sejanus, a trusted advisor, until Sejanus virtually ruled the empire. Tiberius had placed his trust in a poor source, however; Sejanus was ruthless and power hungry, loyal only to himself. After his conspiracy to take the throne was discovered in 31 CE, he was executed, and Tiberius's paranoia and depression increased. By the end of his twenty-three-year reign, Tiberius, who had never returned to Rome, was hated by both the upper and lower classes in Rome.

Shortly before he died, Tiberius named his twenty-five-year-old grandnephew Gaius Claudius Caesar Germanicus, whose father he had adopted, and his fifteen-year-old grandson Tiberius Claudius Caesar Gemellus as joint heirs (and technically, First and Second Consuls). Gaius Claudius was born and grew up in his father's military posts, and wore a little Roman army uniform. He became something of a mascot to the soldiers, who affectionately called him *Caligula*, "Little Boot." He was known by that name for the rest of his life. When Tiberius died in 37 CE at the age of seventy-nine, the Senate voided his will and named Caligula sole emperor. At this point Caligula was still popular with the common people, who knew little of the excesses of his personal life. It did not take them long to become disenchanted. Upon being named emperor Caligula adopted Gemellus as his son, and soon thereafter he had him murdered. Caligula's reign was one of unspeakable horror, and his erratic and immoral behavior was such that many of the ancient writers described him as insane. Stories about him abounded, including that he tried to make his beloved horse Incitatus a senator. Although the veracity of that story is in doubt, other tales, such as that of his incest with his sister Drusilla and his demand that he be worshiped as a god, seem accurate.[19] After a four-year bloodbath of a reign he was assassinated in 41 CE, and died unlamented.

---

19. It was during Caligula's reign that Herod Agrippa I was appointed to a kingdom in Palestine. Caligula's desire to be worshiped as a God did nothing to endear him to the Jews.

Rome's next emperor, Tiberius Claudius Drusus Nero Germanicus, is generally considered one of its best. Claudius was Tiberius's nephew, and by most accounts did not want to be emperor. He was an intellectual, not a politician, and his family had kept him out of the public eye for much of his life because he walked with a limp, had frequent muscular spasms, stammered, and possibly drooled. (Descriptions of him in contemporary writings suggest that he may have been a victim either of infantile polio or of mild cerebral palsy.) Although he was generally considered to be quite stupid, he was in fact brilliant, and had spent much of his early years reading and turning himself into a very proficient scholar.

When Caligula was assassinated there was great confusion and fear about the succession. According to tradition, Claudius was found in the palace hiding under a curtain. Perhaps believing that because he was stupid he could do no harm, the Praetorian Guard (the imperial bodyguard) declared him the emperor. The Senate grudgingly accepted him as emperor under pressure from the Guard. There was at first some talk among senators of trying to restore the Republic, and it is possible that Claudius himself did not want to be made emperor, but in the end the Senate, as had become typical, bowed to the pressure of the Roman military. Had they not, chaos would likely have ensued, since Rome was by this time full of powerful and unscrupulous men who lusted after the throne. Claudius's reign was quite successful, and he managed to restore to Rome much of the glory, honor, and stability that had been lost during Caligula's rule. He also realized a military achievement that no Roman before, including Julius Caesar, had been able to accomplish: he conquered and colonized Britannia, the portion of Great Britain that today is England. In honor of this he named his son Britannicus.

The first Christians began to appear in Rome during Claudius's reign. At first they were considered a sect of the Jews, and as such were an authorized religion. Eventually the Jews rejected them, however, and from time to time this resulted in public disturbances. Despite the fact that his friend Herod Agrippa I was a Jew, Claudius did not understand the difference between Christians and Jews. He finally forbade the Jews from assembling within the city limits of Rome. This meant that they had to leave the city before sundown every Friday to worship, and could not return until after sundown on Saturday. (Jews may not travel on the Sabbath, which begins at sundown on Friday.) Some historians interpret this as Claudius's having expelled the Jews from Rome, but that interpretation is inaccurate.

Claudius's personal life was less successful than his public one. After two arranged and very unhappy marriages, he married Messalina, whom he adored, and who influenced him greatly as an advisor and assistant. Unfortunately, she was also extremely promiscuous, although Claudius was blinded to this by his love for her. After becoming a disgraceful scandal to all of Rome, she finally conspired with one of her lovers to take his throne. She was executed for treason, and after a number of years Claudius married Caligula's sister Agrippina (sometimes called Agrippinilla). He adopted her son Nero, whom he named his heir over his own younger son Britannicus. Since Nero was older than Britannicus, it is possible he did this to avoid problems with the succession, but scholars debate about the reason. This decision turned out to be a bad one; Agrippina poisoned Claudius in 54 CE, soon after he had named her son Nero his heir.

Claudius's choice of heir was certainly the worst part of his legacy, for Nero was a true tyrant.[20] Nero murdered Britannicus, and not long afterward he murdered his mother, Agrippina, and his wife, Octavia. He plundered Rome's riches and was allegedly responsible for ordering the fire that destroyed half of the city and killed thousands in 64 CE. At that time most of Rome was a stinking, ugly, overpopulated city that epitomized urban sprawl, a firetrap made of wood and adobe. Although the fire may have started accidentally and gotten out of control, it is entirely possible that Nero ordered the city torched in order to allow the realization of his dream of building a magnificent city of marble. Whatever actually happened, the people held him responsible. Needing a scapegoat, he blamed the Christians for the fire, declared their religion illegal, and launched a bloody persecution of them. He also taxed the people mercilessly in order to raise the funds to rebuild Rome after the fire. His new marble Rome was magnificent, but hideously expensive. He tried to placate the people with "bread and circuses," regularly giving them bloody gladiatorial games and slaughter of Christians in the arena.[21] While this bought off the people for a while, unrest grew to dangerous proportions. After fourteen years of tyranny and brutality, even the Praetorian Guard finally turned against him. Facing a revolution, Nero fled Rome in 68 CE and committed suicide.

Nero was the last of the Julio-Claudian emperors, all of whom had

20. Some scholars believe that the references in the book of Revelation to the Antichrist and to the Beast whose number is 666 are actually references to Nero. (In the occult science of numerology, the number of his full name is 666.) This was probably not the author's intent.

21. Despite Hollywood's depiction, this was not in the Colosseum (properly called the *Circus Flavianus*), which would not be built until 72 CE by the emperor Flavius Vespasian (the same who ordered the destruction of Jerusalem). Nero's arena was the *Circus Neronis*.

taken the Julian cognomen, Caesar, such that eventually it came to be a ti-tle meaning "emperor." (This has a legacy even into our own day, since the titles Kaiser and Czar are corruptions of "Caesar.") By the end of the Julio-Claudian dynasty the imperial cult had also grown. Reluctantly acknowl-edging the cult's political expedience, Augustus had allowed those in the Roman provinces to worship him as a god, and he was officially named a god after his death. Many of the later emperors claimed to be gods during their own lifetimes. Some believed it, but most used it as a tool to gain the obedience of the superstitious masses. By this time it was clear that Rome's power and wealth had come at a great price; the empire was politically cor-rupt and morally bankrupt. While Roman culture had never had a high re-gard for life, by the end of Nero's reign life was simply a barterable com-modity. Death in the arena was entertainment, and brutal slave labor was a major source of wealth. Notwithstanding, the legacy of Augustus and Claudius would survive. They had laid a foundation of strength that would enable Rome to rule the world for another four centuries.

The reigns of the three emperors who followed Nero — Galba, Otho, and Vitellius — lasted only a few months each, all of them ending with the emperor's death in the year 69 CE. In December of that year Vespasian, a general in charge of putting down the Jewish revolt, was named by the Senate and Praetorian Guard to become the new emperor. He was a plebe-ian, not a patrician, but he had an outstanding record in the army. He left his son Titus in charge of subduing the Jews. The following year (70) Titus solved the Jewish problem. With his father's approval, he launched a mas-sive attack on Judea, crucified tens of thousands of Jews, and leveled the city of Jerusalem, totally destroying the temple. This would be the begin-ning of the end of the Jewish nation until the establishment of Israel in 1948.[22] Despite the less than pretty picture painted above, Vespasian was actually a quite good emperor. A shrewd and firm leader, he ruled well for ten years, and in 79 CE his older son Titus succeeded him without question.

Titus, like his father, ruled well, but his reign lasted only three years. The most significant event during Titus's reign was the eruption of Vesu-vius in 79 that destroyed Pompeii and Herculaneum. He died in 81 CE at the height of his popularity, and was succeeded by his power-hungry and cruel brother Domitian. Domitian demanded sacrifice to the gods as a sign of loyalty to his own divinity, bringing him into a head-on conflict with

22. The final end was in 132 CE, when Hadrian ordered that all the Jews be driven out of Palestine.

The Arch of Titus in Rome was erected by Emperor Domitian in 81 CE to commemorate the conquest of Jerusalem in 70 CE by his father, the emperor Vespasian, and Domitian's brother Titus.    Photo credit: Scala/Art Resource, NY

the Jews and Christians. He launched a bloody persecution of both, but particularly of Christians, whom he blamed for all his troubles. The real source of his troubles was his lavish spending and his cruel reign of terror in which he slaughtered anyone he suspected of disloyalty. He was assassinated in 96 CE.

Domitian was succeeded by the "Five Good Emperors," Nerva, Trajan, Hadrian, Antoninus Pius, and Marcus Aurelius. All ruled with moderation, maintaining good relations with both the Senate and the army. They quelled the threats of civil war and solidified peace within the empire. They built huge numbers of public works, such as highways and aqueducts, and strengthened the Roman frontiers by developing alliances with the peripheral nations rather than trying to crush them.

The greatest of the Five Good Emperors was Marcus Aurelius ( who ruled from 161 to 180). He was a Stoic philosopher and a man of great learning, and by all reports he was gentle and compassionate.[23] Rather than making him appear weak, however, this endeared him to Romans and barbarians alike, because he was wise, consistent, and willing to consider their desires. Sadly, this nonmilitary man had to spend sixteen of his nineteen years of reign in warfare, quelling revolts and uprisings on the frontiers. By the time of his death, however, peace reigned throughout the Roman Empire for the first time in centuries. He died suddenly in 180, possibly assassinated at the instigation of his son Commodus, a ruthless and cruel man. The Roman historian Cassius Dio said that with the ascension of Commodus to the throne "the age of gold turned to rusty iron."

Commodus managed to alienate all the nations that had befriended his father, and instituted an era of cruel warfare. After twelve years of disastrous rule he was murdered in 192 CE, leaving a torn and bloody Rome on the verge of civil war. Many historians consider his reign to be the beginning of the fall of Rome.

For the next fifty years the persecutions of Christians continued, but not on an empire-wide basis. Persecutions were usually localized, at the whim of some governor who because of prejudice or the need for a scapegoat would institute a period of persecution. Most of these were short-lived, although some were incredibly brutal while they lasted. For the most part, the Romans were tired of persecuting a people who would not fight back, and who seemed to be relatively harmless. After about 250 CE there

---

23. His twelve-volume book, *Meditations,* reveals his belief that morality leads to peace, and emphasizes the importance of the virtues of wisdom, justice, fortitude, and moderation.

were few persecutions. Rome seems to have come to a tacit acceptance of the presence of Christians as long as they were causing no trouble.

Over time, the eastern and western portions of the empire had become more and more unlike in traditions and culture, making the empire almost ungovernable. During the subsequent decades, several attempts were made to divide the responsibilities between co-rulers (one superior to the other), and the distinction between East and West became increasingly apparent. Eventually, by the end of the fourth century, there were two emperors, one of the East and another of the West.

The 125 years after Commodus saw sixty-nine emperors, none of whom has any particular significance from our point of view but one, Diocletian (284-305). Politically he was a good leader, but in 303, for no obvious reason, he instituted a persecution of Christians that challenged the brutality even of Nero.

In 313 Constantine ascended the throne in the West, and in 334 took the reins of the whole empire, both East and West. In time he would not only legalize Christianity, but effectively mandate it throughout the empire.


## III. The Christian Era

The first Christians seem to have appeared in Rome during the reign of Claudius, in the mid-first century CE, although there may have been some there even earlier. The book of Acts refers to "visitors from Rome (both Jews and converts to Judaism)" in Jerusalem at the first Pentecost, when Peter preached and three thousand were converted (Acts 2:10-11). Some of those whom Peter converted may well have been Romans, who took their newfound faith back with them when they returned home.

At first the Christians were thought to be a sect of Jews, and probably considered themselves as such. There were thirteen synagogues in Rome at that time, and the Christians worshiped in them. It did not take long, however, for the Jews to reject the Christians as blasphemers. At the same time, the Christians were beginning to accept Gentiles into their ranks, making the separation complete. Christians were suspect because their teachings were quite contrary to the beliefs of the materialistic, superstitious, and bloodthirsty Romans. Nevertheless, Saints Peter and Paul both preached in Rome, and the church there was firmly established. When Nero was labeled an incendiary after the Roman fire, he passed the blame to the Christians and launched years of bloody persecution. No one knows exactly what happened to Peter and Paul, but there is little doubt that they were martyred in Rome under Nero. (Tradition says that Peter was crucified upside-down, and Paul beheaded.)

Paul's letter to the Romans was written before he had ever been to the city, so all he had to go on was reports from others. As a result, it throws little light on the culture of the Christian community in Rome at the time. The letter focuses more on the types of problems that all the Gentile churches were trying to deal with.

In the course of time the Bishop of Rome came to be seen as a primary leader of western Christianity, being the spiritual descendant of Peter, and the bishop of the seat of the empire. He came to be known affectionately as *Papa*, "Dad," which eventually became his official title.[24] By the time the term had worked itself into English it was pronounced "pope." Despite centuries of persecution, the church in Rome remained strong under the leadership of a number of effective popes.

Contrary to the common image, early Christians worshiped in private homes, not in the catacombs. They would gather at the home of one of the wealthier members, simply because those homes were large enough to hold the group, and private enough that the gathering was less likely to be discovered. Their worship was usually very early on the morning of the first day of the the Roman eight-day week, for two reasons. This was usually a work day, and since most Christians worked and most work began soon after sunup, an early gathering was necessary. Also, during the times of persecution they had to slip quietly into the homes one or two at a time in order not to be discovered. This was easier to do in the pre-dawn hours. The service was very short, usually consisting of a few opening prayers of thanksgiving for God's gift of salvation through Christ[25] followed by the telling of the story of the Last Supper, the consecration of the bread and wine, and the Communion of the people. There was also occasionally a service of prayer and preaching that was based on the synagogue worship.

Another common misconception about the catacombs is that they were Roman sewers or drainage tunnels. Many Mediterranean cultures

---

24. This is consistent with the way Jesus addressed God, as *Abba* (Mark 14:36). In Hebrew *ab* is "father," while *abba* is the familiar address by which a child might address his father. It is roughly equivalent to "Dad," and would not generally have been used by Jews to address God, because they would have considered it disrespectful.

25. Thus the name of the service, "Eucharist," which is from the Greek *eucharistein*, "to give thanks."

buried their dead in catacombs, which were tunnel-like underground burial chambers that were dug out and expanded as necessary. The Romans burned their dead with pagan rites, so to avoid any association with this the Christians forbade cremation and dug catacombs outside the city for the burial of their dead.[26] These catacombs have been of tremendous value to archaeologists in discerning much of early Christian history. They were dark, damp, and cramped, however, and the smoke of torches and the smell of decaying flesh would have made them nearly impossible to use as places of worship.

The fourth century CE saw a major change in the directions of both the Roman Empire and the Christian church. The empire was coming apart in the middle, with power diverging toward the two disparate regions of East and West. Because governing the immense empire had become so unwieldy, there were two emperors, one for each half. (At some points there were as many as four, one per quarter.) While the emperor in Rome was technically the head of the other emperors, the emperor in the eastern capital of Byzantium (now Istanbul, Turkey) was becoming increasingly more important and powerful. In 306 Constantine ascended the throne of the western portion of the empire, and two years later Licinius that of the eastern, each taking the title of "Augustus." Each man had to struggle for sole control of his half of the empire, Constantine with his rival Maxentius, the favorite in Rome. Constantine met up with Maxentius and his troops in 312 CE, at a bridge less than ten miles outside Rome. The story goes that Constantine had a vision in which he saw a sign in the heavens and heard a voice saying, *"In hoc signo vinces,"* "In this sign you conquer." The sign he saw was the *"Chi Rho,"* the monogram of the first two Greek letters of "Christ,"[27] intertwined (according to some versions) with a cross. Constantine declared himself a Christian, inscribed the *Chi Rho* on the shields of his soldiers, and defeated Maxentius at the Battle of Milvian Bridge. He thereafter attributed his gaining of the throne to the Christian God, and in 313 he and Licinius issued the Edict of Milan, under which Christianity became a legal and preferred religion in the western empire. Constantine was not baptized until shortly before his death, and scholars have long argued about whether he

26. The tradition of burial became so ingrained in Christian thought that to this day the Roman Catholic Church discourages cremation. This is because of the ancient Christian aversion to pagan Roman funeral practices, not because cremation destroys the body. The condition of the mortal body has nothing to do with the state of the resurrected body.

27. The *Chi Rho* looks like an X superimposed on a P, but it is actually the Greek letters "Ch" and "R."

was ever really a Christian. It is possible that he simply recognized that Christianity was a powerful force in the empire, and that therefore it would be wise for him to ally himself with it in order to enhance his own position. On the other hand, he staunchly defended orthodox Christianity against a number of heresies. He also instituted an ambitious building program, which included what is called "Old St. Peter's," the cathedral on whose site now stands the great domed Saint Peter's Basilica.

Constantine had many disputes with Licinius, not the least of which was that Licinius, who had originally favored the church, had begun to persecute it. After a long power struggle Constantine finally, in 324, defeated Licinius and became the sole Augustus of the whole empire. He then established his imperial capital in Licinius's capital, Byzantium. He renamed it Constantinople,[28] declared it a Christian city, and made it a capital offense to persecute Christians. He rebuilt the city, also building a number of Christian churches. He saw it as the New Rome, although it did not have the constitutional authority of Rome. From then on, Christians were free to practice their religion openly throughout the empire. Unfortunately, they soon began to think of themselves as the preferred group in the empire, and developed an arrogance and self-righteousness that had been previously unknown. It has been said that the cruelest blow that ever befell the Christian church was its legitimization by Constantine. Not only did it give the church an untoward sense of worldly authority and privilege, but it unloosed a series of vicious persecutions of Christians in Persia, because the Christians held what was now the religion of the Romans, Persia's ancient bitter enemies.

The norm in almost every civilization of that time was that the head of state was also the head of the religion. Thus it troubled no one when Constantine declared himself the head of Christianity, and took it upon himself to judge all the church's disputes, including putting down several heresies. The Arian[29] heresy was flourishing at the time, and Constantine called the Council of Nicaea — what became known as the First Ecumenical Council — to deal with it. It was this council that issued the Nicene Creed as a statement of orthodoxy. Constantine was for all practical purposes the final authority in all ecclesiastical matters in the Roman Empire.

28. *Constantinopolis,* "City of Constantine."
29. Arianism denied the doctrine of the Trinity and taught that Christ was created, not divine. Its teachings were very much like those of the modern Jehovah's Witnesses, who honor Arius.

After the death of Constantine the empire was again riven into East and West, with only a few brief periods during which it was united under a common emperor. The strong emperors were almost universally seated in the East at Constantinople, while the western empire in Rome suffered a series of weak leaders.

Christianity stood in danger from the Roman Empire only one more time, and that was brief. In 361 Constantine's nephew Julian became emperor of both the eastern and western empires. He had been raised a Christian, but upon ascending the throne he renounced Christianity and declared it illegal. He restored the worship of the ancient Roman gods as the official religion of the empire, and came to be known as Julian the Apostate. Before any serious persecution began, however, Julian was killed in 363 in a battle with the Persians. Upon his death there again came to be two emperors, eastern and western, and both were Christians.

While the eastern emperors retained their leadership of the church, they often tired of settling disputes between arguing patriarchs, each of whom claimed to have apostolic authority. The pope had no serious rivals, as Rome was the only western church that could claim to be founded by an apostle, but in the east the two patriarchates, Alexandria and Antioch, were at each other's throats when they were not vying with Constantinople for dominance. As a result, they were constantly appealing to the emperor to settle their disputes. As arbiter of ecclesiastical disputes, the emperor's position as head of the church was even more firmly secured. In Rome, on the other hand, the weak political leadership caused the people to seek the pope as arbiter. He had no ecclesiastical rivals, and since the emperors offered minimal leadership, the popes took the reins of state. Because of this and the fact that there was no dispute about his spiritual descent from the apostle Peter, the eastern emperors often sent the disputing patriarchs to Rome to let the pope settle matters. Over the years the people looked more and more to the pope for leadership, rather than to the emperor, and by the fifth century he had enormous power, having become for all practical purposes the head of the state. More than once it was the papal armies that saved Rome from invasion, while the emperor cowered in his palace. Thus, in the East the head of state was the head of the church,[30] while in Rome the head of the church had by default become the head of state. Even so, the eastern church more often turned to the pope for spiritual guidance

---

30. In the East, that situation lasted until modern times. The Tsar of Russia was the head of the Russian Orthodox Church until the fall of the Russian empire in 1918.

than to the emperor. Unfortunately, the wielding of such power inevitably led to the corruption that so tainted the church in the Middle Ages, and ultimately led to the Reformation.

As the western empire weakened, so did the city of Rome itself. It was increasingly harassed by uprisings of local tribes, and as the barbarian incursions from the north increased, so did the danger to Rome. In 376 the Visigoths, fleeing from the Mongolian Huns, crossed the Danube and began moving south. By 400 they were almost at the gates of Rome, and in 410 they captured the city itself. They were finally moved out in 418 when they were given huge tracts of land in what is now France, and were treated as part of the Roman federation. Soon thereafter the Vandals arrived, leaving a trail of destruction and rapine wherever they went. By 475 North Africa and southwestern Gaul (France) were populated mainly by Germans who were totally independent of the Roman Empire,[31] and southeastern Gaul and Italy were ruled by Teutonic (Germanic) tribes who gave their allegiance to Constantinople. In all the western regions that were Christian, the pope had hegemony over the local rulers, but there was no significant trace left of the imperial control that Rome once knew.

In 476 the Germanic tribes in Italy rose up and deposed the emperor, Romulus Augustulus. Although they were technically barbarians, they behaved in a strikingly civilized manner. Rather than killing Augustulus, they forced him to retire on a generous pension, and placed the German Odoacer on the throne. While this is often marked as the end of the Roman Empire, the empire actually continued. Political infrastructure, coinage, taxes, and administrators all remained intact. The common people hardly noticed the change. In the following centuries the power of the western empire slowly moved north into the hands of the Germanic tribes, and eventually segued into the Holy Roman Empire with the coronation of Carolus Magnus (Charlemagne) on Christmas Day, 800 CE.

Though people often speak of the "fall" of the Roman Empire, it never had a true fall in the sense of a defined end. The empire didn't end in a

---

31. Although this fact is not popular with the French, the modern French are primarily descendants of the Germans, not of the Gauls whom Caesar conquered. The Gauls, who were Celts, were mainly pushed out by the Germanic tribes, who are the ancestors of the modern French. One of these Germanic tribes was the Franks, and it is from their name that the name France derives. While some Celts remained and interbred with the Germans, most moved west into the sparsely populated regions of Normandy, Brittany, and the British Isles.

blaze of glory or in a resounding crash; it simply fizzled away. By the sixth century Rome was a shadow of its former self, and most of the power had shifted to the eastern portion of the empire, whose capital was in Constantinople. While this was still technically part of the Roman Empire, it is usually referred to as the Byzantine Empire, after Byzantium, the original name of Constantinople. It could be argued that the real end of the Roman Empire was the fall of Constantinople to the Ottoman Empire in 1453 CE. With that fall, the story of Rome was done.

# Samaria

After Solomon's death in 922 BCE a civil war broke out in Israel, resulting in the division of the United Monarchy into two kingdoms, Israel in the north and Judah in the south. The first king of Israel was the rebel Jeroboam, who ruled the ten northern tribes and took Shechem as his capital. The southern kingdom, Judah, was actually the continuation of Solomon's kingdom. The capital remained at Jerusalem, with Solomon's son Rehoboam as its king, ruling the two tribes of Judah and Benjamin (with a smattering of Danites who had not gone north earlier — see the section on Dan, p. 83).

Over the years the northern kingdom was in turmoil as a result of petty squabbling and jealousies among the tribes, who were not particularly enamored of serving under a single king. Because of tribal pressures the capital moved around to several sites, including Shechem, Peniel, and Tirzah. Finally King Omri, the founder of the Omride Dynasty, after reigning six years at Tirzah, decided that a new capital was needed. He sought a place that would have commercial and military advantages yet would be free of any tribal jealousies. He found the perfect site in the fertile Esdraelon Plain southwest of the Sea of Galilee. It was an undeveloped hill on the convergence of several important highways, it was easily defensible, and it had a plentiful water supply from nearby springs. It was only twenty-five miles from the Mediterranean, and was in one of the best food production regions in Palestine. Best of all, it had no particular association with any of the tribes. In 870 BCE he bought it for two talents of silver from its owner, Shemer, and named it Samaria after him (1 Kings 16:24). He immediately set to building a fortified city there, and as soon as it was habitable he moved his capital to Samaria. Because it was the capital, the new city was immediately thrust into great importance. As a result the whole region surrounding it, as well as the city itself, soon came to be known as Samaria. While this causes some minor confusion in the ancient texts, the context usually makes it clear as to whether the reference is to the city or the region.

The building of Samaria solved the problem of a capital and of the tribal jealousies associated with the other capitals, but it set in motion a social problem that may have been a major contributor to the ultimate downfall of the northern kingdom: The hill was rather saddle-shaped, actually forming two hills, one high and the other a little lower. Omri built his palace on the upper hill, with all the rest of the dwelling areas on the lower. The nobles and aristocracy, as was the custom, lived in the palace, enabling them to shut themselves away from the common people and the prophets. The whole city quickly became divided between the landed aristocracy on one side, and the middle and working classes on the other. The classes drew farther and farther apart, and the class system quickly spread throughout the kingdom, eating away like a cancer at the social structure of what had earlier been a reasonably egalitarian society, at least as far as such was possible in those times. The result was a complete economic polarization, with a fabulously rich upper class who thrived at the expense of an impoverished and oppressed lower class.

The social decay was exacerbated even further by a breakdown of the religious structure. Paganism had infected much of the worship in the northern kingdom from the beginning, but at first the corruption was relatively minor. Over time it increased. Assyrian documents indicate that Omri had an alliance with pagan Assyria, probably to buffer the threat from Syria to the north. Omri's son Ahab married Jezebel, the daughter of the king of Sidon (Phoenicia), thus uniting by marriage these two kingdoms. The Phoenicians were pagan, worshiping the nature god Melkart, whom the Bible calls Baal.[1] Worship of Baal was introduced throughout the northern kingdom of Israel, along with worship of the Middle Eastern fertility goddess Ashtoreth or Astarte, whose worship involved sacred prostitution in the temples and shrines. The social and religious life in Israel became strongly influenced by Phoenician culture. Jezebel, with Ahab's blessing, not only encouraged the worship of Baal and Ashtoreth but even tried to enforce it. Ahab built a temple to Baal in the middle of Samaria. The prophets, particularly Elijah and later Amos and Hosea, spoke out vehemently against the social and religious corruption, but to little avail. They warned that unless the people repented, Assyria would sweep down upon Israel and destroy it. Over the centuries the worst of the idolatry abated, but the Judaism of the northern kingdom remained

---

1. *Ba'al* is actually Hebrew for "lord," and the term applied to any number of nature gods, each of which had its own name, and which collectively were known as the *ba'alim*. The biblical name Baal refers not only to Melkart but also to the whole pantheon of *ba'alim* as well as to other pagan deities such as Ashtoreth.

badly corrupted. It came to be known as Samaritanism, after the capital city, since it was strongest in the regions around Samaria, west of the Sea of Galilee. This corrupted faith was held in contempt by the faithful Levitical Jews.[2] Although it was found throughout the north, by Jesus' time the majority of people in the cities on the west side of the Sea of Galilee were Levitical Jews who looked to Jerusalem rather than Samaria as the focus of their religion.[3]

During Ahab's reign (869-850 BCE) the kingdom of Israel was constantly under attack from Syria, and finally Ahab was killed in battle. His son Ahaziah ruled for two years, then died after falling through a lattice in a second-floor window, probably in a drunken stupor. Ahab's son Jehoram then ascended the throne, and was at least as corrupt as his brother and father. He was overthrown by Jehu, the commander of his army, in a palace coup in which the entire royal family was killed, thus ending the Omride dynasty. Jehu destroyed the pagan temples and killed all the priests and prophets of Baal. Jezebel's own slaves threw her out a window to her death, and her body was eaten by wild dogs. Unfortunately, although he tried to purify the religion, Jehu's reign was a disaster for the kingdom of Israel. He allowed all Israel's political alliances to crumble and lost all his territory east of the Jordan. This was mainly because in the coup he had slaughtered every official in Ahab's government, leaving himself with no experienced statesmen or leaders (2 Kings 10:11). He continued to be attacked by Syria, and his only way to survive Syrian aggression was to become a vassal of Assyria and rely on its protection.[4]

In 786 BCE Jeroboam II ascended the throne, and Israel entered a period of great strength and prosperity during his forty-one-year reign. Samaria was expanded and improved, becoming a beautiful city with magnificent buildings and avenues. On the downside, however, Jeroboam

2. Today the term "Samaritan," because of Jesus' parable, has come to mean an altruistic and compassionate person. When Jesus used the term, however, it had quite a different meaning. He used the compassion of a Samaritan, a heretic and thoroughly despicable person in the eyes of the Jews, to show the lack of compassion of the supposedly righteous Jews who could not be bothered to help the man in need.

In modern times there is a religious group in Palestine who call themselves Samaritans. Their religion is a mixture of Judaism and Islam.

3. This included Nazareth, where Jesus grew up, and Capernaum, where he made his home in his later adult years.

4. His vassalage is recorded on the famous Black Obelisk of the Assyrian king Shalmaneser III.

allowed the polarization between the rich and poor to become even greater, and he permitted the re-incursion of paganism into the religion. He held things together during his reign, but in the twenty-five years that followed his death Israel went into a rapid decline. All the wealth became concentrated in the hands of a small landed aristocracy, and the rest of the population became totally impoverished. The prophet Amos railed against the excesses of the rich. It became the fashion for the rich women, as a public display of their wealth, to become so obese that they could not possibly do any work. Amos called them "fat cows of Bashan" (Amos 4:1) who forced their husbands to oppress the poor in order get the money to meet their excessively luxurious demands. Hosea, in opposition to the sacred prostitution in the temples, claimed that Israel had been unfaithful to her husband God and had become a prostitute to Baal. To emphasize his prophecy he married a prostitute, Gomer, who bore three children, all of whom were symbols that God had forsaken Israel because of its sin (Hos. 1:2-10). Hosea, like Amos, foretold that Israel would be punished for its sins by being destroyed by the Assyrians. Their prophecy was fulfilled in 722 BCE when most of Israel was lost to the Assyrian king Shalmaneser V, and Samaria finally fell to his son Sargon II, who destroyed it.

According to Assyrian records, Sargon deported over twenty-seven thousand Jews to Assyria and slaughtered most of the rest of the population of Samaria. The city and the surrounding areas were repopulated rather quickly by squatters and marauding foreigners, including Assyrians, Babylonians, Syrians, Phoenicians, and Arabs and Jews from the south. The city was rebuilt, but poorly and with little planning. It would never again until the time of the Romans attain the beauty or importance it knew in the days of Omri and Jeroboam II. In 332 BCE it was captured by Alexander the Great, who heavily fortified it but did little to it otherwise. It was destroyed in 107 BCE in the Maccabaean revolt, and remained in partial ruins until the Romans captured Palestine in 63 BCE. They rebuilt it, along with several other ruined cities, into one of the grand cities of Palestine. The emperor Augustus gave it as a personal gift to Herod the Great, who renamed it Sebaste after him (one of Augustus's many cognomens was Sebastianus).

Archaeological research on the city has been extensive, but has revealed disappointingly little. Unlike the development of most sites in the Middle East, the cycle of destruction and rebuilding in Samaria did not result in sequential layers that yield up a wealth of knowledge about the culture and history of the place. Instead, each time Samaria was rebuilt the old ruins were at least partially removed, and the stones used to build the new structures. As a result, each rebuilding destroyed much of the information of the previous city. With the decline of Roman influence in the region in the fourth and fifth centuries CE, Sebaste (Samaria) declined and decayed, eventually disappearing altogether. All that remains today is a nearby village that had no real association with the city, but retains the name Sebastiyeh.

# Sardis

Sardis was the capital of the ancient kingdom of Lydia, in the western part of what is now the Asian portion of Turkey. Lydia, especially under King Croesus, was one of the richest kingdoms in the world in the sixth century BCE.[1] Much of its wealth came from a huge gold lode in the Pactolus River that ran right through Sardis. The city lay on a major trade route that went the length of the Hermus valley. This not only facilitated easy movement and exchange of gold, but also enabled the city to engage in international commerce. The name of the city probably comes from the name Shardani, a tribe who inhabited the region when it was first settled.

The first settlement at Sardis was a heavily fortified citadel over the Hermus valley, built about 650 BCE. It was surrounded on three sides by steep cliffs consisting of such loose rock that they were extremely difficult to scale. For many years the fortress was considered impregnable, but in 546 BCE Persian soldiers, under Cyrus I, scaled the cliffs at night and entered the fort unexpectedly through a weak and poorly guarded entry on the cliff side. Lydia fell, and Croesus was killed. The Persians held Sardis until the entire region of Asia Minor fell to Alexander the Great in 334 BCE. Although the fortress at Sardis was not breached, the city nonetheless fell into Alexander's hands with the rest of the kingdom. In the struggle for power between Seleucus and Ptolemy after Alexander's death, Ptolemy held Sardis for about a century. The Seleucid Antiochus I took it in 214 BCE, using exactly the same tactics as Cyrus had used three centuries earlier. The city continued to flourish another century and a half, until it fell to the Romans in Pompey's march through Asia in 66 BCE. The Romans rarely allowed a city or nation to retain great wealth, so much of Lydia's gold and treasure was shipped to Rome. Although Sardis thrived, it never again attained the glory and riches that it had known in earlier times. In 26 BCE it was considered for the site of an imperial temple. Had it been chosen, this would have thrust it back to fame, but the final decision was to locate the temple in Smyrna instead. Sardis continued for several centuries more, right through the decline

---

1. "Lydian" became synonymous with "rich," and even today we use the expression "rich as Croesus."

of the eastern Roman Empire. It survived, although not as a particularly important city, until it was destroyed by the Mongol Timur Lang ("Tamberlaine" or "Tamerlane") in 1402. It was never rebuilt as a city, but small poor settlements appeared there from time to time. Today at the site is an impoverished Turkish village called Sart, and no significant archaeological discoveries have been made there.

Sardis has a significance in Christian tradition as one of the seven churches listed in the book of Revelation (Rev. 1:11; 3:1-4). It was chastised for the weakness of the faith of many of its residents, yet encouraged in that there were still righteous among the Christians there.

# Sepphoris

The city of Sepphoris[1] is not mentioned in the Bible, and most people have never heard of it. Notwithstanding, it was a very important city in first-century Palestine, and was probably quite important in the early life of Jesus. Ancient tradition identifies it as the hometown of the Virgin Mary's parents and the mother of John the Baptist, although there is no authoritative evidence to support this.[2] Sepphoris was in Lower Galilee, about five miles north of Nazareth. It had a commanding view of the fertile plains below it, making it an ideal location for a military fortification. Although this region was a hotbed of paganism and Samaritanism,[3] there is strong evidence that Sepphoris was a Jewish city, and that it was walled and reasonably well fortified. It fell under the control of Rome in 63 BCE, and a few years later the Syrian proconsul Gabinius placed a Roman Synedrium or Council there. This would mean that there was a strong Roman presence in Sepphoris, influencing both the architecture and the culture of the city.

There is much that is unknown about the history of Sepphoris, although tradition holds that it was first settled during Joshua's conquest of Canaan. Potsherds in the region support this as reasonable. Later potsherds indicate that the city was of some importance during the height of the Persian Empire in the fifth century BCE. Sepphoris achieved its greatest prosperity, however, when the Roman general Pompey the Great captured Palestine in 63 BCE. Although the Jews considered the Roman conquest a disaster, Sepphoris caught the eye of the Romans and was considered a jewel in their crown. Julius Caesar, during his dictatorship, appointed an

---

1. Early Hebrew writings refer to the city as Zeppori or Zephori.

2. The Bible does not mention the names of Mary's parents, although tradition identifies them as Joachim and Anne or Anna. They are honored as saints in the Catholic traditions. During the Crusades the Christians built the huge Church of Saint Anna at Sepphoris. It is not unreasonable to believe that this was the original home of Mary and her cousin Elizabeth, John the Baptist's mother.

3. The Samaritans were followers of a corrupt form of Judaism that was tainted with Phoenician paganism. It arose in the northern kingdom of Israel, reaching its greatest strength under the rule of Ahab and Jezebel. The Jews considered Samaritans heretics and outcasts.

Idumean bureaucrat named Antipater to be the administrator of Palestine. Antipater appointed his son Herod (later called "the Great") as governor of Galilee, which would have included Sepphoris. Thus the Herods were launched as eventual kings in Palestine.

In 40 BCE the Jewish king Matthias Antigonus II was deposed by the Romans and replaced by Herod as governor. He rebelled against Herod and captured Sepphoris. He lost control of it shortly afterward because a snowstorm bogged down his troops (yes, it does occasionally snow in Palestine). With the help of Rome, Herod recaptured the city, effectively ending the civil war. Three years later, in 37 BCE, the Romans placed Herod on the throne as king of Israel.[4] He held Sepphoris until his death in 4 BCE, but during the rebellion there had been terrible destruction. Some rebuilding was undertaken, but neither Herod nor Rome was willing to spend the money to rebuild any more than what fit their own immediate needs and interests.

Upon Herod's death, Rome divided his kingdom among three of his sons, Archelaus, Philip, and Antipas. Antipas was given the rule of Galilee and Perea, with the title of tetrarch of Galilee.[5] The Jewish nationalist Judah ben-Hezekiah, headquartered in Sepphoris, had led another revolt upon Herod's death, however. Publius Quinctilius Varus,[6] then governor of Syria, ordered the complete destruction of the city and the enslavement or slaughter of its population. The order was carried out by his friend Crispus. Varus then ordered the destruction of dozens of cities and towns throughout Palestine, and crucified at least two thousand rebels. The city's ruins and its handful of survivors passed to the control of Antipas.

4. Despite his many monstrous acts, Herod went on to bring a number of improvements to the land, including countless public works, highways, and buildings. His crowning architectural achievement was the rebuilding of the temple in Jerusalem. While he did it for the wrong reason — not to honor God, but to curry the favor of the Jews, who hated him — it was nonetheless a splendid gift to Judaism. This magnificent building was so grand and beautiful that it even eclipsed Solomon's temple of a thousand years before. He earned, perhaps with some justification, the epithet "the Great."

5. It was Antipas who beheaded John the Baptist and presided over part of Jesus' trial. He had the title of tetrarch ("Ruler of a Fourth"), implying that he was one of four rulers of a divided kingdom. This ancient Roman concept no longer was restricted to four, however — Herod's kingdom was divided in three, even though the term "tetrarch" was still used.

6. This is the same Publius Quinctilius Varus who, because of sheer incompetence, lost three Roman legions (about eighteen thousand men) in the battle of Teutobergerwald in Germany five years later in 9 CE. Because of this, Rome lost all her holdings east of the Rhine, and never again regained full control of that area. Varus fell on his own sword as the battle neared its end. His father had been one of the assassins of Julius Caesar.

Antipas, rather than abandoning Sepphoris, decided to rebuild it as his Galilean showcase and established it as his capital. He laid it out and built it beautifully, based on the best architecture and customs of Rome, a place that he loved and admired. The Jewish historian Flavius Josephus described it as the "ornament of all Galilee." Josephus, a knowledgeable military man, also described it as "the strongest city in Galilee." There was a well-planned garrison there, and in the heart of the city were public buildings and private mansions that rivaled those of any well-established Roman city. On the edge of town was a theater carved out of the hillside, where Sepphoran citizens could go to be entertained by plays and orations. The streets of the city were laid out in an orderly grid, and were paved with the latest technology with crushed limestone. There were two markets, the "Upper" and "Lower Market," one selling textiles and hard goods, and the other a wide variety of foods. Public baths were an important part of Roman culture, and Sepphoris had several. There were also smaller baths that were rented out to private groups. There is one document that records the rental of a bath for a year to a group of Jews. Since the new larger city could no longer rely on rainwater cisterns for its water supply, a complex system of aqueducts was built to bring in water from the springs east of the city. An impressive part of this project was the digging of a 700-foot-long underground reservoir a mile away from the city. Sepphoris was located on top of a hill, so it had a commanding view of approaching danger. The light from lamps and cooking fires must have been an impressive sight on the dark Palestinian nights, and the city could be seen for miles. It might well have been of Sepphoris that Jesus was thinking when he said, "A city set on a hill cannot be hidden."

In 20 CE Antipas built a new city on the west shore of the Sea of Galilee. He named it Tiberias (after the emperor Tiberius), renamed the lake the Sea of Tiberias, and moved his capital there. In 61 CE Herod Agrippa II restored Sepphoris and moved his capital back there.

The social structure of Sepphoris was according to the common pattern of the times, stratified by wealth and birth. Most of the Jewish elite were supporters of Herod, on whom they depended for their positions of privilege. (It was significantly unhealthy to be an enemy of either Herod or the emperor.) These were the "rich" against whom Jesus so often railed. The city also had more than its share of the lowest subclasses, including slaves, beggars, prostitutes, and lepers.

Archaeology has confirmed documents of the times that indicate that the majority of Sepphorans were Jewish. Of those who had any significant influence, however, the vast majority were supportive of the Romans, or at least capitulated to them completely. For this reason most other Galilean Jews had little love or respect for the Sepphorans. When the Jewish rebellion took place in the late first century CE, the Sepphoran Jews appealed to Rome for protection. In 66 CE they welcomed General Titus Flavius Sabinus Vespasianus (who would soon become the emperor Vespasian), and asked his help. He sent a full legion (six thousand men and one thousand cavalry) to defend the city, and when the rest of Palestine was destroyed by his son Titus in 70 CE, Sepphoris was spared.

Archaeologists have found no first-century synagogues in Sepphoris, but contemporary writings indicate that most of the population was Jewish, and there is no doubt that there were synagogues there in Jesus' time. There is physical evidence of synagogues in the pre-Herodian city, and two fifth-century ones have been found. Even though the region was strongly pagan and Sepphoran Jews were for the most part capitulators to Rome, they nevertheless worshiped in accord with the Jewish Law and traditions. Beneath the floors of most of the Jewish houses there are remains of *miqvaoth*, Jewish ritual baths.

The rebuilding of Sepphoris took many years, and it required the labors of skilled craftsmen from all over the region. Joseph was a carpenter, and Nazareth would have provided only enough work for a carpenter to eke out a scanty living.[7] It is highly likely that he, like other craftsmen from Galilee, often took on jobs in Sepphoris. It was only a little over an hour's walk from his home, and that would not have been at all an unreasonable distance to travel for a day's work in those times. As was the custom, as soon as Jesus was old enough to begin to apprentice (about the age of nine or ten), he would have accompanied Joseph on his jobs. It is highly likely that Jesus made many trips to Sepphoris as a child, and probably often stayed there for several days at a time. No righteous father would have missed the opportunity to have his son taught in the synagogues there, so it is likely that Jesus received a significant portion of his early religious education in Sepphoris. He also had the opportunity to observe Roman culture, an experience that most Jewish children never had other than to see the occasional Roman soldier or petty official. He might also have picked

7. It is entirely possible that Joseph and Jesus were not carpenters but stonemasons. The word that Matthew and Luke use is *tekton*, which means "worker in hard materials" or "sculptor." Stonemasonry would have been a much-needed skill in the rebuilding of Sepphoris, while carpentry was not a common craft in Galilee because of the scarcity of wood.

up a bit of Latin and Greek, which would have been common languages there.[8] Thus, Sepphoris may well have played a significant role in the development of Jesus' cosmopolitan awareness, a trait that was rare in those provincial times.

Sepphoris, because of its favor with Rome, survived Titus's destruction of Palestine in 70 CE. It also seems to have survived the destruction of the second revolt in 132 CE. The city prospered for several more centuries, becoming a major center of both Jewish and Christian learning. By the fourth century CE, as the Roman Empire decayed, Sepphoris slowly declined into insignificance. It remains today only as the small Arab village of Safuriyya, and as an important archaeological site which has just begun to be seriously explored.

8. Latin was the "vulgar" language, that of the common people of Rome. Greek was the international language of the time, much as English is today — educated people all over the Mediterranean world spoke it. The Roman upper classes spoke Greek among themselves, while the soldiers (except the highest officers) would have spoken Latin.

# Shechem

The city of Shechem played a key role in a number of biblical events, and stood second only to Jerusalem as a religious center of ancient Judaism, being more important even than Bethel. It is located in the central hill country about thirty miles north of Jerusalem and six miles southeast of Samaria, in the valley between Mount Ebal on the north and Mount Gerazim on the south. The site today is a mound known as Tell Balata. It was strategically located at the convergence of several east-west and north-south trade routes, had a generous water supply from a spring at the edge of the mound, and abutted rich farmland in the valley. The site was on a shoulder at the lower slope of Mount Ebal (*Shechem* is Hebrew for "shoulder"), and thus it was open to attack from three sides. Because of this, massive fortifications were built very early in the city's development.

One of the things that made Shechem so important a religious site was that when Abraham entered Canaan, the first place he visited was Shechem. He built an altar there, and there God made the promise, "To your offspring I will give this land" (Gen. 12:7). There also Abraham's grandson Jacob settled down temporarily outside the Canaanite city, and at first had an amicable relationship with the city's people. Soon, however, Jacob's daughter Dinah was raped by the prince of Shechem, whose name was also Shechem. Receiving no satisfaction from the city authorities, Jacob's people attacked Shechem, killing Prince Shechem and his father King Hamor and then sacking the city (Gen. 34). Jacob, whose household had reverted to paganism, buried all their idols and magic talismans there and rededicated his household to God (Gen. 35:1-5). Following the Exodus, Joseph's body was brought out of Egypt (Exod. 13:19) and buried at Shechem in a burial plot that Jacob had purchased (Josh. 24:32).

The two mountains bracketing the city, Ebal and Gerazim, had great religious significance at various times in the region's history. Shortly before his death, Joshua built an altar and held a major covenant renewal ceremony at the base of Mount Ebal, with half the people standing at the base of Mount Gerazim and half at Mount Ebal. There he reviewed the entire Law as it had been given to Moses, and reaffirmed Israel's commitment to the Mosaic Covenant. He then gave his farewell address (Josh. 24:1-28).

Two centuries later, after Rehoboam ascended his father Solomon's throne, he was anointed king in Jerusalem. He then went to Shechem to be anointed again there (1 Kings 12:1). This was doubtless to emphasize that he was the king of the entire United Monarchy, not just of the south. The southern tribes were firm monarchists, but the ten northern tribes had strong anti-monarchical tendencies. Soon after Rehoboam's ascension Jeroboam waged a revolution that resulted in the division of the monarchy into two, Israel in the north, which accepted Jeroboam as its king, and Judah in the south, which remained loyal to Rehoboam and the Davidic dynasty. Jeroboam established Shechem as his capital, and immediately encouraged pagan worship there. A few years after the division of the United Monarchy Samaritanism, a corrupted form of Judaism, began to flourish in the northern kingdom. The Samaritans revered Mount Ebal instead of Mount Sinai as "The Mountain of God,"[1] maintaining that it was there that God had given the Law.

Shechem was founded as a village sometime around 3500 BCE, although there was nothing of significance at the site until about 1800 BCE when a fortified city was built there by the Canaanites. It reached its height of prosperity during the Hyksos period, around 1700 to 1550 BCE.[2] During this time the fortifications were greatly strengthened, the earlier walls were filled in, and a fortress-temple was built on top of them. Soon after 1550 BCE the city was destroyed; it is not clear by whom, but it was probably the Egyptian forces of Amhose I, the pharaoh who led the revolt that expelled the Hyksos from Egypt and drove them back toward Syria. About 1450 BCE Shechem, including its massive wall and temple-fortress, was rebuilt. At some point in about the twelfth century BCE it fell into Israelite hands, but seems to have been undamaged in the process. This indicates that it probably surrendered to the Israelite forces with little resistance.

Although it was a major religious shrine because of its association with the patriarchs and the tomb of Joseph, it remained politically unimportant with only a few changes until it was selected by Jeroboam to be the capital of the northern kingdom of Israel in the late tenth century BCE. The

---

1. The modern-day sect of Samaritans still revere it as such, and on the Day of Atonement each year they hold their rites and ceremonies on Mount Gerazim, looking over to where Joshua built the altar on Mount Ebal.

2. The Hyksos were a northern Semitic people who conquered most of Palestine and eventually conquered Egypt, holding it for about 150 years until they were defeated and expelled by the Egyptians. During this time Palestine, including Shechem, was considered a part of Egypt.

area, although technically Jewish, was already rife with pagan and idolatrous worship, and Jeroboam exacerbated the problem through his own practice and encouragement of paganism. This made the city hateful to the Levitical Jews, even though they honored the patriarchal shrines there.

After the capital was moved from Shechem the city began to deteriorate, and around 722 BCE it was destroyed by the Assyrians when they conquered Israel. It was not rebuilt as a city, but squatters and nomads eventually settled there permanently, and Shechem served as nothing more than a village of farmers and shepherds for almost four centuries. As the Samaritan sect grew in the area they focused on Shechem, and with the advent of the Hellenistic influence in the late fourth century BCE the village was revived and thrived as a Samaritan shrine. There is a continuous record of Seleucid (Graeco-Syrian) coinage there from 325 to 108 BCE. When the Maccabaean revolt drove out the Seleucids, the Judean high priest John Hyrcanus destroyed Shechem and all its pagan shrines, and at that point the town ceased to exist.[3]

In 72 CE the Roman emperor Titus founded a new Roman city on the site of Shechem, in honor of his father, the previous emperor, Vespasian. Vespasian was of the minor nobility, of the ancient Flavian family, but by becoming emperor he had elevated the Flavians to the highest social rank. Titus named the city Flavia Neopolis, "Flavia the New City." It thrived for many centuries, being generally known only as Neopolis. By the time the Arab Muslims captured it in 636 CE, the name had become corrupted to Nablus. Today it is more commonly known as Nablus. Modern Nablus is a major commercial, industrial, and agricultural center in the West Bank. It manufactures a soap made from olive oil, which has been a Nablus specialty for over 250 years, and it is also famous for its goldsmiths and pastries.

3. Some believe that Sychar, where Jesus met the Samaritan woman (John 4:5), was the same as Shechem, although most scholars reject this. There is no record of any habitation in Tell Balata after 108 BCE, and the only signs of any Roman occupation are a few relics indicating that Roman troops passed through the region. Sychar may have been a village nearby.

# Shiloh

Shiloh was a town of little political or commercial importance, but with huge religious significance to the Jews. Its location is recorded in Judges 21:19, making it reasonably sure that it was at the site of the modern Seilun, a ruin about eight miles north of Bethel. There was a heavily fortified city there in the middle Bronze Age (about 2100-1550 BCE). It was either destroyed or abandoned after that, but the site seems to have been a shrine to which offerings and sacrifices were brought during the fifteenth century BCE. This would have been pagan worship, as the Hebrews were still in Egyptian slavery at that time. An Iron Age settlement appeared there in the twelfth century, but it was destroyed by fire in about 1050 BCE. This might have been done by the Philistines following the Battle of Ebenezer (1 Sam. 4:1-3), after the ark of the covenant[1] had been retrieved from Shiloh (1 Sam. 4:4). There was a small settlement on the site from that time through the time of the Roman occupation, after which it appears to have been abandoned.

Shiloh was the site of the Tent of Meeting[2] during the early stages of Joshua's conquest of Canaan (Josh. 18:1), and during the period of the Judges it was the primary religious center. The Israelites always carried the ark of the covenant with them into battle, and when they were not in battle it was kept originally at Bethel, and later at Shiloh. By the high priest Eli's time in the twelfth century BCE, a proper temple stood in place of Joshua's tent shrine at Shiloh. It was in this temple that the prophet Samuel grew up under Eli's tutelage. No archaeological relics have been found to confirm the existence of this temple, but this does not mean that it did not exist. While there is no biblical record of its destruction, there is archaeological

---

1. The ark of the covenant was the great chest built by Moses and Aaron to contain the stone tablets of the Law that Moses brought down from Mount Sinai. Its eventual resting place was in Solomon's temple in Jerusalem. At the time of the Babylonian conquest in the sixth century BCE, it was lost. Some believe that it still exists, hidden in a long-forgotten place somewhere in the labyrinth of caves and passageways in the rock below where the temple stood.

2. Tent meetings and revivals in tents were a very common occurrence among the early American Baptists. This is why such a large number of Baptist churches are named "Shiloh."

The cistern of Shiloh remains to mark the town that served as the religious center of Israel during the period of the Judges. By the twelfth century BCE, the temple where the prophet Samuel grew up stood in Shiloh.

Photo credit: Erich Lessing/Art Resource, NY

evidence of later massive destruction at Shiloh. This is consistent with the Bible's references to Shiloh as an example of the people's wickedness (Ps. 78:60-61 et al.). As has been noted, this destruction may have occurred in the wars with the Philistines. They captured the ark at the Battle of Ebenezer, when Eli's sons Phinehas and Hophni were killed (the news of which killed Eli) (1 Sam. 4:17-18). The ark was recovered a few years thereafter, after the Philistines suffered a terrible plague. Blaming their ill fortune on the ark, they returned it to the Israelites.

After the destruction of Shiloh, the center of the priesthood was moved to Nob, and Shiloh ceased to be a shrine or place of sacrifice. Several later biblical references indicate that there was still some kind of settlement at Shiloh, but it was never again a place of any particular significance.

# Sidon

It is difficult to examine the city of Sidon without also considering Phoenicia (also called Sidonia), the federation of independent city-kingdoms of which Sidon was a member. For information on Phoenicia's origins and nature, I refer the reader to the section on Phoenicia (p. 163).

Sidon, along with Tyre and Byblos, was a major seaport with two deep harbors. Since it was only about fifty miles west of Damascus, it was a major hub for commerce between Syria and the other Mediterranean nations. The Phoenicians earned the reputation of being the best seamen in the world. Sidon had a particular advantage in that there was a string of small islands just outside the harbors. This served not only as a breakwater to provide calm waters in the harbors, but also as a windbreak, shifting the winds and currents in several predictable routes. Because of this, ships could maneuver into whatever wind and current direction they needed to set sail for their destination. The region inland of Sidon was a fertile plain that provided excellent agriculture. This also enriched the city, which became a major exporter by sea of agricultural produce. The city was famous for its fishing industry, and for metalworking and glass-blowing. Throughout its history, from ancient times right into New Testament times, the primary religion of Sidon was worship of Eshmun, the god of healing. There was a huge temple to him in the middle of the city, where there was also extensive worship of Melkart, Ashtoreth, and the Baals.

Archaeological research in Sidon is very limited, because the thriving Lebanese city of Saïda rests directly atop the ruins of the ancient city. (The city was also badly damaged during the Arab-Israeli conflicts in the early 1980s.) It is not known with certainty when Sidon was originally settled, but excavations nearby indicate habitation in the fourth millennium BCE. It is mentioned in Genesis 10:19 as the northernmost city in Canaan. At some time around the fifteenth century BCE, while Phoenicia was still under Egyptian rule and Sidon professed loyalty to Egypt, the city allied itself with the rebel Amorites in order to try to gain control over the neighboring city-states, particularly Tyre. While this was never entirely successful, it was not seriously blocked by the Egyptians because the Hyksos rule in Egypt fell at about that same time. The turmoil weakened the Phoenicians enough, however, that when the Philistines invaded at the end of the thirteenth century BCE Sidon's resistance was insufficient, and the Philistines plundered the city. Many of the people of Sidon fled to Tyre for protection.

The Philistines were a Hellenistic people, most likely having originated in Crete and the Aegean. They were known commonly as the "Sea People," and they eventually migrated throughout the whole of Palestine,[1] well inland to the east and as far north as Phoenicia. They spread themselves too thin, however, and their strength soon waned on the outskirts of these regions. Their power eventually was concentrated in the southwest of Palestine in the territories surrounding the area that is now known as the Gaza Strip, and their influence deep inland and in Phoenicia was minimal. By the twelfth century BCE Sidon had fully recovered from Philistine incursions and the flagging Egyptian control, and it became the leading city of the Phoenician alliance. It was during this period that the Egyptian influence became weak enough that the Phoenician cities, under Sidonian leadership, managed to throw off the Egyptian yoke completely and become independent. Sidon was able to resist Israelite incursion (Judg. 10:12), but was not able to protect Laish (later to become Dan) in the upper Jordan (Judg. 18:7, 27).

The Phoenicians met strong Assyrian opposition to their expansion under Tiglath-Pileser I, who, although he did not invade Phoenicia, intimidated the port cities to the extent that they paid him tribute (not unlike the Mafia "protection racket"). The only city that was exempt was Sidon, because Sidon was useful to the Assyrians as the ruling city. It was in Sidon's interest to assist Assyria in exacting the tributes from the other cities, not only because it kept the city exempt from tribute, but also because the pseudo-alliance with Assyria enhanced Sidon's position of strength over the others. By the end of the eleventh century BCE, however, Sidon's leadership had slipped, and Tyre, under the rule of Hiram, became the controlling city-state of the Phoenician confederation.[2] In 880 BCE the Assyrian king Ashurnasirpal II claimed Sidon as a vassal and demanded tribute from it as well; and in 841 Shalmaneser III descended on the region and exacted tribute from Tyre, Sidon, and the northern kingdom of Israel. This is depicted in cuneiform and carvings on the Balawat temple gates, now in the British Museum.

1. The name Palestine is a corruption of Philistine.
2. It was at this time that Hiram and David became allies and then personal friends, and a few years later that Hiram aided Solomon in building the temple at Jerusalem.

Despite its woes at the hands of the Assyrians, Sidon remained a wealthy and prosperous city until about 739 BCE, when the Sidonians became tired of paying tribute and rebelled. Tiglath-Pileser III marched on Phoenicia and captured Tyre and Sidon and forced their submission. A few years later they rebelled again, and this time Sennacherib attacked. As he approached the city the king, Luli, fled to Cyprus and died in exile there. After Sennacherib's death Sidon rebelled once more, and this time the Assyrians had had enough. Sennacherib's son and successor, Esarhaddon, destroyed the city and slaughtered or enslaved most of its population. He then rebuilt the city at a new location nearby as Kar-Esarhaddon, and populated it with prisoners from Elam and Babylonia.

With the decline of Assyria, Sidon rose again, regained its independence, and eventually absorbed Kar-Esarhaddon. Its troubles were not over, however. In the early sixth century BCE Sidon got caught in the middle of a dispute between Egypt and Babylonia, and in 587 BCE it was captured by Nebuchadrezzar II. It fell into Persian hands when Cyrus conquered Babylonia in 539 BCE, but this turned out to be a much easier yoke. The Persians appreciated Sidon's importance as a port and the Phoenician seafaring skills, and made the most of them. Under Xerxes I, the greater part of the Persian fleet was built at Sidon and manned by Phoenicians.

Sidon remained under Persian rule, but in 350 BCE it allied with Egypt to lead a rebellion against Artaxerxes III. At first the city had the upper hand, but Egypt betrayed them and not only failed to provide the promised support but evidently even helped the Persians. Artaxerxes burned the city to the ground and put forty thousand Sidonians to the sword. Not only was the city in ruins, but the spirit of the Sidonians was broken. The fortifications were never rebuilt. Seventeen years later, in 333 BCE, when Alexander the Great approached the city, Sidon surrendered without lifting a sword, and then helped Alexander take Tyre. After Alexander's death his general Ptolemy gained control of Phoenicia and rebuilt and refortified Sidon. In 197 BCE it fell into the hands of the Seleucids. In 64 BCE Pompey the Great conquered the whole western part of the Middle East for Rome, and Sidon became a city of the Roman province of Syria. The Romans made it a free city, which meant that it had local autonomy with its own senate, and was free of much of the oppressive Roman taxation. It was of value to Rome because of its importance as a port, and because the Phoenicians still had great skill as seamen.

There are twenty-three references to Sidon in the Old Testament, and eleven in the New. It played a significant role in many of the Old Testament prophecies, particularly those regarding the impending threat of the Assyrians and Babylonians. It was also important in New Testament times. Jesus visited there, and it was near Sidon that he healed the Syro-Phoenician woman's daughter (Mark 7:24-30). Herod Agrippa I acted as a mediator in a squabble between Tyre and Sidon, receiving ambassadors from them at Caesarea (Acts 12:20). When Paul was on his way to Rome to be tried by Nero, his ship stopped at Sidon, and he was allowed to visit friends there (Acts 27:3). By New Testament times Sidon had become known as a center of philosophical learning, and most of its inhabitants were Greek or thoroughly Hellenized Semites.

Today Sidon survives as the Lebanese city of Saida. Its most popular tourist attraction is the ruins of a crusader castle.

# Sinai

The name Sinai refers to two things, the Sinai Peninsula and the Holy Mountain of God. The Sinai Peninsula is the triangular peninsula between the Gulf of Suez and the Gulf of Aqabah that joins Africa with the Middle East. It has a harsh and uninviting terrain and climate, making it an effective buffer zone between African Egypt and the Middle East. Throughout most of history it was a part of Egypt.[1] In the Bible, the distinction is made between what is called the Desert of Sinai and Mount Sinai. The location of both is something of an enigma, because the Desert of Sinai clearly does not mean the whole peninsula, but only an undefined portion of the interior desert in which Mount Sinai was located. The Old Testament often calls this the Wilderness of Sin,[2] and both the peninsula and mountain derive their names from this. Mount Sinai is also called Mount Horeb in the Old Testament, but not in the New. Neither the Desert of Sinai nor Mount Sinai has ever been specifically located. There are several mountains in the interior that various scholars have identified as Mount Sinai, and there are strong arguments pro and con for each. One of the favorites, however, is what is now called Jabal Mûsá (Arabic for "Mountain of Moses"), a mountain about twenty-five miles north-northwest of the southern point of the peninsula. Ancient tradition identifies it as the site of Mount Sinai, and its imposing granite scarps fit the descriptions in the Bible. Notwithstanding, the true location may never be positively known. The book of Exodus (19:18; 20:18) speaks of smoke and fire at the top of the mountain, suggesting that it might have been volcanic. There are no sites in Sinai, however, where there was any volcanic activity at any time even remotely close to when the Hebrews were in the region.

According to the book of Exodus (19:1) the Hebrews[3] reached Sinai

---

1. In ancient times Egypt's borders varied, depending on the political situation at any given time, from most of North Africa and Palestine as far as central Syria, to approximately the same borders as the country has today. The entire Sinai Peninsula was captured by Israel in the Six Days' War in 1967, but by a treaty of 1979 it was returned to Egypt, with the last Israeli troops withdrawing in 1982.

2. "Sin" here has nothing to do with moral transgression. The Wilderness of Sin was a region holy to the cult of the Egyptian moon god Sin or Shin (also known as Nanna).

3. It is customary to refer to them as Hebrews until after the covenant was sealed at

three months after leaving Egypt. This Sinai refers to the interior desert, not the peninsula itself, which they probably entered after only a few days. They camped at the base of the mountain, while Moses went to the top to commune with God. There he received the Ten Commandments (and by tradition the rest of the Mosaic Law). Upon returning to the people, after the incident with the golden calf (Exod. 32), he built an altar and made sacrifice, binding the Hebrew people to God as one people. This is the first indication of any real sense of unity among the twelve tribes, the descendants of Jacob's twelve sons. While many scholars reject the authenticity of this story, it is one of the most deeply ingrained of all the traditions of the Jewish people. One of the reasons for rejecting it is that there is no archaeological evidence of the forty-year trek through Sinai before entering Canaan. It is argued that thousands of people living in the same area for forty years[4] would have had to leave some traces, none of which have ever been found. On the other hand, the Bible is clear that they wandered about, never settling in any one place and never building. About all that they would have left behind would be decomposable waste and the remains of campfires, and these do not leave traces that would last twenty-five hundred years until they could be discovered by modern archaeologists. The tremendously strong Old Testament emphasis on the significance of Mount Sinai and the importance of the tradition as a keystone of the Jewish faith lend a powerful note of authenticity to the story.

---

Sinai. There is evidence that by the time they left Egypt, most had lost any contact with the simple religion of their ancestors Abraham, Isaac, and Jacob, and had fallen completely into the religion of the Egyptians, and that even those who retained the ancestral faith practiced it only primitively and with pagan corruptions. This is why they demanded that Aaron make them images of the old gods when they became frightened and discouraged in the desert (Exod. 33:1). After the giving of the Law and the sealing of the covenant, the Hebrews embraced an essentially new religion, and thereafter are called Jews.

4. Forty is a Hebrew idiom for a very large amount, and was understood to be an exaggeration. It is rather like the modern expression "I've told you a thousand times." Thus we have the forty days and nights of Noah's rain, the forty years of wandering of the Hebrews, and Jesus' forty days of fasting in the desert. The Jews would have understood this as simply meaning "a tremendously long time."

# Smyrna

Smyrna was a prosperous city in the Roman province of Asia, located on the Aegean coast of what today is Asiatic Turkey. The first settlement in the vicinity was a very ancient Greek colony, but it was captured and destroyed by Lydians sometime around 6000 BCE, and was not resettled again until the late fourth century BCE. Sometime around 300 BCE the Thracian king Lysimachus,[1] when he was briefly also king of Macedonia, refounded the city on its present site. With an ideal location as a port on the Aegean, and a plentiful supply of food from the fertile farmlands inland, it flourished and became a major commercial center and one of the most prosperous cities in Asia Minor. It allied itself with Rome in the middle years of the Republic, long before Rome was a major influence in world affairs. During the Roman imperial period Smyrna retained its loyalty to Rome, and thus received many favors. The Romans assisted it in becoming an outstandingly beautiful city, and helped in the construction of several magnificent public buildings. Smyrna not only survived but prospered during the Byzantine and Ottoman periods. Today it is known as Izmir, one of Turkey's most important ports and industrial cities.

Smyrna has a particular religious significance to Christians. Christianity arrived there very early, probably brought by missionaries from Ephesus (Acts 19:10), and it apparently grew rapidly and remained faithful to the teachings of the early evangelists in spite of serious opposition and even persecution from the Jews (Rev. 2:9) and later the Romans. Smyrna and Philadelphia are the only two of the "seven churches in Asia" (Rev. 1:4ff.) that are not chastised for their shortcomings, but are praised and encouraged to bear up under their tribulations. Smyrna's last notable event in Christian history was in about 155 CE, when Saint Polycarp, the eighty-six-year-old Bishop of Smyrna, refused to recant and was martyred there.

---

1. Lysimachus was one of Alexander the Great's generals who vied with the other generals, particularly Ptolemy, Seleucus, and Antipater, for a piece of the empire when Alexander died. He managed to take the regions around the Aegean, but did not hold them for long.

# Sodom and Gomorrah

Sodom and Gomorrah are two of several cities believed by many to have been located in southern Palestine where the Jordan broadens into a fertile plain just before it flows into the Dead Sea. The other cities in the plain were Admah, Zeboiim, and Bela (Zoar) (Gen. 14:2), but we can only hypothesize about their location and history. Many other scholars believe that the ruins of Sodom and Gomorrah lie under the water at the southern tip of the Dead Sea, where there is also a plain. Both of these possible locations are borne up by several descriptive passages in Genesis, many using geographic terms whose meaning is no longer clearly understood, such as the "Plain of Jordan." It is not known whether the ancients considered the Dead Sea to be part of the Jordan, in which case the plain at the southern tip could also be considered part of the Plain of Jordan. To add to the confusion, Genesis indicates that the whole region of the Dead Sea was fertile and well-watered until the destruction of Sodom and Gomorrah, after which it became desolate. This claim of fertility is not supported by geological evidence, however.

The destruction of these cities (Gen. 19) is also something of an enigma, although there is a logical explanation for it. The conventional wisdom of the time was that their residents were very evil. The Bible accuses them of corruption and sexual perversion, particularly homosexuality. Their destruction, therefore, was God's judgment on them. However that may be, the means of the destruction was "fire and brimstone." The region around the Dead Sea is prone to earthquakes, and beneath the area there are large oil and natural gas deposits. It is perfectly reasonable that an earthquake destroyed the city and ruptured the rock that capped a gas or oil deposit. With a rush of natural gas meeting a spark or cooking fire, the entire city would have been engulfed in a searing holocaust. The coastal area could have then sunk as a result of the earthquake, plunging the ruins under the waters of the Dead Sea.[1]

1. Werner Keller, in *The Bible as History,* takes it even a step further, postulating that Lot's wife, looking back at the horror, might have died of fear. Such a cataclysm would have stirred up great turbulence in the Dead Sea waters, and when this happens, the spray can be carried for miles on the wind. When it lands on any object in that arid climate it evaporates instantly, leaving the object encrusted with salt. This would explain Lot's wife being turned into "a pillar of salt" (Gen. 19:26).

# Succoth

The name Succoth refers to two places, whose names derive from the Hebrew *sukkoth*, "booths."[1] One of the sites is a city of the tribe of Gad (Josh. 13:27). It was near two important sites associated with the building of Solomon's temple, the quarry at Zarethan[2] where the stone was cut and dressed and the clay grounds in the Jordan plain between Succoth and Zarethan. These clay grounds were where Huram (Hiram) the artisan built the foundry that cast all the massive bronze-works of the Temple (1 Kings 7:46). Succoth was the home of a large number of the workers in both places.

The other Succoth was the Hebrews' first stop in their journey out of Egypt (Exod. 12:37). Many scholars believe that it was the same place as Pithom, where the Hebrew slaves had been severely oppressed in an earlier building project (Exod. 1:11). It was from here that God guided them with a pillar of cloud in the day and a pillar of fire in the night (Exod. 13:21). This Succoth was something of a portal between African Egypt and the Middle East, in a wadi near a mound called Tell el-Maskhuta. Egyptian documents (especially the Papyri Anastasi V and VI) indicate that it was a place through which runaway slaves and refugees commonly passed, probably because it was well off the usual routes of passage.

1. "Succoth" is also the name of a Jewish feast, often called the Feast of Tabernacles, that each autumn commemorates the Hebrews' forty years of wandering in the desert, living in tents or "booths." It is also a harvest festival, tied with the early Canaanite and Israelite custom of remaining in the fields during the harvest, living in booths or small huts.

2. Zeredatha in the King James translation.

# Tarsus

Tarsus, the birthplace of Saint Paul, is one of the oldest cities in the world. Its earliest detected settlement goes back to the late Stone Age, possibly as early as 5000 BCE. The city still exists today in Turkey, and still bears the name Tarsus.

The first settlement was a fortified town on the Cydnus River in Cilicia in Asia Minor. It had become an important trading center by 2300 BCE, when Troy was first beginning to flourish. The Hittites recorded its existence as Tarša in the second millennium BCE, and there is evidence that it bore this name from the beginning. It may have been the capital of the Hittite province of Kizzuwatna, and was certainly under the control of Hittite Anatolia.[1] The city was located by the sheltered harbor of Rhegma, whereby Tarsus had an easy access to all the Levant[2] and the Semitic countries, and developed a flourishing maritime trade.

Around 1200 BCE the city was raided and destroyed by maritime marauders. It was resettled, according to Tarsian legend, by Mycenaean Greeks from the Trojan War. Priam's Troy (the Troy of the *Iliad*)[3] fell at about that time, so there may be some grain of truth to the legend. At any rate, the city was resettled, grew, and flourished again.

In 832 BCE the Assyrians under Shalmaneser III captured Anatolia, but their conquest did not extend as far as Tarsus, which continued a successful maritime trade. In 698 BCE, however, Sennacherib took the city and looted it clean. Archaeological evidence indicates that for the next two centuries there was a continual inflow of Greek settlers into Tarsus, which prospered during that period of immigration.

Little is known of what happened to Tarsus when the Assyrians fell to the Medes and Babylonians in 609 BCE. There is evidence that it was ruled

---

1. Anatolia and Asia Minor are synonymous terms, referring to the portion of Turkey between the Mediterranean and the Black Sea.

2. "The Levant" means all the countries of the eastern Mediterranean coast from Turkey, through Palestine, to Egypt.

3. This would be what archaeologists call Troy VIIa, which is believed to have been destroyed by a war. That particular level of Troy is probably the basis of the Homeric legend of the Trojan War.

by native princes for some time, and that this local rule continued even after the Persians annexed the region into their empire. Inscriptions on coins indicate that it was under Persian control by 401 BCE, and that it was administered by a Persian satrap. There is no reason to believe that the city did not continue as an important trading center during this time.

Some unknown event turned the Persians against Tarsus, and in 333 they tried to burn the city, but it was saved by Alexander the Great. The probable explanation is that as Alexander approached Tarsus in his campaign against Persia, the Tarsians threw their allegiance to him against their old captors. Alexander stayed in Tarsus for several weeks recuperating from an illness that he supposedly got from bathing in the cold river.

After Alexander's death his general Seleucus wrested control of the territory extending from Asia Minor to what is now Pakistan. Not much is known of what happened to the city under Seleucid rule. Around 175 BCE its name was changed to "Antioch-on-the-Cydnus" in honor of the Seleucid king Antiochus IV Epiphanes. (He was the oppressor of Judea who was driven out by Judas Maccabaeus). In 171 BCE there was a minor revolt because Tarsus and the nearby city Mallus were to be given to one of the king's mistresses. This event is reported in 2 Maccabees 4:30. By the first century BCE the only remaining part of the crumbling Seleucid Empire was the province of Syria, which included Cilicia and thus Tarsus. In 67 BCE the Roman general Pompey defeated the Seleucids, annexed Cilicia as a Roman province, made the city its capital, and restored its name to Tarsus. In 50 BCE Cicero was appointed governor of Cilicia (perhaps to get him out of the way of Julius Caesar — they despised each other). The people loved him because of his gentle and liberal rule. Julius Caesar and Marc Antony were charmed by Tarsus, visiting frequently. Although Tarsus was not particularly important historically, one of the most spectacular events in the memory of the city was when Cleopatra, dressed as the goddess Aphrodite in full regalia, sailed her royal barge up the Cydnus River into Tarsus, where she first met Marc Antony, who refused to meet her on Egyptian soil. She claimed that he had done so, because her barge was Egyptian. They eventually became lovers. More important historically was the foundation of a university which produced many brilliant scholars, including Octavian's teacher and friend, the philosopher Athenodorus.

After Pompey's death a major political council met with Caesar at Tarsus, and the city assumed the name Iuliopolis ("City of Julius") in his honor. Cassius, who would become one of Caesar's assassins, was given civil authority over Cilicia, although he was not the official governor.

Shortly thereafter Caesar was assassinated, and Tarsus gave a significant amount of aid to Antony's army in opposition to Cassius. Cassius imposed a huge fine on the city, and then tried to collect it with brutal measures. When Antony regained power in the region he rewarded the city by exempting it from all taxes. After Augustus assumed power he restored the name of Tarsus and granted it all the rights of a free city. This meant that it had its own senate and could engage in international trade.

One of the city's important industries was the production of *cilicium*, a goat-hair fabric that was highly prized for the making of tents. As many of the inhabitants of the region were nomadic, tent-making was also an important industry, and Saint Paul (then Saul of Tarsus) was trained in the art (Acts 18:3). As the fertile fields outside the city produced excellent flax, linen-making was also a lucrative industry for the city.

It is not known how large a Jewish population there was in Tarsus, although Jews lived in all the major cities around the Mediterranean. The fact that most of the names were Greek means little, because in Hellenic cities like Tarsus most people used Greek names regardless of their ancestry.

Tarsus had a peaceful, prosperous, and largely uneventful history during most of the rest of Roman rule. There were occasionally local disturbances and economic challenges, but they were usually overcome and the city would continue comfortably. Tarsus was of military importance in the Parthian Wars in the third century CE. It fell to the Parthians (Iranians) in 260, but was soon recaptured by Rome. The emperor Julian the Apostate was buried in Tarsus in 363.

In later years the region was torn by East-West conflicts, among the cruelest of which were the Crusades. It was finally incorporated into the Ottoman Empire in the fourteenth century, remained Turkish after the fall of the Ottomans, and is still a Turkish city today.

# Thessalonica

The correct name of this city is Thessaloníki, meaning "Victory over Thessalia." Thessalia (Thessaly) was a vast plain adjacent to ancient Macedonia. In Greek mythology it was the home of the Centaurs and the land ruled by Jason (of the Argonauts and the Golden Fleece). By the time of Philip II of Macedon, Alexander the Great's father, Thessalia had become so bitterly oppressed by the tyrant Jason of Pherae and his successors that the people appealed to Philip for help. He attacked and conquered the country with the blessing of its populace, then annexed it to Macedon, more than doubling the size of his realm. He then founded the city of Thessalonica as a token of triumph — a symbol of Macedonia's having been thrust into a position of leadership in world affairs. The city not only prospered, it flourished, rapidly becoming one of the most important and wealthiest cities in the Macedonian Empire. It had a perfect location for international commerce, being situated on the Gulf of Thermaïkós at the intersection of the main trade route between Italy and the East, and the main route from the Aegean to the Danube. This gave it easy overland and sea access to the whole known world of the time. These routes remained major highways throughout Roman times and the Middle Ages, and as a result Thessalonica has been a prosperous and peaceful city from its creation in 344 BCE right up to modern times. Thessalonica was rather like a successful merchant who never gets involved in politics, carefully caters to the needs and wants of his customers, and avoids trouble at all cost. Because of this the city was never the focus of any wars, and made few significant contributions to culture or history. As a result it remained prosperous for two millennia regardless of who the ruling power might have been at any given time.

To Christians, what makes Thessalonica particularly important is the church that Saint Paul founded there. It was the first city to which he preached in which he was well received not only by large numbers of people but also by many socially prominent ones (Acts 17:4). His opponents, who had been able to silence him in other places by appealing to the ruling powers, failed to garner that influence in Thessalonica. They therefore resorted to trying to stir up mob violence, with only minimal success. The rulers of the city were trapped between their liking for Paul and the threat of the people, so they managed to urge Paul to leave the city with a minimum of discomfort to him, and to avoid trouble to his followers he left. He wrote two letters to the Thessalonian Christians. The first commends them for their dedication to the faith in the face of anti-Christian hostility and contains several doctrinal teachings. In the second, it seems clear that Paul had received reports that the Thessalonians, believing that the end was coming very soon, had stopped working and were focusing only on the end things. He urged them to be always prepared, but to cease spiritual laziness and continue meeting their secular and spiritual responsibilities.

Thessaloníki, also known as Salonika, still thrives today as a city and port in northern Greece.

# Thyatira

Thyatira was originally a frontier garrison in the west of Asiatic Turkey. It was built in the late fourth century BCE by Seleucus I, one of Alexander the Great's successors, to protect his western frontier. In the ongoing power struggle between Alexander's generals after his death, it eventually changed hands and became a protective fortress on the eastern frontier of Lysimachus's kingdom of Pergamum. In 133 BCE it fell into Roman hands. Thyatira was located on an important highway connecting the Hermus and Caicus valleys, and as a result it began to get involved in commerce and trading. It developed into an important manufacturing city whose main industries were dying, clothing manufacture, pottery, and brass-working. One of its specialties was the dying of cloth with a reddish-purple dye known as "Turkey red." It is extracted from the madder root and is still manufactured today in the area. It was of a similar hue to Tyrian purple, but vastly less expensive.[1] Saint Paul, when he was in Philippi, met the Thyatiran lady Lydia, a "seller of purple" (Acts 16:14). It is likely that she was an agent of a Thyatiran dyer, selling the popular purple woolens.

Thyatira's religious significance is that it was one of the "seven churches in Asia" of Revelation 1:11. John commends the Thyatiran Christians for their spiritual growth and the fidelity of many of them, but he also condemns them for listening to "that woman Jezebel," apparently a self-proclaimed prophetess who was leading them into heresy and immorality.

Thyatira thrived throughout the Roman, Byzantine, and Ottoman periods, and still stands today as the Turkish city of Akhisar.

---

1. Tyrian purple is a reddish-purple dye extracted from a rare mollusk shell found only off the coast of Tyre. It was so valuable that in some regions it was illegal for anyone but royalty to wear it. It has come to be associated with royalty, as is indicated in the expression "born to the purple." It even became the name of a late Byzantine emperor, Constantinus Porphyrogenitus, "Constantine Purpleborn." It is of a reddish hue, and should not be confused with the bluish-purple dye that was made from grapes and berries and was quite inexpensive.

# Tiberias

The city of Tiberias is mentioned only once in the Bible (John 6:23), primarily because it was founded only about five years before Jesus began his ministry. It was built by Herod Antipas and named after the Roman emperor Tiberius. Located on the southwest shore of the Sea of Galilee, which Antipas required be called the Sea of Tiberias, it was one of nine important cities around the sea, and the only one which is still an active city today.

In 20 CE Antipas decided to move his capital from Sepphoris, and to build a new capital city from scratch. It is not entirely clear why he chose to do this. He felt the hatred of the Jews in Sepphoris, although there is little indication that any of the Herods (with the possible exception of Herod Agrippa I) cared much what the Jews thought of them as long as it did not erode their favor among the Romans. Perhaps it was nothing more than that he so much enjoyed rebuilding Sepphoris from ruins that he decided to build another city just for the fun of it. Also, being an unconscionable sycophant to the Romans, he would have polished the emperor's apple by building a beautiful city and naming it after him. He chose the site for three reasons. First, it was by a high rocky crag that was readily accessible yet easily defensible and gave a commanding view of both the lake and the surrounding valleys. This was an ideal site for his palace, and yet the city below, also easily defensible, was on a level with the lake, giving ready access by boat to any of the other major cities on the Sea of Galilee. Second, it was at a point of convergence of several international highways, providing a powerful commercial advantage and easy mobility of military forces. Third, it was near a spring of hot mineral waters that was already well-known, and was a popular Roman spa and bath. There were also miles of fertile plains just to the north, guaranteeing a plentiful food supply.

From the Jewish point of view, the site of the city was an abomination. It included a large graveyard, which made the whole city ritually unclean. Any Jew entering the city would have to be ritually cleansed upon leaving it (a complex process that could take up to several days), and could not participate in Jewish worship or any other religious or social rituals during the period in which he was unclean. The west shore of the Sea of Galilee had a reputation of being an unsavory region, heavily populated by Gentiles and nonbelievers.

There is no record that Jesus ever visited Tiberias. As a faithful Jew he would have been loath to enter the city because of its uncleanness, although that is not likely to have stopped him if he had felt a reason to go there. The city was primarily populated by Gentiles — few Jews lived there, and those who did were probably those who did not take their religion very seriously. Antipas offered many enticements to Jews to populate the city, including free houses and land. Those who accepted were obviously willing to put their purses ahead of their religion, although some who moved there were forced to do so by extreme political or social pressure exerted on them by Antipas. Because Jesus dedicated his early ministry almost exclusively to faithful or repentant Jews, there was little call for him to go to Tiberias.

Much of the early history of Tiberias has been lost, mainly because of the extreme turmoil of a very rebellious Israel during the first and second centuries CE. It remained the capital of the Galilean tetrarchy until Herod Agrippa II moved the capital back to Sepphoris in about 61 CE. In the great rebellion of 66 to 70 CE, Tiberias was captured by the rebel leader Flavius Josephus,[1] who prepared for the inevitable onslaught of Roman troops. When the general Vespasian (who would soon become emperor) attacked the city, Josephus and the rebels opened the gates and surrendered. Because the city and fourteen surrounding villages had been given by Nero to Herod Agrippa II as a personal gift, and because the rebels did not resist, they were freed, and the city was allowed to remain under Jewish rule for another thirty years. Jerusalem and the temple were completely destroyed in 70 CE, and the Romans massacred thousands upon thousands of Jerusalem Jews. At that time the chief rabbis moved their seat of activity to Tiberias. Following the second Jewish revolt (100-135 CE), the emperor Hadrian decided to remove any Jewish influence in the city by repopulating it entirely with Gentiles. In spite of that a large Jewish population remained, and although their political influence was virtually nil, their scholarship became highly respected. Strangely enough, despite the original position that the city was unclean, Tiberias became an important Jewish center of scholarship.[2] In about 150 CE the Sanhedrin, the ruling body

---

1. This is the same Flavius Josephus who was a famed Jewish historian. He was both a historian (although his histories are strongly biased) and an accomplished general.

2. The rabbinical interpretation of the Law may have allowed that sufficient time had

of the Jewish theocracy, moved from Sepphoris to Tiberias. The Mishnah was compiled there in the third century CE, and the Talmud in the fifth. At some point in that period the Tiberian vowel pointing system was developed, marking a major move forward in the writing of Hebrew.[3] The first-millennium Jews considered Jerusalem, Hebron, Sepphoris, and Tiberias to be the four sacred cities in Palestine. The importance of Tiberias is highlighted by the fact that some of the greatest Jewish thinkers are buried there, including Rabbis Akiba, Judah the Prince, and Yahonan of the second century, and Rabbi Maimonides, the great Spanish theologian of the thirteenth century.

Because Tiberias has been an active city continuously since its founding, there has been little archaeological research there until recent times. In 1990 a full-scale dig was begun under the current city dump. This and other digs indicate that ancient Tiberias was a typical Roman-Jewish city, but much is yet to be learned of its physical details.

---

passed since the graveyard had been used that it was no longer a ritual necessity to consider the site unclean.

3. Until then, Hebrew was written with only consonants. Since the majority of Jews were literate and oral tradition was still extremely strong, this was not a major problem in earlier times. Reading the Hebrew Scriptures would be like reading Genesis 1:1 as "N TH BGNNG GD CRTD TH HVN ND TH RTH." If you knew what you were reading, this would be no real problem, but it would be quite difficult if it were an unknown text. The Tiberian vowel pointing system places dots and lines beneath the consonants to indicate the vowel that follows.

# Tirzah

The Song of Songs (6:4) extols Tirzah as one of the most beautiful cities in Samaria, the region southwest of the Sea of Galilee surrounding the city of Samaria. The city's ruins are in a mound called Tell el-Far'ah, about six miles northeast of Nablus (Shechem). Tirzah is at the head of the Wadi Far'ah, a dry riverbed along which passed the main trade route from Samaria to Nabatea on the east side of the Jordan. There was continuous settlement there from the late fourth millennium BCE until the rise of Nebuchadrezzar's Babylonia in the seventh century BCE. Tirzah was captured from the Canaanites by the Israelites in the thirteenth century BCE, and was given into the hands of the tribe of Manasseh (the descendants of Joseph's son). It was a prosperous city, although not particularly significant until the ninth century BCE, when Baasha, king of Israel, moved his capital there when the Judeans attacked the northern kingdom. When Baasha died his son Elah became king, and he was overthrown in a palace coup by Zimri. He, in turn, was overthrown by Omri, and died when he burned down his own palace while he was in it. The whole sordid story of the corruption of the pre-Omride kings in Tirzah can be found in 1 Kings 15:9–16:20; the kings of the Omride dynasty were not much better. In about 870 BCE, after reigning six years in Tirzah, Omri built Samaria and moved his capital there. One more Tirzah-based coup took place in about 752 BCE when Menahem came up from Tirzah and overthrew King Shallum, who had managed only a very brief reign in Samaria as king of the northern kingdom (2 Kings 15:13-14).

Archaeological digs have shown several levels of Tirzah in great detail. What is called Level III is in complete accord with the biblical accounts of the social problems in eighth-century Israel (see the section on Samaria, particularly p. 202, for more details). The city contained a huge administrative building — essentially a palace — surrounded by several large and lavish houses; separated from these were a large number of tiny, very poor houses, confirming the economic and social polarization of the society of Israel against which the prophets Amos and Hosea railed so strongly.

The city survived the Assyrian invasion and seems to have continued, although contributing nothing of importance, until the fall of the Assyrian

Empire at the end of the seventh century BCE. Tirzah was destroyed at that time, probably at the hand of Nebuchadrezzar's forces as they swept through on their way to the conquest of Judah. There is no evidence that it was ever rebuilt again.

# Tyre

It is difficult to examine the city of Tyre without also considering Phoenicia (also called Sidonia), the confederation of independent city-kingdoms of which Tyre was a member. For information on Phoenicia's origins and nature, I refer the reader to the section on Phoenicia (p. 163).

When they gained their independence from Egypt, the Phoenician cities prospered, and Tyre rose to prominence. Over the decades it vied with Sidon to be the ruling city of the Phoenician confederation. During the twelfth to the ninth centuries BCE the Phoenicians became the best merchants, craftsmen, and sailors in the ancient world. Their influence spread throughout the Mediterranean and extended to the Atlantic, and they established colonies all over the Mediterranean. Many nations vied to get Phoenician mercenaries to fight in their navies, and they hired Phoenician builders to erect great monuments. Some scholars believe that Stonehenge may have been built by hired Phoenician engineers, and there is evidence (but not strong enough to be compelling) that they may even have reached America.

There are indications that Tyre was a very ancient city, although little is known of its origins. The Greek historian Herodotus puts its foundation at the twenty-eighth century BCE, but more reliable evidence puts it closer to the fourteenth, about the time Egypt was losing its hold on Phoenicia. Tyre probably began as the town of Ushu on the mainland, and was likely started as a colony of Sidon. It expanded onto an island just off the coast, and that position made it easily defensible and able to control shipping between Palestine to the south and the other Phoenician cities to the north.

When the cities' rebellion against Egypt was increasing, Tyre remained loyal to Egypt. The Egyptians made several sorties into Phoenicia, but Tyre, because of its loyalty, was never harmed. In the thirteenth century Ramses II[1] marched as far as Berytus (Beirut), but again left Tyre unmolested. These forays weakened the other cities, and allowed Tyre to increase in strength until it became the ruling power by the time independence from Egypt had been achieved in 1100 BCE.

---

1. Many scholars believe that Ramses II was the reigning pharaoh at the time of the Exodus.

In about 1000 BCE King David joined the tribes of Israel into the United Monarchy, controlling a huge territory in the Middle East. He did not reach into Phoenicia, however. He developed a relationship with King Hiram (or Huram) of Tyre that seems to have been a personal friendship as well as a political alliance. Some scholars have suggested that Israel was a tributary of Tyre, but there is little evidence to support this claim. It is more likely that they simply developed a strong relationship of mutual help. When David's son Solomon ascended the throne, he dedicated himself to the building of a temple to God. He enlisted the aid of Hiram, who provided materials, skilled architects and builders, and craftsmen in exchange for wheat and oil, while Solomon provided money and labor.[2] Hiram provided a craftsman (also named Hiram, or Huram-abi)[3] who may have been the finest bronze-worker in the world at the time. His castings of the huge temple vessels and the two twenty-six-foot bronze entrance pillars would be considered extraordinary achievements even today.

In Tyre, King Hiram built a breakwater at the openings of the harbors, making them the best in the Mediterranean. He developed an active trade with Cyprus and Spain, and his navy was the finest in the known world.

In the ninth century BCE, Tyre founded the colony of Carthage on the north coast of Africa (where the city of Tunis now stands). Carthage was originally a strong ally of Rome, but it eventually became Rome's most formidable enemy and was destroyed by the Romans in 146 BCE. Later in the ninth century Tyre purchased immunity from the Assyrian emperor Ashurnasirpal II, but only a few years later it joined in an alliance with several other nations, including Ahab's Israel, to resist Ashurnasirpal's son Shalmaneser III. With this alliance Tyre and Sidon joined under one king, Ethbaal. The alliance failed, however, and Tyre and Sidon were forced to pay tribute to Assyria. At the same time Jezebel, Ahab's queen, the daughter of Ethbaal, introduced the worship of the pagan Phoenician god

2. For all his wisdom, Solomon made some incredibly unwise moves: he virtually enslaved twenty thousand Jews to serve as forced laborers on the temple and on his palace, and he gave twenty cities of Galilee to Hiram (1 Kings 9:11-14). This meant that Jewish cities were voluntarily turned over to pagan rule. The cities did not please Hiram, and he returned them, but many remained under pagan control thereafter. This caused an unrest that may well have contributed to the revolt that broke up the United Monarchy after Solomon's death.

3. Huram-abi (or Huram abu) was the son of a Phoenician bronze-worker and a Jewish woman of the northern tribe of Naphtali. It is not known whether he practiced the Jewish faith or was a pagan.

Melkart into the northern kingdom of Israel, permanently corrupting Judaism there.[4]

In the eighth century BCE Shalmaneser V of Assyria captured Ushu, the mainland portion of Tyre, but was unable to get a foothold on the island portion before he died in 722. His successor Sargon II was successful, however, and Tyre yielded. As Assyria declined, Tyre regained a significant degree of independence, and prospered.

In 585 BCE the newly re-ascending Babylonian Empire, under Nebuchadrezzar II, began a siege that lasted thirteen years. Finally Tyre was forced to yield to Babylonian suzerainty in 573. When the Persians defeated Babylon in 538, all of Phoenicia fell under Persian rule, and remained so for two centuries.

In 333 BCE Alexander defeated the Persian emperor Darius III, then marched south toward Egypt. As he passed through Phoenicia he demanded that the cities open their gates to him in order that the Persians might not have use of the Phoenician navies. The citizens of Tyre refused to do so, and in 332 he laid siege to the city, easily taking Ushu, the city's mainland portion. He used the rubble of Ushu to build a two-hundred-foot-wide mole across the straits, turning the island into a peninsula. It has been a peninsula ever since. Alexander obtained 324 ships from all over his empire, blockaded the city, and attacked from all sides. After seven months Tyre fell. In retribution, he slaughtered ten thousand Tyrians and sold thirty thousand into slavery.

After Alexander's death, Tyre remained under Hellenic rule until it was captured by the Romans in 68 BCE. Jesus visited Tyre and Sidon (Matt. 15:21-28), and Paul and Mark spent a week in Tyre while their ship was provisioned (Acts 21:3-7). Tyre's main industries during Roman times were the manufacture of silk and of Tyrian purple, an extremely expensive purple dye extracted from a mollusk that grows off the Tyrian coast.

By the second century CE Tyre had become the see of a bishop and housed an important Christian community. The Christian scholar Origen was buried there in 254, and Eusebius of Caesarea preached there in 323. In 638 the city was captured by the Muslims, who held it until it fell to the

---

4. Melkart was usually called *Baal*, "Lord." Baalism swept through Israel, the northern kingdom. Although it was fiercely resisted by the prophet Elijah and his followers, it permanently infected Judaism in Israel. The religion that ensued was a mixture of Judaism and paganism. It came to be called Samaritanism after Ahab's capital city, Samaria. From this time on the Jews of the southern kingdom, Judea, spurned the Samaritans as heretics and social outcasts.

crusaders in 1124. The crusaders built a cathedral there, and when the Holy Roman Emperor Frederick I Barbarossa drowned in Tyre in 1190, he was buried in the cathedral. In 1291 the Muslims recaptured the city and destroyed it. It was never again to rise to any level of importance. The city still stands today as the city of Sur, but it is insignificant except for the archaeological digs in it.

# Ur of the Chaldeans

Ur of the Chaldeans, believed to be the ancestral home of Abraham, played a major role in the early development of Mesopotamia.[1] For centuries there has been argument as to the location of Ur, and many scholars even doubted that it ever existed, claiming that it was purely mythological.[2] One reason it took so long to find the ruins is that archaeologists were looking for them near the mouth of the Euphrates, which has since moved far away. Also, Genesis 11:31 says that Abraham's family left Ur and settled in Haran. Many scholars identified this with the city of Haran in northern Mesopotamia, and thus assumed that the Ur of the Bible was nearby Urfa (Edessa). The problem with this is that the Bible calls it Ur of the Chaldeans, yet the Chaldeans, a Semitic tribe, lived in southern Mesopotamia and never settled in the north. This was answered by claiming that it was a misinterpretation, and that the reference was not to Chaldea but to Haldai, a section of Armenia to the north. While some scholars place Ur in upper Mesopotamia near the city of Haran, most locate it on the banks of the Euphrates in the lower region. When it was in its prime, Ur was a major port on the mouth of the Euphrates, very close to the Persian Gulf. Over the millennia the gulf coast has moved back and the Euphrates has shifted its course, flowing about ten miles east of the now-inland ruins of the city.

Today it is generally accepted that Tell el-Muqayyar in the southern part of Iraq is the biblical Ur. The ruins there date back to 5500 BCE, with levels indicating that the city was finally abandoned about 300 BCE. One fascinating level is a heavy layer of alluvial silt that many scholars believe was deposited in the Great Flood described in Genesis and the Gilgamesh Epic.[3] Thousands of building inscriptions and inscribed tablets provide

---

1. Mesopotamia, literally "Between the Rivers," is the region in the Middle East that lies between the Tigris and Euphrates Rivers. The upper portion covers much of what is present-day Iraq.

2. Many made the same claim about Troy. Archaeology has proven the existence and location of that city, even though much of the legendry surrounding the Trojan War is unquestionably mythological.

3. The Gilgamesh Epic is a second-millennium BCE Babylonian epic of the adventures

detailed information about the society, economy, and religion of the city over the five millennia of its existence. The city was oval in shape because of its location on a sharp bend of the river.

From its first settlement in about 5500 BCE until the advent of the Sumerian culture about two thousand years later, Ur was an insignificant fishing and farming village. By the end of the fourth millennium it began to flourish, developing writing and a simple but refined architecture. With the rise of the Sumerians, Ur became an important city, assuming a leading role in politics and commerce. Its location on the river and its easy access to the Persian Gulf made it a key trade center. With the dominance of the Sumerians, southern Mesopotamia came to be known as Sumer. Politically, beginning about 3000 BCE, Ur was ruled by a number of dynasties, at some times being the ruling city and at others being ruled by the kings of neighboring city-states. One of these kings was Gilgamesh, the king of Uruk[4] (the biblical Erech), about whom the great mythological epic was written.

The third dynasty of Ur arose about 2150 BCE, established by Ur-Nammu. He was a great warrior, and under his leadership Ur became the ruling city of most of Mesopotamia. He and his son Shulgi developed extensive irrigation systems, eased travel and inland commerce by building roads and canals, and established worship centers, temples, and ziggurats all over Mesopotamia. Under the inspiration of Ur-Nammu and Shulgi the arts, philosophy, and mathematics flourished, as did engineering and medicine. Ur was a worship center of many pagan religions, especially the worship of the moon god Nanna,[5] and idol-making was an important industry there. It was probably during the third dynasty that Abraham's father, Terah, a pagan, moved his family from Ur to the city of Haran in the north. According to tradition Terah was an idol-maker by profession.

---

of the king Gilgamesh and his friend Enkidu. It contains an account of the Great Flood almost identical to that of Genesis. Many ancient Middle Eastern legends tell of a great flood.

4. The modern name Iraq may be a corruption of Uruk.

5. Another name for Nanna was Sin or Shin, and the Wilderness of Sin, where the Hebrews wandered after fleeing from Egypt, is believed to be a desert region in the northwest Sinai Peninsula dedicated to the god Sin. Nanna/Sin was widely worshiped throughout the Middle East. He was a god of fertility, with special providence of husbandmen and orchard growers, and had a secondary role as the god of the dead. His worshipers believed that as the moon waned he increasingly attended to the underworld, and that he returned to the surface as the moon waxed. His wife Ningal also attended to fertility as the goddess of cowherders. She was also the goddess of marshes and reeds.

After the end of the third dynasty, Ur's fortunes began to ebb. It remained an important trade center, and it was the primary shrine of Nanna, but its political influence waned significantly. In 1740 BCE it was destroyed by barbarian raiders. It was quickly rebuilt, but it never regained its former importance. The population remained stable for centuries, but in about 325 BCE a meander in the Euphrates caused the river to shift its course several miles away from the city. Losing the river trade was the final blow to the city. It fell into a rapid decline, and was finally abandoned in about 300 BCE.

One of the most striking buildings in Ur was the Great Ziggurat[6] of Nanna in the center of the city. This was buried under the sands for millennia and is quite well preserved. Another important archaeological find, also well preserved, is the royal cemetery of the third dynasty, which provides a trove of information about burial practices and religious beliefs of the time. Royals were buried in much the same way in Ur as they were at the same time in Egypt. The third major find is a number of family houses of the era of 2000 to 1750 BCE, apparently belonging to middle-class people. They were two-storied, brick, with wooden framing and supports. The design consisted of a central open courtyard surrounded by several small rooms. A wooden stairway led to the second story, whose rooms were accessed from a railed balcony on the courtyard side. Archaeological finds indicate that family life was highly valued in the social structure of Ur.

Although there are still many questions about the relationship of Abraham to Ur, it is not at all unreasonable to believe that he was born and raised there. Despite the common erroneous image that he was some kind of wandering ascetic, Abraham was in fact a very rich and powerful tribal leader. It is entirely possible that his father, Terah, was also a wealthy and influential man in Ur during the third dynasty.

6. A ziggurat is a stepped, truncated pyramid, usually built as a temple to an important god. At the top was an altar of sacrifice, often designed for human sacrifice. Early ziggurats were almost certainly the inspiration for the great pyramids of Egypt. Interestingly, ziggurats of almost identical design are also found in the ruins of the Mayan, Aztec, and Inca cities of Central and South America.

# Maps

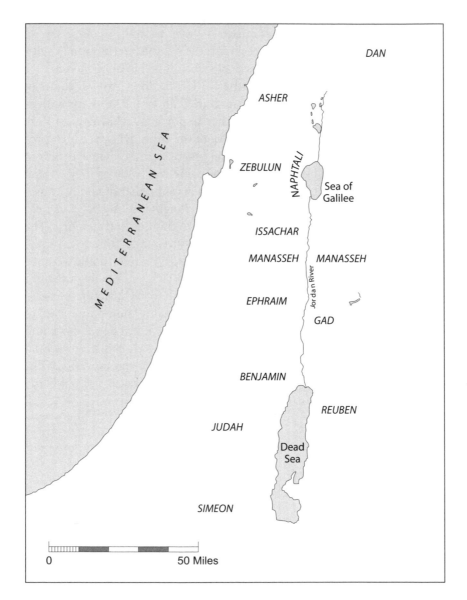

The Twelve Tribes of Israel

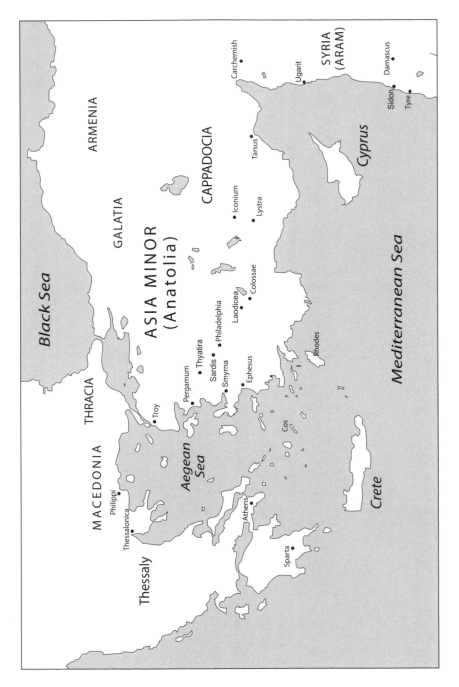

Ancient Asia Minor (Anatolia)

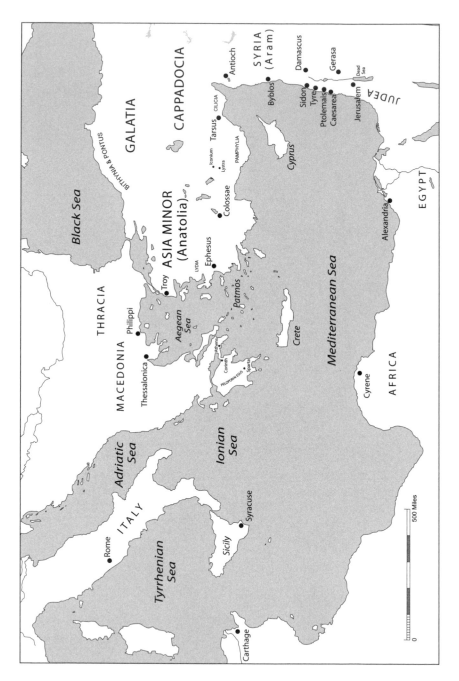

The Mediterranean World of the New Testament

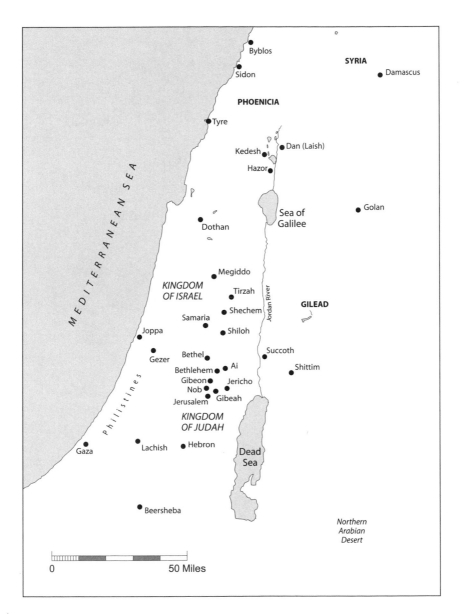

Palestine in Old Testament Times

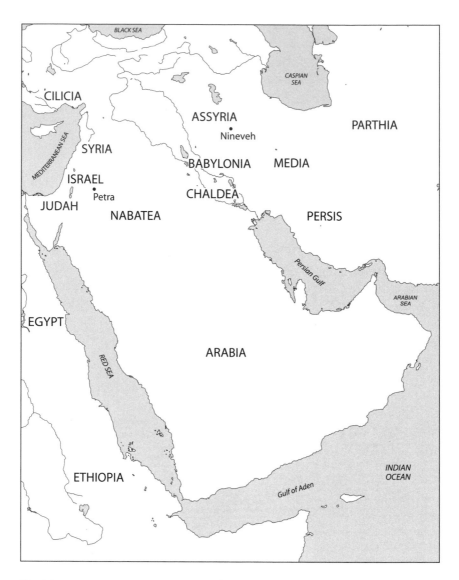

The Kingdoms and Empires of Old Testament Times

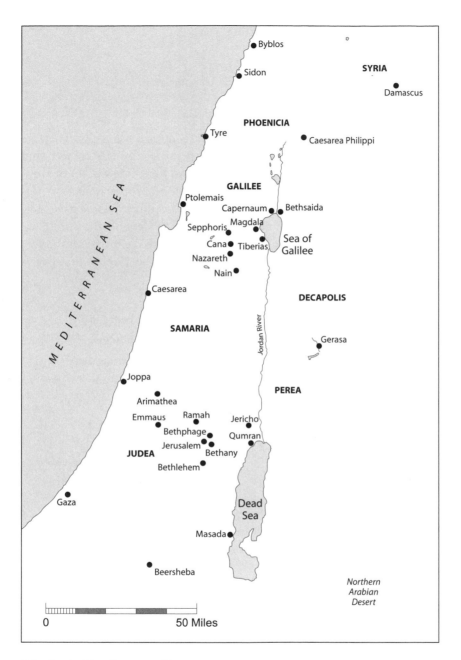

Byblos

Sidon

SYRIA

Damascus

PHOENICIA

Tyre

Caesarea Philippi

*MEDITERRANEAN SEA*

GALILEE

Ptolemais

Capernaum • Bethsaida

Sepphoris • Magdala

Cana • Tiberias

Sea of Galilee

Nazareth

Nain

Caesarea

DECAPOLIS

SAMARIA

*Jordan River*

Gerasa

Joppa

PEREA

Arimathea

Emmaus Ramah

Jericho

Bethphage

Qumran

Jerusalem

Bethany

JUDEA

Bethlehem

Gaza

Dead Sea

Masada

Beersheba

*Northern Arabian Desert*

0          50 Miles

Palestine in New Testament Times

# A Guide to Pronunciation

The following pronunciations are those in common use today. They are not necessarily those used in ancient times, or the exactly correct (but rarely used) currently accepted pronunciations. It is often a point of argument, for example, whether we should Anglicize proper nouns or pronounce them according to their own language. In some cases we have indicated both. There is no sound in English equivalent to the sound we indicate with <u>ch</u>. It sounds like an airy "k" formed in the throat on the very back of the tongue. Vowels may be assumed to be short unless they bear a long mark; "g" is hard.

| | | | |
|---|---|---|---|
| Achaean | uh-**kee**-an | Bethphage | **beth**-fuh-jee |
| Aegean | uh-**gee**-an | Byblos | **bib**-lōss |
| Ai | **eye** (Yiddish **oy**) | Byzantine | **biz**-un-teen |
| Antioch | **an**-tee-ahk | Byzantium | buh-**zan**-tsee-um |
| Antiochus | an-**tī**-uh-kuss | Caesarea | sess-uh-**ree**-uh |
| Antipater | an-**tih**-puh-ter | Calvary | **cal**-vuh-ree |
| Armageddon | ar-muh-**ged**-un | Cana | **kay**-nuh |
| Assyria | uh-**seer**-ee-uh | Capernaum | cuh-**per**-nee-um (not |
| Baal | **bay**-ul (anciently | | **cah**-per-nawm) |
| | bah-**all**) | Carchemish | kar-**chem**-ish |
| Babylon | **bab**-uh-lon | Colossae | kuh-**law**-see |
| Babylonia | bab-uh-**low**-nee-uh | Croesus | **kree**-sus |
| Beersheba | beer-**shee**-buh | Cyrene | sī-**ree**-nee (anciently |
| Bethany | **beth**-uh-nee | | kee-**ray**-nay) |
| Bethel | **beth**-el (anciently | Decapolis | duh-**cap**-oh-lus |
| | pronounced like two | Dothan | **dō**-thun |
| | words, **Beth el**) | Emmaus | uh-**may**-us |
| Bethlehem | **beth**-luh-hem (an- | Ephesus | **ef**-us-us |
| | ciently pronounced | Esdraelon | ez-dray-**ee**-lon |
| | like two words, | Euphrates | you-**fray**-teez |
| | **beth le**-<u>ch</u>em) | | |

| | | | |
|---|---|---|---|
| Gadarenes | **gad**-uh-reenz | Mesopotamia | meh-zō-pō-**tay**-mee-uh |
| Galatia | guh-**lay**-shuh (anciently guh-**lah**-tsee-uh) | Nabatea | nah-bah-**tee**-uh |
| | | Nebuchadrezzar | neh-boo-kuh-**drez**-zer |
| Galilee | **gal**-uh-lee | Nineveh | **nin**-uh-vuh |
| Gaza | **gah**-zuh | Palestine | **pal**-uh-stīn (not **pal**-uh-steen) |
| Gerasenes | **ger**-uh-seenz | | |
| Gezer | **gee**-zer | Patmos | **pat**-mōs |
| Gibeah | **gib**-ee-uh | Peloponnesian | pel-ō-pun-**ee**-zhun |
| Gibeon | **gib**-ee-un | Peloponnesus | pel-ō-pun-**ee**-sus |
| Gilgamesh | **gil**-guh-mesh | Peniel | **pen**-ee-el |
| Gilead | **gill**-ee-ad | Pergamum | **per**-guh-mum |
| Golgotha | **gall**-go-thuh | Petra | **peh**-truh |
| Gomorrah | guh-**mor**-uh | Philippi | **fil**-up-pī |
| Goshen | **gō**-shun | Phoenicia | fuh-**nee**-shuh |
| Hanukkah | **hah**-nook-kuh | Ptolemy | **tol**-uh-mee (the "p" is silent) |
| Hazor | **hay**-zor | | |
| Hebron | **hee**-brun | Qumran | **koom**-rahn |
| Hyksos | **hix**-us | Rehoboam | ree-uh-**bō**-um |
| Idumean | id-you-**mee**-un | Samaria | suh-**mah**-ree-uh |
| Ishmael | **ish**-may-el | Sardis | **sahr**-dis |
| Jericho | **jer**-ih-kō | Seleucid | suh-**loo**-sid |
| Jehoshaphat | jee-**hosh**-uh-fat | Seleucus | suh-**loo**-kuss |
| Jeroboam | jer-uh-**bō**-um | Seljuk | **sel**-jook |
| Judah | **joo**-duh | Sepphoris | suh-**for**-us |
| Judea | joo-**dee**-uh | Shechem | **sheh**-<u>ch</u>um |
| Laodicea | lay-**ah**-dis-ee-uh | Shiloh | **shī**-lō (anciently **shee**-lō) |
| Lycurgus | lī-**kur**-jus | | |
| Maccabaeus | mack-kuh-**bee**-us | Sidon | **sī**-dun |
| Macedonia | mass-uh-**dō**-nee-uh | Sidonian | suh-**dō**-nee-un |
| Magdala | **mag**-duh-luh | Sinai | **sī**-nī (anciently **see**-nī) |
| Mameluke | **mah**-muh-luke | | |
| Masada | muh-**sah**-duh | Smyrna | **smeer**-nuh |
| Megiddo | muh-**gid**-dō | Sodom | **sah**-dum |

| | | | |
|---|---|---|---|
| Thessalonica | thess-uh-luh-**nī**-kuh or thess-uh-luh-**nee**-kuh (but not thess-uh-**lon**-nih-kuh) | Tirzah | **teer**-dzuh |
| | | Tyre | **tire** |
| Thyatira | thī-uh-**tī**-ruh | Ur of the Chaldeans | **oor** of the kal-**dee**-uns |
| Tiberias | ti-**beer**-ee-us | Zion | **zī**-un |

# Index

Page numbers in bold refer to main entries.